History in My Life

History in My Life

A Memoir of Three Eras

Ivan T. Berend

Central European University Press
Budapest – New York

© 2009 by Ivan T. Berend

Published in 2009 by Central European University Press
An imprint of the Central European University Share Company
Nádor utca 11, H-1051 Budapest, Hungary
Tel: +36-1-327-3138 or 327-3000
Fax: +36-1-327-3183
E-mail: ceupress@ceu.hu
Website: www.ceupress.com

400 West 59th Street, New York NY 10019, USA
Tel: +1-212-547-6932
Fax: +1-646-557-2416
E-mail: mgreenwald@sorosny.org

All rights reserved. No part of this publication may be reproduced, stored in a retrieval system, or transmitted, in any form or by any means, without the permission of the Publisher.

ISBN 978-963-9776-48-7 cloth
ISBN 978-963-386-701-3 paperback

Library of Congress Cataloging-in-Publication Data

Berend, Ivan.
History in my life : a memoir of three eras / Ivan T. Berend.
p. cm.
Includes bibliographical references.
ISBN 978-9639776487 (cloth : alk. paper)
1. Socialism--Europe, Eastern. 2. Socialism--Europe, Central.
3. Intellectuals--Hungary--Biography. I. Title.
HX240.7.A6B474 2009
335.092--dc22
[B]
2009021684

Table of Contents

Introduction and Acknowledgement	1
My Family in Budapest in the 1930s	5
With my mother, father and brother Ervin in 1935.	7
The End of Childhood	21
Dachau—and the Südosteuropa-Gesellschaft's Conference in Munich	31
The Gebirgsjägerschule in Mittenwald	39
Where is My Home?	43
The 1956 Revolution in My Life	59
My Universities	75
A Widening World, Learning by Traveling	95
In the International Community of Historians; Friends all Over the World	107
Experiencing and Writing History: a Special Friend, Books and Debates	119
Teaching in Two Different University Systems	155
My Globalized Family	169
In the Establishment	175
In the Storm of Regime Change	207
Leaving Hungary for Los Angeles	233
America	243
References	275
List of Photos	277

I dedicate this book to my generation who experienced "the best of times and the worst of times," the tragedy, pain, success, and happiness of the 20th century. However, I recommend it most to Western readers, who are often taught oversimplified interpretations of life behind the Iron Curtain.

While writing my memoirs, I thought a lot about the past: about my late parents, grandmother, and brother, I though about my friends, who are very important for me, but also about the thousands of students I have taught in Hungary and the United States during my more than half-century career as a teacher.

However, my thoughts soared even more often to the future, to the life of my beloved family, wife, daughters and grandchildren, who may compare their life experience with mine, and who may learn that we can cope with the most dramatic challenges of life.

Introduction and Acknowledgement

I bear witness to the most horrible times of twentieth-century Central Europe: its industrialized mass murder, genocide, oppression, hyperinflation and poverty, its revolutions and struggle for a better life. I was born at an unfortunate time in an unfortunate place, Budapest, Hungary during the Great Depression. The authoritarian regime became a close ally of Hitler, shifted more and more to the Right, then established a Nazi system, which sent me the teenager to Hungarian prisons and Nazi-German concentration camp.

I survived and returned to a Hungary that turned to democracy, land reform, and free elections, but in a few years, under Soviet occupation, introduced a terrible Stalinist-communist regime. After a decade, a heroic and bloody revolution destroyed it, but it was soon reestablished by the Soviet Army. Stalinism, nevertheless, was replaced with a more moderate, reform-oriented system with freedom to travel and research. After a third of a century a new, this time peaceful revolution destroyed communism and established real democracy. I became part of a historical experiment to cope with traditional backwardness, experienced major failures, and learned important lessons from them.

In the most troubled but interesting of historical times, I became a historian who did not remain a passive witness but decided to take an active part in those changes. Now, I am presenting my own history to illuminate life in a Central European country during fascism and communism. Western readers often have an oversimplified view of the Cold War decades; they do not differentiate between the Eastern countries and the various periods under communist rule, as if all of them had been the same, without any real difference between the 1950s and 1980s. What I experienced and the way I reacted to those experiences may help a better understanding of a unique and extremely interesting chapter of twentieth century history.

When the best known Hungarian dissident, George Konrád, recently published his memoirs, one writer noted on the back cover of the book: "to read *A Guest in My Own Country* is to experience the recent history of East-Central Europe from inside." That is only partly true; inside, yes, but from a certain angle. Nevertheless, one may approach this history from several viewpoints. Here I will present the experience of history from my own.

I have a special advantage to tell this story to the Western readers because my life, with a sudden change, continued in Los Angeles. I made a career in a communist country and then a second one in the United States. Writing my memoirs in the latter they may offer a better comparison and understanding. Besides, it allows me to share my impressions of my new home country as I see it parallel from within and without.

My presentation here is not a strict chronological record: the past history of our life is always part of our present, and the future incorporated into our past. My childhood experiences became a part of my professional life, strongly influencing my way of thinking, while my high-school studies have determined my entire life. The historical events became part of my work as a historian, and as a historian I felt inspired to try and influence history. I consider myself lucky and enriched by the experience of hard times.

Autobiography is a subjective genre. It reflects my perception of events, and my role in the history I experienced. I am sure that some readers will disagree with some of my views and my interpretation of certain historical events and phenomena. I tried to be as frank as possible regarding my motivations, my way of thinking, and my actions, and I checked my memory against the historical record when sources allowed that. This memoir is full of history: it is the memoir of a historian, but it is still not a history book.

I am strongly indebted to those who have read the manuscript and offered their views and even editing contributions. As always, I am most grateful to Kati, my wife and most honest critic of my manuscripts, including this one. A number of wonderful friends also made important critical remarks and good suggestions regarding certain parts and chapters, but I would like in particular to mention David Summers, who polished the first version of the manuscript, and Priscilla Heim, who also volunteered to thoroughly edit the entire manuscript.

My Family in Budapest in the 1930s

During the first decade of my life between the Great Depression and the beginning of World War II, I was not aware of horrible times, existential fears and dangers. I was born in December 1930 in Budapest. This was one of the worst years of the devastating Great Depression in Hungary and world-wide. Unemployment, bankruptcies, and poverty reached peak numbers everywhere. The world's industrial output declined by 30 percent, grain prices by 60 percent; twenty million Europeans became unemployed.

Life expectancy at birth was less than 60 years in the United States and about 55 in Hungary. It was a very different world from the one we know today. Even small amounts of money had huge value. As a popular Hungarian song of those years put it, *"havi 200 pengő fixszel az ember könnyen viccel,"* (with a monthly salary of 200 pengő it easy to make jokes, i.e. easy to live). The dollar value of that amount was roughly $40. This was quite a universal phenomenon: the price of a new house in the United States was about $7,000 and the cost of a gallon of gasoline 10 cents, although the Texas oil fields had just been discovered that year.

My parents were certainly somewhat disappointed not to have a baby girl, as they had hoped, after already having a son. According to the family annals my grandmother went out to the corridor in the apartment house where my family lived and informed the entire house by shouting: "we waited for a girl but got a second boy!" The future was uncertain, and fear

History in My Life

At the age of three,
the first photo on me in 1933.

penetrated all of life. Nevertheless, although it was not the best time for family expansion, they were happy with my arrival.

I was one year old when Japan attacked China, hardly more than two when Hitler gained power in Germany, three when Hungary signed a special trade agreement with Hitler that made the country wholly dependent on Germany; and five when Mussolini attacked Abyssinia. I was six years old when the Spanish Civil War began, seven when Guernica was bombed by Hitler, eight when Hungary introduced a five-year plan for war preparation. During those years of my life, about ten million people died in the Soviet Union in consequence of the brutal, forced collectivization and the famine it generated; while Stalin's show trials followed one after the other in Moscow. I was eight years old when the *Kristallnacht* in Germany and the first anti-Jewish laws in Hungary foreshadowed the coming Holocaust. When the war erupted, I was nine years old. When Regent Miklós Hor-

With my mother, father and brother Ervin in 1935.

thy's Hungary joined Hitler's Germany, attacking Yugoslavia first, then the Soviet Union, bringing the war to Hungary, I was somewhat more than 10 years old.

Those were frightening times in Hungary. There had been two consecutive revolutions immediately after World War I, a democratic revolution in 1918 followed by a communist revolution in 1919. After 133 days the communist regime was brought down by military intervention organized by France and executed by the Czechoslovak and Romanian armies. Following these stormy years, a "White Terror" campaign was launched by Admiral Miklós Horthy in retaliation for the preceding "Red Terror." Though formally a parliamentary system with multi-party elections, the regime established by Admiral Horthy was fully authoritarian. As Horthy's Prime Minister, István Bethlen declared: "secret balloting would be unsuited to the open character of the Hungarian people." For the quarter of a century of the existence of this regime, opposition parties never had the slightest chance to win.

The political system, already right-wing, nationalist and anti-Semitic, rapidly shifted even farther to the right in the 1930s. From the moment of its birth in 1919, the Horthy regime was strongly anti-Semitic. Bloody pogroms were launched in the countryside during the early 1920s in retaliation of the 1919 communist revolution. The regime introduced the first anti-Jewish legislation in Europe limiting the number of Jews admissible to universities (*Numerus Clausus* legislation). Beatings of Jewish students became an everyday phenomenon. Later on, however, Horthy made some adjustments to more accepted European standards, and official anti-Jewish measures were removed.

All the phenomena of those extremist early 1920s, however, returned during the late 1930s. Horthy immediately allied up with Hitler in 1933, and in 1935 a united and powerful Hungarian Nazi Party was founded, the third largest in Europe after those in Germany and Romania. In 1938, and then in 1939, two anti-Jewish Laws excluded Jews from equal citizenship rights. The First Jewish Law in 1938 restricted the number of Jews in liberal professions, administration, commercial and industrial enterprises to 20 percent.

In 1939, the Second Jewish Law, which copied the Nazi Nuremberg Laws, and defined Jewishness on a racial rather than a religious basis, further limited the livelihood of Jews by restricting their numbers to five percent in the professions and economic life. Of the roughly 450,000 Jews in the country's 1938 territory, 250,000 lost their business, employment, and income. In 1941, intermarriage was banned as well.

Jews were no longer accepted by universities. In the early 1940s, a family who had lived on the ground floor of our apartment house for at least two decades was rounded up by the police and taken away. I think they were Galician Jews by origin and lacked Hungarian citizenship though they were fluent in Hungarian. We later learned that it was the overture of the Holocaust in Hungary because several thousand non-citizen Jews were deported to Kamenets Podolsk and killed. After 1939, Jewish men of military age were not called up for regular military service but drafted to "labor battalions." My father was one of them. After 1941, many of them, including my favorite uncle, were sent to the Russian front with the deliberate goal of eliminating them. Very few returned.

A wave of nationalism swept the country. Hungary's foreign policy was determined by irredentist border revision goals from 1919 on because the country was truncated by the Trianon Peace Treaty, part of the Versailles arrangement, which cut off two-thirds of the country's territory and 60 percent of its mostly minority, Romanian, Slovak and Croat pre-war population. However, also nearly three million Hungarians found themselves having become citizens of neighboring enlarged Romania, newly established Czechoslovakia, and Yugoslavia. When I started school in 1937 we began each day with a prayer: "Rump Hungary is not a country, Great Hungary is heaven. I believe in one God, I believe in my only Fatherland, I believe in the resurrection of Hungary!" In each classroom, a huge map of Great Hungary as it had existed before World War I hung on the wall, marked with the borders of rump Hungary.

Between 1938 and 1941, in alliance with Hitler, Hungary enacted the first revisions of the Trianon Treaty and began the re-annexation of some of its lost territories. First, in connection with Hitler's attack against Czechoslovakia and due to the first Vienna Award of Hitler and Mussolini in 1938, the mostly Hungarian-inhabited southern strip of Slovakia was reattached to Hungary, followed by the annexation of Subcarpathia, and then, based on the second Vienna Award of 1940, the northern half of Transylvania. When Hitler attacked Yugoslavia, and Hungary joined, the Voivodina region from Yugoslavia was also reoccupied in the spring of 1941. The territory of the country nearly doubled between 1938 and 1941, and its population increased from less than 9 to more than 14 million people.

Euphoric nationalism made the Horthy regime popular. I still have my history copy-book from the fourth year of elementary school and it clearly illustrates the nationalist interpretation of Hungarian history that was fed to us. The first page was a full photo of Regent Miklós Horthy, Hungary's head of state. On the last pages I wrote all the irredentist slogans about "rump Hungary" beside photos of Horthy riding a white horse as he entered Kassa (Košice) at its reoccupation in 1938, as well as the main facts about the territorial enlargement of the country.

I was enthusiastic over the territorial enlargement. In 1939, when I was nine years old, I ran home from the street where I played soccer with my friends with this happy news, "Mussolini has declared that Transylvania belongs to Hungary!" I learned it from the newspaper-man who shouted the news with a bunch of dailies under his arm. I actually misunderstood and thought "we" had already got Transylvania back. There was no escape from the atmosphere of that nationalist wave. As a young kid, I was not

History in My Life

My grandmother, concierge in the late 1920s in Akácfa utca 32. She had run our household during the first two decades of my life.

able to predict that the greatest part of my family would soon drown in this filthy flood.

Our three-generation family, my natural environment, sheltered me, and I had a sense of security and warmth. My father and mother could not have been more different in character. My father was a man for all seasons. He had strong convictions and expectations, lived a hard working life, and had a universal aptitude. Strangely enough, I do not know much about his family. When he was alive and I could easily have got all the information, I never asked. During my childhood he went with my mother to visit his family in the village every year, but they went without my brother and me. As a consequence, I met only one of his brothers, a cabinet maker, who lived in a suburb of Budapest and was killed in 1944, but not with his siblings, my grandmother, and several of my cousins. The only thing I know about the history of the family is that my great-grandfather was a rebel during the revolution of 1848. I do not know my grandfather's occupation, probably because he died early, when my father was only six years old. Then my father's oldest brother, twenty years his senior, became the head of the family. What I do know about them is that none was educated beyond elementary school level.

Born into a poor family in a village in East Hungary and half orphaned at the age of six, my father was first trained as a cabinet maker, and then retrained all by himself as a teacher. Before I was born, however, he established a small paint and chemists shop. For additional income, he made wooden toys which he painted. He could fix everything, worked long days in the shop, and edited a journal of the organization of the retailers in his field.

Most of all, he was highly intellectual and owned a large library that covered a room from floor to ceiling. He was intensely interested in psychology and studied Freud, Adler, Jung, and Ferenczy. He developed a skill in graphology admired by everybody, but his main passion and ambition was literature. Throughout his life he wrote novels and dramas. However, except for a small volume of short novels which came out a few years before I was born, he never published them. His manuscripts, as I remember during my entire childhood, were always rejected, but he never lost his drive to try again.

He was hard-nosed and honest, unable to compromise, always said what he thought and, of course, made several enemies. My mother often told me the story of a friendly gathering around a table with colleagues and friends at which my father turned to my mother sitting next to him and said: "No use kicking my legs; I'll still tell him the truth!"

My mother was very different. Warm and loving, ready to adjust and keep her opinions to herself, she was also a hard worker in the shop where they worked together without outside help. When my father spent years in labor service during the war she did everything alone. The shop was shut down because of the anti-Jewish legislation of 1939. My mother learned how to make artificial flowers and sold them. That is how she kept the family alive. She was a very pragmatic person and not an intellectual. Her family moved to Budapest in the late nineteenth century from the north Hungarian town Eger. No one was educated in her family either. I do not know anything else about my mother's family, except that her parents became concierge in an apartment house. She also lost her father early in her life. Continuing her studies was out of the question, and as a teenager, she began working as a secretary during the difficult post-World War I years of hyperinflation. She liked reading, but mostly popular bestseller books.

History in My Life

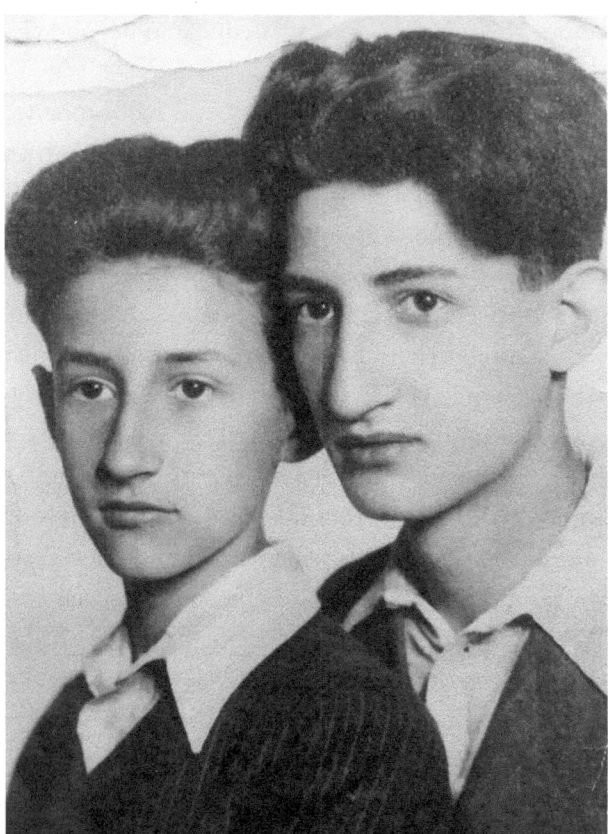

The last photo with
my brother Ervin
in the summer of 1944.
In a few months
he was dead
and I was in Dachau.

These two different persons, however, formed an ideal couple. I never heard an argument or frightening debate between them. My mother was six years younger than my father, and once, without joking but not realizing what she said, she told me: "if one of us, your father or I, dies before the other, I will move to another apartment." Nevertheless, she died fifteen years before him. Decades later, already widowed and in his eighties, my father told me that he never had any affairs during their forty-year marriage, because he did not want to cause pain to her. I regret it now, he added with a smile.

I was somewhat afraid of my father's rigor and expectations. I remember telling my mother at the age of seven or eight that I had a frightening dream at night: I entered the classroom in my school and—what a terrible bewilderment—my father was the teacher. I became my mother's son, while Ervin, my brother who was four years older, soon turned into my father's intellectual partner. He was much better than I at everything. He discussed with my father the political situation he had read about in the newspapers, wrote history studies, tutored the children of the wealthy, and emerged as a promising sculptor. I still have two of his small figures made of clay at the age of eleven or twelve: the figure of an old peasant lady carrying something in her apron and a shoemaker fixing a shoe. Both demonstrate his talent.

He was a rebel and in many senses similar in character to my father. I loved him and felt high respect for him. Almost weekly, just the two of us, went to the nearby Buda and Pilis mountains, and did long hikes together. For me, he was a genius and would probably have been so for the entire world had he not been killed by Hungarian fascists at the age of seventeen in 1944. He is alive in our memories. None of my daughters knew him personally, but my older daughter Zsuzsa gave his name as middle name to her younger son Daniel and my younger daughter Nora dedicated her first book to the memory of her unknown uncle. As I write this he would be eighty years old.

The only area where I bested my brother was sports. I was a poor student, preferring to play soccer in the street with my friends. When my father suddenly appeared and caught me there, he would order me to go home and study. At that time, learning to play a musical instrument was a natural part of a middle-class education, even when lower middle-class. We had a huge piano, and in the 1940s I took regular piano lessons from a teacher who came to our home. But I did not like to play, and after three years I was happy to stop.

During all those years I was probably a good-for-nothing in my father's eyes. I knew the names of all of the famous soccer players, built a button-soccer-team and played championships with my seven close friends in the four-story apartment house where we lived. Our other regular play was "wild West" cowboy fight. We made wooden "colts" and "Winchester" guns and two teams fought against each other. Sometimes we were unable to agree about our "shots," whether the enemy was killed or only wounded. In secret I read detective and cowboy stories. These booklets were often confiscated by my father. My other favorite readings were American Indian stories from James Fennimore Cooper and the German author Karl May. I loved the romantic stories of the last of the Mohicans and others. This feeling was still with me when nearly half a century later I visited Mesa Verde and climbed the ladder to see the structures that were built into natural caves. I was overcome with the same enthusiastic, romantic feeling again.

During one summer vacation after the second or third year in elementary school I wrote a short novel. I still have this copybook. The first sentence tells it all: "Maud, the daughter of the sheriff, had blue eyes and blond hair." The location of the story was Kansas, a state whose name I picked up from one of the cowboy stories, but have yet to see for myself. I definitely was a naughty boy, but better at socializing than my brother who was a loner.

My behavior, of course, was not a deliberate and conscious reaction to the challenge of being a second, younger sibling. In retrospect, however, I see certain motivations, especially because of my experiences with my grandchildren. The younger sibling has to cope with the fact that the older one is "ex officio" bigger, stronger, and smarter. How to compensate for that? How to compete? Although there are no general patterns, you have to be different. I became wilder, more extroverted, much more athletic, and physically far more active. This instinctive competition motivated me regardless of the love and solidarity that closely united me with my brother.

In the large apartment house where we lived I had several friends and we spent most of our time together, all like extended members of each other's families. Built in the first years of the twentieth century, the four-story building had twenty-four apartments around a large, paved courtyard with a stand in the middle used for beating carpets—an ideal structure for this communal life. From time to time housewives and maids took the rugs there and beat out the dust. Corridors circled the floors on each level with six apartments opening from each corridor. Most of them faced the inner courtyard and only six faced the street, one of them ours, with a small balcony. At each end of the building there were staircases, the front one for the tenants, and a spiral staircase in the back for delivery men and maids. The ground floor apartments shared a common toilet, but each apartment on the other floors had its own bathroom and toilet. In the attic a common washroom was available for family wash day, usually once a month. It was a major event in my family when an old lady, Emma, arrived and assisted my grandmother in the work. I liked to help hang the washed bed-linen in the attic.

This structure fostered a natural community of people living there, not only because of the common facilities, but because everybody's life was exposed to everybody else. We ran in and out of our friends' apartments. We knew about family fights, whether somebody left or arrived, if somebody had guests. On the fourth floor my friend "fat Miki" lived with his mother and three unmarried or divorced aunts. They often washed themselves in a bowl in the kitchen, and never hid their half naked bodies. "You have surely seen similar," they repeated. Sometimes we even witnessed the sex life of our neighbors. Once I was sitting at the Friday evening dinner when my teenage friends knocked the door and urged me to come out because in one of the illuminated and un-curtained ground floor apartments, a couple was making love in full sight. We watched eagerly from the second floor. There were no secrets in our building.

Curiously enough, my loose lifestyle did not destroy my good relationship with my rigorous father. Though not greatly successful, he never gave up trying to educate me. His opinion of me changed only after the war when, in high school and university, I began to work and became successful, and finally, at the age of 30, after publishing my third economic history book co-authored with my close friend, György Ránki, we shared the Kossuth Prize, the highest scholarly award of the country. Then my father and I became good friends and talked about everything from international politics to my work. When he was in his seventies, already widowed, one leg amputated, I visited him often. After the artificial leg, we took walks together, the roles changing in our remaining family, and he became more and more dependent on me. It was a painful experience to see him, the high authority in my early life at that humiliating stage. When my mother was diagnosed with breast cancer and had surgery, according to the custom of the day in Hungary the doctor told this terrible news only to me, and I kept the secret from both of them until she died at the age of 63. After this tragedy he became even more dependent on me until he died at the age of 84.

From the late 1920s until her death in 1952 our household was run by my maternal grandmother, widowed long before I was born. She was a simple but wonderful soul who dedicated her life to serving the family. Although she did not have any private life or fun, she never complained. Her two sons, Andor and Jenő, two and five years younger than my mother, also lived with us. This was wonderful because Jenő, my favorite uncle, twenty years my senior, was also my close friend. He had a fine sense of humor, a caring, warm character, and was always ready to play with me. I was about five years old when he built a red wooden car for me, driven by pedals. I was very proud of it. None of my friends had anything like it. He was good at sports and taught me skiing at the age of ten. Andor was different and I did not have much interaction with him.

My father, a *paterfamilias,* took care of his brothers-in-laws, and from the small amount of money they earned he established a paint-and-chemist's store for each of them. When my uncles married in 1937 and 1938, they moved out and established their own homes. Until that time, however, my brother and I lived not only in the same apartment at 36 Akácfa utca (Acacia street), but in the same room with my uncles for eight years.

The seventh district of Budapest, including my street, was a markedly Jewish-populated neighborhood. Between one-fifth and one-quarter of Budapest's population was Jewish before the war. Only three non-Jewish families lived in our building. In June 1944, when Hungary was already under Nazi-German occupation, the separation and isolation of the Jews began by the establishment of about 2,000 "Jewish Houses." A large yellow Star of David on the entrance door signaled that our house also became formally "Jewish." On June 25, a curfew was imposed, and we were allowed to leave the building only in a few hours in the morning. Later in the same year, when the walled Budapest ghetto was instituted, all the remaining Jews of the city were resettled in the ghetto area—I was already in prison in the west Hungarian cities of *Veszprém* and then *Komárom*—and thirty-six people were jammed into our apartment.

Apartment number 14 on the first floor (second in American terms) was about 800 square feet, with three rooms. From the entrance a long corridor connected all the facilities and rooms and opened onto the kitchen, a storage cabinet room, the toilet, the bathroom and two of the rooms. A third small room opened onto the bathroom. I have to confess that I played soccer in that corridor when nobody was at home. One of the rooms was for my parents and one for my grandmother, two uncles, my brother and me. Ervin and Andor slept on two separate sofas, my grandmother, Jenő and me in a double bed, and I lay across the bed at their feet. The third room was sub-let to the Katz family, a couple with two adult sons. All of us shared a single bathroom, toilet, and kitchen. Nevertheless, in a small servant-room attached to the kitchen, we almost always had a domestic servant, a young girl from the countryside who helped my grandmother with everyday work.

In the kitchen we had a coal-heated oven, and an icebox filled with ice, which was replenished once a week. When the iceman arrived and shouted in the courtyard, "itt a jeges a jeges!" ("the iceman, the iceman's here!"), I ran down with a bucket, and bought a piece. Beggars also visited the building and sang or played on some instrument in the courtyard. We knew them all, including a blind man, wounded in the First World War, who always sang the same folksong, "az a szép, az a szép, akinek a szeme kék..." ("beautiful, beautiful are those with blue eyes"). We packed some small change in paper and threw it down into the courtyard.

In the winter wood-heated tile-stoves warmed the rooms, but the stove in our room did not work well, and we added a small coal-fueled iron stove. Wood and coal were delivered in the fall and stored in the basement. This event was always exciting, because horse-driven coaches packed with coal or wood, drove into the courtyard and two men delivered the stuff to the basement in huge buckets they carried on their backs.

All the shops we needed were close by. Izsák Bandel's grocery store was in the next house, and the dairy shop was opposite. I sometimes went with my mother to a special cheese and butter store in a neighboring street. Two buildings away was a small shabby restaurant where Rezső Seres played the piano. He was well known at that time as the composer of the widely popular melancholy song, "Gloomy Sunday," which became a hit all over the world. It inspired dozens of people, even more than usual, to commit suicide, a wide-spread, mysterious phenomenon in Hungary anyway, which always ranked among the first three countries with the highest suicide rates in the world ever since modern statistics exist. This restaurant is still in operation, and a few years ago became world famous from a German movie *Gloomy Sunday*, based on partly real, and partly made-up stories.

A few buildings away was a farmers' market, one of several similar iron and glass market structures built in the city at the turn of the century. Three buildings away was the barber who cut my hair, the only non-Jewish business-owner in the neighborhood. And at the corner of our street, the tobacco shop, where I often dropped in to buy fine Turkish tobacco and cigarette paper for my father, who was a heavy smoker and rolled his own cigarettes. Within a few hundred yards of each other there were two pubs, which I never entered. On the other hand, Uncle Winter's coal and wood shop was in the basement of the building just opposite. He sometimes hired me and a few friends of mine to carry down wood. The whole world was wrapped closely around us.

Life was well structured and simple. My parents went to work early in the morning but my father would always come home for lunch and a short nap. He developed this habit during World War I when, at the age of 18, he was called up and sent to the Italian front. His company had a commanding officer, who—what a different war it was!—took a quick five-minute nap every day after lunch. It made quite an impact on my father who imitated this habit in his entire life. He tried to pass it on to me too, and before I started school, he often ordered me to have a nap with him. I didn't like that and usually refused.

The main meal was lunch, almost always the same menu for a given day. Wednesdays, for example, we had bean soup and sweet poppy-seed pasta, which remains one of my favorite dishes. In the evening we had something light. My grandmother only had some chicory coffee with milk with some biscuits. (This coffee substitute was my regular breakfast with bread and butter. I always hated drinking it, and even nowadays, although I am a coffee addict, I never drink latte.) Friday evening was an exception; we had a festive Sabbath dinner: chicken soup, meat, and dessert. Thursday afternoon the copper stove in the bathroom was stoked up and we had the weekly bath.

It was a small and friendly world. Besides family members and the apartment house "community," our social environment consisted of a few friends of my parents, most notably Margit and Miklós Salamon. He was a painter and taught me drawing.

For years, I rarely strayed farther than two or three blocks away. For me Budapest ended two blocks north at the *Erzsébet* Boulevard, and the National Theater, at the eastern end of our street, where I waited at the actors-exit to collect autographs. At the western end of the street, also two blocks distant was Saint Teresa Catholic Church. Every year at a festival there I rode the carousel, enjoyed the Lilliputian theater, and tasted some "oriental" sweets. One block away and there was my parents' shop with its wonderful smell of the mixture of chemical substances (which I still like). Smells stay with us throughout our lives. Because I always watched and admired the asphalt pavers work as they knelt to level the fresh asphalt layer on the street, I still love inhaling the smell of asphalt and tar. That was the first job I longed for in my childhood.

I enjoyed walking to my parents' shop and seeing my parents there, and I often did so, especially because of my brother's English lessons from Miss Bertha Beavis, an English spinster who lived in the neighboring street in a very small hotel room and made her living by teaching English. She hardly spoke any Hungarian and was a heavy drinker. When Ervin had his lessons I often accompanied him, sitting on the floor and making drawings. Once, around the age of five, I managed to embarrass my mother terribly. She sent a small bottle of eau de Cologne with me to Miss Beavis as an Easter present, and when I gave it to her I repeated what my mother had said: "She probably will drink it too."

Next to my parents' shop was a pub, owned by Mr. Csejtei, a huge man with an impressive belly. He was a "Schwab," as we in Hungary called people of German origin. I learned after the war that somebody denounced him to Russian soldiers in the very first days of street battles in the city, and that they shot him dead on the spot.

From this close environment of a few blocks, the only major "excursion" was to take the tram and travel for one hour to the town of *Pestszentlőrinc*, administratively independent, but in reality a suburb of Budapest [as it would formally become in 1949], where my father had bought a small plot of land and, together with one of his brothers, built a one-room adobe summer cottage with no running water and no electricity. An outhouse, which my uncle Jenő painted red with a small landscape on its side, stood at the other end of the garden. A well, ninety-foot deep, produced cool water, and also served as a cooler. Ervin and I spent our entire three-month-long summer vacations there with our grandmother. On weekends, Ervin and I would walk to the terminal of tram number 50 and wait for our parents who came to spend the weekend with us. I naturally picked up gardening skills from my father by helping him water the plants, pick fruit, and plant tomatoes, peppers, and even flowers in a small vegetable garden next to the house. We bought goat milk from our neighbor who had a funny goat, Mici. From time to time, I took her out for grazing.

The old apartment at Akácfa Street actually remained my home and *Pestszentlőrinc* my summer vacation place until well after the war, right until

1960. I became thirty years old that year, was already assistant professor, married with one child, but could not even dream about an apartment of my own, let alone expensive vacations, during the Stalinist 1950s. By then, my grandmother had died. We lived in one of the rooms, and my parents in the other, while the third small room became a kind of storage place.

I wanted to show the 36 *Akácfa utca* building to my close friends when six of us visited Hungary from Los Angeles in 2006. My wife Kati and I led a "guided tour" through the former Jewish ghetto for Cindy and Gary Nash, Ruth and David Sabean. The street was a shocking spectacle. Nowadays, since the Jewish inhabitants are gone, it is mostly inhabited by Roma (Gypsy) people from the countryside. The houses have lost most of their plaster, still show war damage, and haven't been renovated since the war. Nevertheless, it was still my *Akácfa utca*, and my friends realized that.

The End of Childhood

In normal circumstances it is hard to assign the end of someone's childhood to an exact date. In my case, however, childhood ended on October 31, 1944. Both history and our family situation turned from bad to worse then. *Hungary* joined Hitler's war in 1941 and declared war not only against the Soviet Union but—it is still hard to understand—also against the United States. Because Regent Miklós Horthy, head of state and deliberate collaborator with Hitler, secretly initiated separate armistice talks with the Allied countries in 1944, in spite of the alliance between Germany and Hungary, on March 19 of that year, the *Wehrmacht* launched "Operation Margarethe" and occupied Hungary.

Horthy's position regarding the war had changed after the battle of Stalingrad. Stalingrad became the turning point in the war. In the summer of 1942 a huge German army of more than one million soldiers, 1,200 planes, and approximately 700 tanks closed in on Stalingrad, and attacked the city in September, occupying part of it in hand-to-hand combat. The Soviet army, also consisting of more than a million men, 1,500 tanks, and 1,300 planes, initiated a counter-attack in November, and encircled the Germans who, in the end, surrendered in early February 1943. We learned that fantastic and encouraging news, but the end of the nightmare was still far away.

The battle of Stalingrad became a major tragedy for Hungary. On January 15, 1943, Soviet troops crushed the Hungarian army that assisted the Germans at Voronezh. Roughly 50,000 Hungarian solders died, some 60,000 were wounded, and 28,000 fell prisoner of war. The Hungarian army was eliminated. From that time on, the Soviet army launched major offensives and began reoccupying the Soviet territories. In the summer of 1944 the Red Army advanced 240 miles in a single month, and arrived at the borders of Poland and Romania. That was when Horthy looked for a separate peace.

The Hungarian army and government were deeply penetrated by Hitler's spies, and the secret armistice talks did not remain secret. Hitler invited Horthy for a meeting to discuss issues, and meanwhile the *Wehrmacht*, on a sunny Sunday, occupied the country. I was visiting a schoolmate's home when his parents told us the news and sent us home. (In the mid-1970s, I took part in a conference in Germany and, along with a few other participants, was invited by an elderly German colleague to his home. During the friendly discussion he turned to me with a big smile, and said: "you are living in a beautiful city. One of my nicest memories is when as a German soldier I entered Budapest in March 1944. What a wonderful day it was!" I was unable to resist to answer that it was, indeed, a beautiful sunny day but considering its consequences in my life, it was one of the worst days in my life. He suddenly changed the topic.)

Horthy returned from Germany and appointed one of Hitler's puppets prime minister. My father, like all adult Jews, was already in a labor battalion. My uncle Andor was lucky: with his new wife he was able to escape Europe on the last boat headed for Mexico in 1940. My favorite uncle Jenő, however, was already dead. His labor battalion had been sent to the Soviet front a few days after his daughter was born in November 1941. He died on this journey in 1942.

In May and June 1944, the deportation of the Hungarian Jews from the countryside, except Budapest was accomplished. That time, because the territorial enlargement of the country between 1938 and 1941, the number of the Jewish population increased from roughly 450,000 to 850,000. About 440,000 were deported to Auschwitz. Among them, my father's entire family, his blind ninety-year-old mother, five brothers and sisters, and several nephews and cousins who lived in the countryside. We learned only after the war that thirty-two members of my family were killed along with the 565,000 Hungarian Jews who had died.

The deportation and eradication of the Hungarian Jewry—the last chapter of the European Holocaust roughly eight months before the end of the European war—did not include the Jews of Budapest. Horthy was warned by President Roosevelt that he would be considered a war criminal if deportations continued. Nevertheless, the adult males were in labor battalions, and many of them like my uncle, already dead. After October 15, 1944, the Fascist Arrow-Cross take over, labor service was extended to boys over sixteen years old and men until the age of sixty. My brother Ervin was also called up and sent to dig trenches in the Trans-Danubian region. He was not a strongly built seventeen-year-old, and—as we again learned only later—died within a few months near the western Hungarian city of Győr where he was buried in a mass grave.

In 1947, a memorial statue was erected in the Jewish cemetery of Győr, and my parents and I went there to see the graves. The victims were buried in four mass graves. All of a sudden the wind whipped the small black shawl from my mother's head and covered a part of one of the mass graves. "Here lays Ervin," said my mother, convinced.

In the summer of 1944 we were still quite hopeful. We always tried to listen to the BBC's radio broadcasts, which were heavily jammed, but sometimes came through with important information. When a quarter of a century later I met with Elmer Macartney in Oxford, and visited him at his home, I told him, how extraordinarily important his frequent BBC radio analyses about the war situation had been for us. He spoke Hungarian with a very thick accent and introduced himself as Professor Macartney Elemér, placing his Magyarized first name last, and last name first, according to Hungarian custom. We were able to follow the movements on the Eastern front, and feel some optimism after the devastating defeat of the Germans at Stalingrad in early 1943, and then at Kursk in the summer of that very same year. In the summer of 1944 we knew that the Soviet Army was nearing the Hungarian border. And at last we became euphoric when we learned about the Allied landings in France. It was clear that the war could not continue for long. Nevertheless, there was still far to go. That exact summer of 1944 and the developments that followed became the most devastating time for our family.

In the frightening war years my mother enrolled in a course and studied Indian astrology from a well-known expert. She calculated and made horoscopes for everybody in the family whose exact hour and minutes of birth were known. My brother's horoscope was not promising and signaled a very short life. My horoscope, on the other hand, gave her some reassurance since it showed professional success signaled by the triangle contact between the Sun and Jupiter. It also indicated two marriages in the seventh "house" of my horoscope. I never forgot that forecast in my life. When my first marriage went bad, this astrological prophecy forecasting my destiny became in some way self-fulfilling. It helped me to make a difficult decision.

After the German occupation of the country in the spring of 1944, Allied bombing began. We had to run to the house basement, which was set up as a shelter. In certain periods, the sirens screamed almost every evening, and we picked up our small prepared packages and ran down to the shelter. From summer on, heavy bombing did serious damage to the city. The bloc's civilian air-defense commander formed a youth brigade, which ran to help firefighters extinguish fires and search for wounded people under the rubble when the sirens signaled the end of the bombing. Once we were sent to the elegant part of the sixth district, where an orphanage was hit. There I saw the first dead man in my life when we dug out the body of a middle-aged man from under the wreckage. Once I was slightly wounded while we tried to extinguish the fire in an apartment building but had to leave running when it began to collapse. I proudly arrived home with a big bandage on my left hand.

Against all odds, however, my life still seemed easy. Following the segregation of the Jews into appointed "Jewish Buildings," we were forbidden to leave the house except for two hours in the morning, thus we lived a closed communal life in our apartment house. We played cards and the extremely popular new parlor game called "Capitaly" (a version of "Monopoly") through the long afternoons and evenings. With my friends we even performed shows in the shelter during air raids. Most memorably, I fell in love for the first time in my life at the age of thirteen, and enjoyed chatting in the fourth-floor corridor, where the ten-year-old but quite mature-for-her-age Vera lived.

But a new, radical change endangered our life even more than before.

On October 15, 1944, Regent Horthy proclaimed in a broadcast radio message that Hungary had made a separate armistice and finished fighting. Happy people swamped our street, but the euphoria was soon replaced by a frightening shock: Horthy was arrested and Hitler placed Ferenc Szálasi and his Hungarian National Socialist Party, or as it was nicknamed after its symbol, the Arrow Cross Party in power. Szálasi became *Nemzetvezető* (Führer), and his armed Fascist mob ruled the entire country. Although the Jews had already been deported to Auschwitz from the countryside, the Budapest Jews were still safe, except for the adult men who were already serving in labor battalions. Now the Budapest Jewry fell victim to a wave of uncontrolled, brutal terror. "Death Marches" were ordered and decimated the Jewish population of the city. Many were taken at random to the bank of the Danube and shot into the river. After the war I met a girl, Agnes Mandelovits, a year younger than I, who had been shot into the Danube. Although she dropped into the icy river, she had escaped and survived. She bore a healed gunshot wound on her shoulder as a mark of the experience.

Thousands were beaten and killed at the Arrow Cross headquarters at *60 Andrássy Boulevard*. Several Jews of a more venturesome spirit tried to escape by buying genuine or fake Gentile personal documents—the official Hungarian documents always contained the religion of the person—and went to the countryside with the false document as refugees from the Russian-occupied territories of the country. My aunt, Ili, wife of my Uncle Jenő did so with my cousin, Ági. Although they were lucky to survive, I was shocked to learn their story. Ági, three years old that time, had to learn her new name and a place they had lived before, if asked. It was not easy for her to tell a different name since she said her real names for more than a year and could not understand the situation. Any mistake, however, might prove fatal. My aunt trained her asking hundreds of times the same question in various situations, and if she mistakenly told her real name, she was slapped in the face. It remained a painful memory for her entire life. My first wife's stepmother also tried the same trick with her five year-old daughter. In a faraway village, however, somebody, visiting from Budapest, recognized and reported her to the authorities. They were killed. Thousands of personal tragedies increased the numbers of victims. All the remaining Budapest Jews, closed into a walled ghetto, starved and were decimated. Until the city was liberated by the Soviet Army, 98,000 Budapest Jews were killed.

I did not see any of that murderous terror. For early in the morning of October 31, Miki Tóth, the son of the concierge, one-year-older than

I and my friend and playmate for ten years, arrived at the building with a bunch of German soldiers. Miki had already joined the Hungarian Nazi Arrow Cross armed militia, and he arrived in his black uniform with its striped red and white Arrow Cross armband. We were forced down into the courtyard. Men over sixty who had not been doing labor service and the boys who were there, actually just the two of us, fourteen-year old Józsi and myself—since all the others, a couple of years older, were already away—were pushed to the top of a German truck. My mother and grandmother watched us in shock, and as I later learned, my mother had a nervous breakdown. We left.

The Germans also picked up others from other buildings in the neighborhood. The truck stopped in a neighboring street, in front of a building where one of my schoolmates lived on the second floor, but I did not have the courage to sneak out since my name was on a list in the Germans' hand. That was probably my last opportunity to avoid my destiny. I could have spent the day and the night in my friend's apartment and then walk home the next morning when we were allowed to go out into the street. I still feel some shame that I did not take my destiny into my hand and instead remained sheepishly on the truck. Much later, when I already had my first child, I deliberately tried to teach her not to follow every order. I taught her to run on the grass if a sign showed that it was forbidden.

Sitting on the back of the truck, we were taken to *Lepsény*, a small Trans-Danubian township near Lake Balaton, which I saw then for the first time. Accommodated in a barn, we were put to work the next morning in the depot, a six-storey building next to the railroad used by the German army as a storehouse. We had to unload long trains full of military winter clothing, boots, and warm blankets, carry the heavy bundles on our shoulders to the upper floors, and carry them down again the next day to reload into military trucks, which distributed the goods to the troops. Because of the unusually hard physical work in two days I was in pain, and could hardly move my body. Herr *Obersturmführer* Ludwig, the commander of the depot, a jovial elderly soldier, allowed me to rest in the barn for a day. Moreover, he asked me whether I was able to count in German and wanted to put me, the youngest and skinniest in the entire group, in the "administration." Unfortunately, I did not know German at that time, and had to return to carrying the heavy loads.

The End of Childhood

36 Akácfa utca in Budapest, where I lived in the first 30 years of my life.

At the end of November the Russian army, which had entered Hungary in September from two directions, the east and the south, neared *Lepsény*. We could hear the promising noise of the cannons. The *Wehrmacht* closed the depot and we were taken over by the infamous and brutal Hungarian gendarmerie. They escorted us to Veszprém, a hilly township in the middle of Trans-Danubia where I was imprisoned in a single cell in the county jail. It was a strange feeling: I was escorted by a guard down several floors, although we entered the building on the ground floor. I thought we were descending into a catacomb several stories deep, but this was not the case. There was a small barred window in the wall of the cell and when I looked out, I realized that I was several floors above ground. The prison was built on a hillside, with one floor on the entrance side, and several floors on the opposite.

Fortunately enough, the bishop of Veszprém, József Mindszenty, was imprisoned because of his conflicts with the Arrow Cross regime in the same building and on the same level with a few of his priests. Mindszenty later became the famous cardinal of Hungary, who was imprisoned in 1948, freed by the revolution of 1956, and played an important role in it. Their cell doors, unlike mine, were open, and they were allowed receive visitors every day, mostly nuns who brought food for them. In the evenings, they knocked on my cell door and through the small door-window gave me food. Here I lost my friend Józsi, his father, and all the others with whom I had been living and working for the Germans. I don't know how this separation happened. I never saw them again. A year later I learned that, except for me, none of those who were taken from 36 *Akácfa utca* survived this "excursion." Miki Tóth, the former friend who was responsible for their deaths, escaped to West Germany after the war, but his parents, equally active members of the Arrow Cross Party, were jailed. I later learned that Miki's sister married a member of the Stalinist secret police in the early 1950s and had a hard time during the 1956 revolution when secret policemen were hunted and often lynched. The story of the Tóth family was a characteristic episode during that period of Hungarian history.

The Russian troops soon closed in on Veszprém (which afterwards changed hands several times as Hitler sought to defend German territory on Hungarian soil). All the criminals were released from the prison, but Jews were handed over once again to the gendarmes and another march followed to *Komárom* nearer the western border. We spent a terrible night at the Arrow Cross headquarters. Some of us were taken to the basement. A strong light from a flashlight was directed in my face. I did not see anything, but heard the question: "why is your Star of David—the yellow star, every Jew had to wear—loose on your coat? Did you try to escape?" Before I could have answered the question, a strong blow hit my face and I fell. Several of us were badly beaten. One of the Fascist militiamen confiscated my good hiking boots (my mother insisted I take them), but I was fortunate enough to get a shabby pair of shoes instead.

It felt like salvation when the next morning we were escorted to the *Komárom Csillagerőd* prison, an old Austrian military building from the 1850s that was rearranged as an internment camp in 1944 and served as a transitional station for deportation to Germany. Political prisoners, mostly communists from the Budapest *Margit körút* prison, had been moved there from October, followed by arrested trade union leaders, miners, gypsies and

Jews who arrived in November and December. More than a hundred prisoners were jammed into a huge cell. Keeping ourselves clean was impossible and the straw, which served as bed, was full of bugs. In a few days I was both scabious and infected with lice. Somebody explained to me that washing the skin area with urine can get rid of the scabies. It worked. On December 11, 1944, I "celebrated" my fourteenth birthday in that environment. Lunch that day was beans, and I found a big piece of salt like stone in my portion. I put it into my pocket as a birthday present to keep for bad times.

A few days later the entire prison population was escorted to the railway station and jammed into cattle cars for our six-day trip to Dachau. The last transport, as I later learned, was sent to Germany on December 27. Most of those who were arrested later were killed at the bank of the Danube.

(Jorge Semprun wrote a fascinating novel about his six-day trip from the French resistance to a German concentration camp. In the mid-1980s this renowned Spanish writer, who became a politician in democratic post-Franco Spain, sat next to me in a private room of a restaurant after his official visit to the Hungarian Academy of Sciences. I turned to him and mentioned that his novel describing his six-day trip inspired me a few years before to write about my own trip. My experience and feelings were strikingly similar to his. Unfortunately, and what a disappointment, my short novel was too much like his novel, a kind of reworking of it. Semprun laughed and assured me that this was the best tribute to his novel.)

Dachau—and the Südosteuropa-Gesellschaft's Conference in Munich

When the Russian troops neared Komárom all the prisoners were taken to the railway station and pushed into cattle cars, seventy or eighty of us to a wagon. In one of the corners, a slop-pail for all of us. The doors were closed and our trip began. Everybody received a loaf of bread for the entire trip. In a wooden box there was a piece of hard marmalade for the entire group, to be cut and distributed by one of our "fellow travelers" who, on finishing, washed his sticky hands in his own urine above the slop-pail. We had no idea where we were going or how long we would travel. The winter of 1944–45 was one of the coldest in years and the cattle car was ice cold. The train progressed slowly toward its unknown final station. The first day we sang folksongs.

During one of the endless nights, three young men broke the floor of the freight-wagon, and one after the other jumped under the train between the rails. I was horrified, especially when a few seconds later we heard gunshots. The train stopped and soldiers ran in and hit those who were next to the hole with their rifle butts. "We killed all of them," they shouted menacingly. The door was closed again and we continued. An old man who had seen better days and had traveled in Europe, watched the stations we passed, and sometimes where we stopped in the middle of the night, from the small, barred window and quietly stated: "we are going to Munich." I can still hear his voice as he pronounced München, the German name of the city.

Dachau where I spent the terrible winter and spring of 1944–45. The photo was made by the Seventh American Army unit that liberated the camp in April 1945.

After a terrible six day trip we arrived. From the camp's railway station we were accompanied by SS soldiers to a building. We had to take off our clothes and wait naked in the cold December evening outside the building. After a while we had to go to a huge shower room where we got our prison clothes. Our heads were shaved and our underarms and genitalia were smeared with some corrosive chemical, against bugs. I received a number that became my name from that time on, and each day before dawn I had to shout *jawohl*, signaling my presence when it was called at the *Appell-platz* (the court yard of the roll-call).

We were ordered to keep our shoes, but mine had been stolen when I was in the shower. Our group marched on the central road of the camp, edged with old poplar trees, between the thirty barracks. I went along surrounded by people from the transport. I did not know anybody near me. I had been lost. Barefoot in the frozen evening among unknown people, I cried loudly without being able to stop. We were assigned to Block 23 where I shared a bunk on the first level of the three-level bunk structure with another prisoner, a relatively young Hungarian communist miner from *Tatabánya* whom I had never seen before. We were lying on the wooden bunk and two of us got a rug. He tried to calm me down and produced a jar of strawberry jam—I could not imagine how he smuggled it in—and ate the entire jar using two fingers as spoons. It tasted heavenly, though I had never liked strawberry jam before.

Later I shared a different bunk with an older man, Tibor Varga, a teacher from the West-Hungarian town of *Kapuvár*. He was a convinced communist and talked a lot about the unjust system of capitalism, which evidently led to Hitler. Most of the time, however, we switched the topic and talked about food. We were starving. Block 23 was a quarantine barrack and we were isolated because severe diseases, mostly typhoid fever and diarrhea, decimated the *Häftling* (prisoner) population. Since we did not work, we got hardly any food. In the very early morning we were awakened with the shouted order, *aufstehen, essen holen,* get up and take your food. In reality it was a piece of bread and some *ersatz* coffee in the morning, and some almost empty soup as the main dish at noon and evening, which left us always extremely hungry. In a few weeks we lost a lot of weight, and were soon reduced to skin and bone. During the long days, we talked about food. Even the memory of good eating caused some satisfaction.

The company of Tibor Varga was pleasant and he definitely wanted to politically educate me. He talked about politics, the war, and the Soviet Union as a savior. A few months later, however, I witnessed his terrible last days when he lost his mind, and it became frightening to stay next to him. I asked for permission to go to another bunk, but few days later he died.

In those months the camp became even more overcrowded. Dachau, established in March 1933, was built for 6 to 8,000 prisoners and that was the average *Häftling* population until the war. At the peak in 1944, however, the prisoner population reached 60,000. That was the reason that two and even three of us had to share the same bunk and also that diseases decimated us in those last months. During the last three months, according to records, 13,000 to 15,000 people died. When the camp was liberated, 32,500 prisoners were alive. Our evacuated transport of 4,000 was not counted.

When I was ordered to share a bunk with two Polish Jews they did not accept me because I did not speak Yiddish. They did not allow me to occupy the legitimate one-third of the bunk but forced me to stay at the lower end at their feet. I could not understand such behavior and learned to hate this tribal attitude.

In a few weeks more and more people died every day. Our barrack was decimated by dysentery and typhoid fever. In one morning I saw the dead body of György Goldman, the sculptor collapsed into the bare toilet, his mouth and eyes open. I did not know at the time that he was a very gifted sculptor, but saw some of his works much later. Goldman, with a few of his comrades, arrived from the Komárom prison in the same transport as I. Although quite a few years older than me, this group of young communists also talked to me occasionally. I learned about the Hungarian Communist Party, which was dissolved in the last period of the war and reestablished as Béke Párt (Party of Peace). I learned about the *Margit körút* prison where they spent some time after being arrested in Budapest. I heard about tortures and the use of electric shock to force prisoners to make confessions and name names.

Two comrades took me to the *Appell-platz* at 5:30 in the morning each day when I could not stand, hear, and burned with temperature from typhoid fever. I was very lucky to contract the disease soon after my arrival when my body was strong enough to cope with it. Those who helped me in those difficult days stood faceless before me. Without their help I could not have survived. I am very grateful to the middle-aged Austrian prisoner, the former *Stubeältester*, or room-commander that often gave me some remaining food from his own portion, and asked me once about my home city. When he heard "Budapest," he encouraged me: we will go home together, at least as far as Vienna, his home town. He was shot dead a few days before the liberation. I was mourning my deceased comrades who surrounded me.

Those comrades in distress who helped me, or at least cared, also remained with me. A Hungarian gendarme colonel surprisingly shared our fate. He certainly would not have talked to me at home, but tried educating me in the first days of our stay in Dachau. He tried to convince me not to retaliate after the war because it would cause social warfare. I well remember the metaphor he used: "don't forget, my son, if we survive and return home we may not throw the ball against the wall because it will bounce back." I remembered the French prisoner of war with whom I shared a bunk at one time. Although we could not and did not talk to each other or have any verbal communication, he involuntarily "helped" me. The western POWs—as I learned recently from a report written by Colonel William W. Quinn of the Seventh American Army, who liberated Dachau on April 29, 1944—were considered to be political prisoners and represented a relatively large group, nearly 4,000 French at the time of the liberation of the camp. They had a tremendous and strongly envied privilege—they received food-packages from the Red Cross. Food was the most valuable item for us. He never shared anything with me, but once I had the opportunity to steal a piece of marmalade from his well-guarded package. I know it was not a decent act, but even today, I do not regret it. I still feel the heavenly taste in my mouth.

When I recognized my stolen shoes on somebody's feet sometime in March, I asked for help from a young Yugoslav POW who helped me by mobilizing the prisoner-commander of the room and I got back my shoes at last, after several months spent barefoot. I have the fondest memory about my Yugoslav, mostly Serbian comrades in Dachau. (Colonel Quinn recorded 3,200 Yugoslavs in the camp.) They were the most helpful people and preserved humanity and solidarity with others, a rare asset in the inhuman circumstances. My later readings about Tito's partisan army, which, with terrible losses, survived eleven Nazi offensives between 1941 and 1945 and liberated their country, strengthened my sympathy. I definitely developed a better understanding of their difficulties, and still feel strong sympathy with them.

Once I asked a Russian POW to teach me Russian and he began to do so. Much later I realized that he taught me Ukrainian. (There were 4,258 Russians, or better to say Soviet citizens, because a great many among the liberated prisoners were Ukrainians.)

A young Hungarian officer assured me as the youngest among the hundreds of prisoners in our quarters, that he would adopt me after the war, if we survived. Some of these people have no face any longer in my memory, but they are still with me. The memories of these rare cases of solidarity in a period when virtually all of us lost decency and animal instincts dominated our behavior are very important for me.

Colonel William Quinn's report describes what he and the first liberating American troops saw: "Our troops found sights… horrible beyond belief, cruelties so enormous as to be incomprehensible to the normal mind. Dachau and death were synonymous. No words or pictures can carry the full impact of these unbelievable scenes… The most horrible sight at

Dachau is the corpses who are still actually alive." (Quinn, [1945] 2000, 5, 13–5, 48, 101–4)

Yes, Dachau has stayed with me for my entire life, fortunately not in the form of permanent health problems—although some joint problems in my knees emerged after my return and had to be cured in the later 1940s and from time to time resurfaced during the sixties and seventies, they have not bothered me permanently. Strangely enough, Dachau in my memory and as a built-in instinct is not a nightmare, an experience of horror in my life. It had, most surprisingly, a positive internalized impact. I feel much richer with this experience. I think I understand human character and the fragility of civilized behavior much better. I know that in hard situations humanity may evaporate and I learned the importance of solidarity. These lessons are deeply rooted in my mind. I learned to hate tribal exclusion. I learned to hate hatred.

The Dachau experience, paradoxically, made me optimistic because it generated a deep feeling that I could cope with deadly difficulties and challenges. It taught me to love and enjoy life, and this has become a kind of basic attitude and instinct, which do not leave me even in difficult situations. I do not like complaining and feel no reason to do so. It has made me a fatalist: I do not have to worry; a good outcome from the most difficult situation might already be on its way. All these are internalized feelings without thinking and speaking about Dachau.

These feelings became coded in my mind and helped me to cope with frightening situations, such as two major sport accidents I experienced in my thirties. Both from playing sports, and both were nearly fatal. In 1961, with a broken fifth vertebra, which might have paralyzed me from the neck down, I spent an entire summer in a cast from the top of my head down to my hips. On the very first evening I asked the doctors to remove the terrible cast because I could not sleep and it was difficult to move. Fortunately all of them refused and I soon found my peace. The only tolerable position was sitting at a desk and leaning a bit forward. I was not depressed, but looked for a positive outcome and spent most of the time writing my new book on postwar reconstruction, and memorizing an entire German dictionary.

In 1967 another sports accident led to an operation on my skull to remove a huge hematoma as big as a child's fist next to the brain. With a

In cast from head to hips for two-and-half months after a major sport accident in 1961

large bandage on my head, I asked the surgeon whether I would be able to travel to the Netherlands in a few weeks' time, and deliver a lecture at a conference. If you are sure they will not hit your head after your lecture, he jokingly answered, you may, and I went.

Following the harsh years of the closed society and hermetically closed borders of Stalinism, Hungary's borders were opened from the early 1960s on, and people were allowed to get a passport. For the first time in my life I could travel abroad freely. This was the best timing for me: I received an invitation from the Südosteuropa-Gesellschaft to participate at their conference in Munich, and so with two other colleagues I arrived at the Munich *Hauptbahnhof*. Hardly had I stepped onto the platform when I heard my name on the loudspeaker. People were waiting for us, and insisted on carrying my luggage to a car that drove us to an elegant hotel. A strange, triumphant feeling came over me. The elegant arrival, I felt, was a kind of rehabilitation.

The Munich I returned to was in much better shape than after the war, when I saw it in ruins. How strange that later it would become one of my favorite cities and I often visited it. Most important, the 1961 invitation made it possible for me to visit Dachau, virtually a suburb of Munich, where the concentration camp was located. I went out alone by tram on the first free half day of the conference. The camp had not changed at all. All thirty of the long barracks remained intact, and German refugees, probably those who were expelled from Poland or Czechoslovakia, were accommodated in them in transit. I went to both blocks, number 23 and 30, where I had stayed, and I could not stop crying. All my lost comrades were with me and I mourned them. My later visits to Dachau with my daughters and again with Kati, my wife, were not as shocking as that first one. All the blocks but one had been removed by that time. Only the stone building of the SS-guards, the crematorium, the watch towers, and the remnants of the barbed wire fences were parts of a memorial museum.

More than 40 years later I had a triumphant feeling again when I was awarded also in Munich the Konstantin Jirasek Gold Medal of the Südosteuropa-Gesellschaft for my research on the history of Southeast Europe. I did not go to see the camp again.

The Gebirgsjägerschule in Mittenwald

The Yugoslav prisoner of war who worked for a Bavarian farming family shook my shoulder. "Wake up and look outside!" I emerged from the warm straw and went to the small window of the barn. What a triumphant feeling! My endless nightmare had ended! An American soldier stood in the middle of the small square, a box of hand-grenades next to him. White flags were hanging all over the houses of the small Bavarian village. May 1, 1945. The war was over for me.

Soon all five of us, 14 to 15 year-old boys stood outside the barn: a strange group of young people with close-cropped heads, thin as corpses, dressed, at least partly, in Yugoslav military uniform pants or jackets. We had received the clothing the evening before from the Yugoslav prisoners of war when we came out of the forest where we had been hiding for the previous four days. Better to get rid of the prisoner uniform, one of them suggested. It was already a happy feeling to drop the Dachau concentration camp uniform and the burden of the frightening memory of the past half a year.

I did not fully understand what happened in Dachau's Block 30, where I had been only a few days before. We did not know anything about the outside world and the war situation. Strange things were happening to us. First, we heard rumors that the "Blockältester" and "Stubeältester"— the prisoner block- and cell commanders who were German and Austrian communists and long-time Dachau prisoners acceding to a kind of prisoners' command position—had been shot dead the previous day. Then hundreds of us, including me, were selected and put on a regular passenger train. I lay down in the corridor and fell asleep. When I woke up early next morning I realized that we had been transported from the camp to the nearby Alps. I was ordered with another prisoner to carry a dead body from the train when we arrived. Excrement dropped from the dead man on my pants. I looked around and realized that we had arrived nowhere. It was not another camp or a city, but the wilderness. We were surrounded by SS guards and escorted to a place bordered by a curve of the fast running Isar River. On the other side, there were guards with machine guns. We waited for hours in apathy. After a while, when darkness slowly descended, I lay down on the stony ground. Hungry, weak, and tired, I fell asleep. One of my friends wakened me: hurry, the guards have vanished and we should go and hide somewhere before they come back! After a few days of hiding in the forest, moving during the night, knocking on the doors of peasant houses and asking for a piece of bread and a glass of milk, which we would always receive, we arrived at last at the German village where we met the Yugoslavs who immediately offered their help.

Recently I learned from Colonel William W. Quinn's report what fate had been planned for us. On April 27, a couple of days before the liberation of the camp, orders came to evacuate the entire camp and kill us all in order to eliminate witnesses. However, only a single transport of 4,000 prisoners, our group, was evacuated in the direction of Tyrol. This "large transport of special prisoners" consisted of Russians, Poles, Germans, and Jews. I belonged to that group of "special prisoners." In the chaotic last days, the guards were unable to dispatch the other roughly 28,000 prisoners. Fortunately, our guards also decided to escape rather than execute the order (and us).

I also learned much later, reading the memoir of Marcel Reich-Ranicki, that the SS long had a similar practice to eliminate witnesses. When Soviet troops neared the Poniatowa labor camp in Poland, for example, the "SS units drove all the prisoners out of their huts to ditches dug near the camp. There they were mowed down by machine-guns. Altogether the SS murdered 15,000 prisoners at Poniatowa camp that day." (Reich-Ranicki, 2001, 220)

Thus, when I saw the first American soldier I realized that my Golgotha was over. An American jeep stopped in front of us and an officer, who easily

The Gebirgsjägerschule

The Gebirgsjägerschule, Mittanwald on a Nazi picture-postcard. The German barrack was rearranged as a recuperation camp for liberated Dachau prisoners by the American Army. I almost died in that building, but gradually recuperated during May and June of 1945.

understood who we were (close shaved and about seventy pounds of skin and bone), pointed toward a township within walking distance where the American army had arranged shelter for liberated prisoners in a German military school. The *Gebirgsjägerschule*, the mountain *Jäger* training barracks in Mittenwald, was indeed near and easy to find. We received civilian clothing, food, and a bed in one of the barrack's sleeping quarters. The enormous complex was still almost empty. A few of us went around and searched some well-furnished but empty apartments which seemed to have belonged to officers' families. We all began to collect useful things when an agitated middle-aged woman stormed into the apartment. *"Es ist meine Wohnung!"*—"this is my apartment!" she shouted and we left.

My euphoria was short-lived. In two days I was about to die. Unable to manage the food after the long months of starvation, my body could not cope with the sudden change, and an almost fatal diarrhea hit me. I lay in bed without the strength to sit up or even raise my head. How strange. During the previous months I never thought about dying, although death surrounded me in quarantine Block 23. Our regular duty in the morning, after the hours-long *"Appell"* standing in the *Appell-platz* in the ice-cold weather, was to carry the dead bodies from the block to the courtyard and pile them in layers. Four in one layer and then four more, stacked in the other direction. There, death was the natural environment but I never thought it might happen to me. Now, it seemed to approach, and I waited in deep resignation. Not so my friends, who mobilized the Americans, who arranged for me to be placed in caring hands and thus to be saved.

I am walking in the long corridor of the *Gebirgsjägerschule*. A German general, the commander of the military school accompanies me and politely asks whether I remember which room I slept in. I was not sure. The corridors and the rooms were very similar. Maybe this one? Who knows after more than fifty years? It is nevertheless a euphoric feeling. It is 1996, and next to me are my wife, Kati, and the Schönfelds, Renate and Roland, our wonderful German friends who arranged this visit. How strange and how very exceptional that we are walking here together. Kati was not yet alive when I was here before. Roland, only ten days my junior, was a member of the *Hitlerjugend* and then a child soldier in Hitler's army at that time. But the barrack is still a barrack, the same *Gebirgsjägerschule* as half a century before. Miraculous continuity and astounding changes.

A couple of years later, in 1998, as part of a tourist trip to the Austrian Tyrol, I went back again for a few hours with Kati just to walk in the streets and sit on the terrace of a coffee shop. We did not return to the *Gebirgsjägerschule*. Only then did I realize what a beautiful Alpine township Mittenwald was! The painted houses with murals were in excellent shape. Everything clean and rich. What a great, well organized and prosperous country. It is good to be here, still with that strange triumphant feeling in my soul.

Where is My Home?

After the period in the hell of prisons and the concentration camp, after the miraculous escape from certain early death, it took me four months to fully recover. From Mittenwald, we were soon sent over to another rehabilitation camp set up by the American army in Feldafing, next to the Starnberger See, a beautiful lake in the lower slopes of the German Alps. The summer arrived and I had no responsibility other than to recuperate. The free atmosphere strongly helped my return to normal life. I even learned to swim in the lake. I started smoking cigarettes as well. I am grateful, however, that the American military police stopped my smoking, the consequence of a funny incident. Next to our camp was an American military base. Trucks and jeeps were left unguarded and some of us regularly visited the military base to "collect" things from the vehicles. I returned once with several cartons of Camel cigarettes that I kept in my closet. One day the military police searched our rooms because somebody had taken guns from the jeeps. They found the Camels, confiscated them, and arrested me. That evening I was released, but I stopped smoking and never tried again. It was a pleasant and easy time.

But what next? Where to go? In the camp, the International Red Cross, and several other agencies opened small offices, invited us to discuss our plans and offered various possibilities to go to Sweden or other countries. A Zionist organization tried to attract people to Palestine. It was a dilemma that could have determined my entire life. At the time, however, I did not see it that way. I was only fourteen years old and did not consider the future consequences at all. I just waited. In such a situation inertia becomes decisive. I had no idea and was in no mood to choose. I read the long list of names on the wall which appeared from time to time telling about survivors in other recuperation camps, but I did not find the names of my parents and had no idea what became of them.

One afternoon in August, as I sat outside my living quarters, a young man approached me and asked whether I was from Budapest. I had never seen him before, and he had not seen me either. He had just arrived from Budapest where he looked for his sister Helen, who had come to the city from the countryside during the war years, and stayed with my family. He did not find his sister, but he met my father and mother and recognized me because of my similarity to my father. They were alive!

I immediately decided to return to Budapest. I talked to my few Hungarian friends, all teenagers liberated together, and suggested that we go home together, and all joined. We did the paperwork, received documents and food-stamps, and four of us took the train traveling through destroyed Germany. We did not have to pay for the trip, only show our documents. The trip from Munich to Budapest which takes only ten hours today lasted nearly a week. We had to stop several times and could not take the shortest way. We crossed borders, sometimes, as in the case from Vienna to Bratislava, on the top of the coal wagon behind the locomotive. At the main station in Bratislava, somebody hearing us speak Hungarian whispered that we should keep silent. We had seen a young man being beaten and carried away. Our new patron told us that he had spoken in Hungarian and was attacked by the mob.

On August 31, 1945, we arrived at Budapest's East Railway Station. We all went our separate ways, and I did not see any of my comrades for sixty years. But in 2004, when I was invited to deliver a lecture on Budapest television as a part of a popular lecture series, a man approached me after the lecture, and I immediately recognized him as János, one of the boys from our group. He has lived in Budapest during the entire postwar period but we never even ran into each other.

I took a tram and then walked the two blocks from the station to my home. I rang the bell, and my father opened the door. They had no news about me at all. My mother survived the Arrow Cross regime in a safe

Where is My Home?

Budapest in ruins when I returned from Dachau in August 1945.

haven, in a "protected house" in Budapest. Several protected houses, as they were called, were established by Swedish, Swiss and other initiatives. Although these houses were often raided by the Fascist mob, she was very lucky to stay there until the city was liberated. My father, whose labor battalion marched to Germany to the Mauthausen concentration camp, returned only a month earlier. My grandmother remained in our apartment when it became part of the ghetto and also survived. The family was all together—except for my brother. I learned that day about his death and the decimation of our relatives.

I had arrived home. But was it really my home? Hungary was no longer the same country for me as before. I remembered the faces I had eagerly scrutinized during our forced march through Trans-Danubia from one prison to the next, escorted by gendarmes, the yellow Star of David on my overcoat. I had thought of escape and looked for faces expressing some sympathy. I did not see a single one as we passed along the streets of small settlements.

I learned now that Józsi, my friend from *Akácfa utca,* never returned, and neither did his father or the elderly men with whom we were taken. Although from the 850,000 Jews in the territory of enlarged, 1941 Hungary, some 260,000 survived the Holocaust, and about half of them were citizens of Budapest, my friends, Robi and Gyuri died. "Fat" Miki survived but after the camp he spent some time in France before returning. Bandi, a next door neighbor, and Tomi left for Israel. On the other hand, some of my old neighborhood friends such as Miki Tóth and Lajos Bíró—the last named lived in the opposite house, but were part of our "gang" had joined the armed Arrow-Cross militia and were now war criminals. Innocence was lost, my friends had disappeared, and my social environment drastically changed.

After my arrival I had to go to an office to report my return. According to a government measure, everybody who returned received 1,500 pengő in aid. It was a huge amount of money before the war, but now, in the middle of runaway inflation, it was just enough to go to a pastry shop and buy two small cakes. It was humiliating, and I decided that I would never accept anything from anyone in "compensation." I kept this pledge and did not apply when the German government later decided to pay more significant compensation.

But what should I do? Go back to school? That seemed obvious, but I had no appetite for it. In the end, however, I did return to school, passed the exams for the fourth grade I missed, and entered the fifth grade of my old "gymnasium," as high schools are called in Hungary after the German model. I was depressed, not enthusiastic at all, and it was only later that I realized that it was an excellent old-new environment with a very good group of students and some superb teachers.

At the moment sports offered an immediate escape from my deep apathy. I played tennis, soccer, and became a pillar of our school handball and basketball teams. At the age of 16, I joined the Fencing and Athletic Club, and started playing in the second league of the Hungarian National Basketball Federation. Next year I joined the bench of the Club's first league team. It was time consuming but a relief: we had training or games virtually every day, sometimes even on Sundays and in the countryside. The movie theaters played American movies and classic Soviet films which had not been accessible before. The world of theater, concert and opera opened for me. Tickets were cheap and I enjoyed a cultural delicatessen.

One day the students of all Budapest schools were ordered in shifts to the city's largest movie theater to watch a documentary on Nazism. To my shock, an ovation erupted when Hitler appeared on the screen. After all that happened, it was frustrating and deeply disappointing to meet with the remnants of the Fascist past. I tried to find my identity and a friendly community. In the nearby *Síp street* Hanoar ha Zioni, a Zionist youth organization established its headquarters. I went there to look around and found friends. I also met a girl, Rózsa, who later became my wife. It was a pleasant environment and a new experience. I learned about the struggle to establish the Jewish state and retrain the Diaspora Jewry to cultivate land. However, I soon realized that I did not want to leave Hungary. I became much more interested what was happening here and after a few months I left the organization.

The political atmosphere in the city was tense. The first free elections in November 1945 led to the absolute victory of the Smallholders Party, with 57 percent of the vote, attracting, besides the landed peasantry, all the various anti-communist and anti-socialist elements of the population. It became a reservoir of almost the entire right wing from the Horthy regime. A harsh political struggle ensued, and a left bloc was established by the communists, social democrats, and a small left-wing peasant party. The country was sharply polarized. Many, especially young people and the victims of Nazism, were worried about anti-communism which they saw as a trend leading to pro-fascism.

During that period István Bibó, an outstanding scholar and political thinker, published enlightening political essays. Bibó was an extremely smart democrat, a rare political animal in the polarized Hungarian society. Because of his role in the 1956 revolution his destiny was to be tragic. He spent years in prison and then was marginalized by the Kádár regime and worked as a librarian. Once he wittily remarked that after his death he wants the epitaph "Here lies István Bibó, lived from 1945 to 1948" on his grave, signaling that those years were the ones he really was alive. In the 1980s, after his death, his political genius was recognized and celebrated by the dissidents.

In one of his essays Bibó concluded that in postwar Hungary the political Right amalgamated three main political emotions, anti-Semitism, anti-communism, and anti-poor peasantry, i.e., the reconstruction of the "úri Magyarország," an almost untranslatable term for a Hungary ruled by the same conservative-Christian-noble-middle class elite that dominated it in the interwar decades. "Therefore it is hopeless to think about anti-communist democracy without anti-Semitism, and national policy without the restoration of the socio-political establishment of the Horthy regime." (Bibó, [1945] 1986, 34) Influential Italian and French intellectuals, I later learned, expressed similar feelings about anti-communism at that time.

The air was filled with hatred. I must also quote Bibó, as the best analyst of those years. In an essay in 1948 on *The Deformed Hungarian Character and the Dead End Street of Hungarian History,* he sharply attacked the dominant national ideology. According to the leading conservative ideologues, writers, and historians of the times, the reasons for the failure and tragedy of the country in the last century was the result of the "deformation of the Hungarian character." It was considered to be partly a consequence of long foreign occupation, especially the four-hundred-years spent under Habsburg rule, and partly the result of the assimilation and "foreign influence" of alien minorities, Germans and Jews, which had transformed the society. (Bibó, [1948] 1986, 572–5)

In several Central and East European countries during the nineteenth and twentieth centuries, national ideology expressed in literature, poetry, and historical studies generally blamed outside forces and factors for their failures. In Hungary, the hundred and fifty years of Ottoman occupation of the middle of the country and four hundred years of Habsburg rule. In the Balkan countries, explaining backwardness, social problems and negative values one often heard: *Petstotin godini pod tursko igo,* five hundred years under Turkish yoke.

Bibó sharply challenged this ideology and looked at internal social and political deformations. His views were not popular, and the blame for the country's tragedy in its alliance with Hitler was shifted partly onto the country's German minority. Czechoslovakia and Poland were flooded with violent hatred against their significant German minorities, and expelled millions after the war. Between 100,000 and 200,000 Germans were expelled from Hungary as well, even though most of those families had lived in Hungary for two or three hundred years. (Sixty years later in Los Angeles, after his lecture and before a pleasant dinner, I asked Joschka Fisher, the former vice-chancellor and minister of foreign affairs of the Federal Republic of Germany, about his family story. He was born in 1948 in Germany. But his ethnic German parents who, like several generations before them, had been butchers in Hungary, were among the deportees. He told me that though his parents established a butcher shop in their new German homeland, they never ever fit in and always felt like outsiders.)

I also felt like an outsider in my own country after my return. Hatred was specifically targeted against Jewish survivors of the Holocaust. We often heard that "more returned than were here before!" In two countryside cities, Miskolc and Kúnmadaras, spontaneous anti-Jewish pogroms erupted in 1946, the same year that a similar pogrom occurred in Kielce, Poland. The populist right-wing was warning of the danger of Jewish revenge. In the most bizarre way, the influential populist writer and political thinker, László Németh, had forecast that idea already in 1943, a year before the Hungarian Jewish Holocaust, in a famous speech, stating that he had to be deaf who did not hear that "Shylock already sharpens the knife." (Németh, 1943) After the war this idea gained ground in populist circles. The Nazi concept of *Judeo-Bolshevism* that equalized communism with the Jewry was widespread. Communism was actually considered a Jewish response, and they proved their view by naming the members of the leading *quadriga* of the Communist Party, Mátyás Rákosi, Ernő Gerő, Mihály Farkas, and József Révai, all Jews. (A few decades later, as a clear sign of the small-country syndrome, the grandson of László Németh became one of my most talented and favorite students at the University in Budapest. I mourned him when he committed suicide and died in the mid-1980s.)

Major trials and hangings were also part of life and the daily news in those years. Leading fascists such as Ferenc Szálasi, László Endre and László Baki, and prime ministers of war governments such as Béla Imrédy, László Bárdossy, politically responsible for the alliance with Hitler, the war and the death of nearly one million citizens, altogether roughly three hundred war criminals were tried and executed.

Demonstrations followed one after another. Hyperinflation left the currency valueless. In the spring of 1946, the prices increased by 12 percent per hour. In the summer of 1946, 47,000,000,000,000,000,000,000,000,000,000 paper pengő was equal to one prewar gold pengő, the Hungarian currency unit. This is not a misprint; this astronomical number with thirty zeros expresses the scale of inflation exactly. Nobody accepted money any longer. The country was in ruins. More than a quarter of the houses of Budapest had been destroyed or heavily damaged. My mother exchanged pieces of clothing for flour and vegetable oil.

If we continue living here, we must create a new country! The communists used the strongest rhetoric to eliminate, to "sweep away" the hated past, and in my impression offered the strongest safeguard against Fascism. They promised a comprehensive solution to social, economic and political ills. After such a horrific past I developed a strong social sensitivity and a longing for social justice. It was a defining period of my life, in spite of my youth. Hungary's past was loaded with exclusions and discrimination and I felt sympathy for all those excluded and victimized in any way. Like most of the less developed peripheral countries of Europe, Hungary had the sharp polarization of a nineteenth-century class society. The majority of the population, the peasantry, was excluded from society. About 60 percent of them were landless or owned only a tiny parcel of one to three hectares, not enough to make a living. Urban poverty was also very visible and deep.

I understood that well, and during the postwar years I began reading the excellent sociographic writings published by peasant-intellectuals, the *népies* (populist) writers of interwar Hungary. Gyula Illyés' *Puszták népe* (People of the Puszta) from the early 1930s was an indictment of the country of big estates, landlessness, and the humiliations of the people of the countryside. Illyés described a few minor but shocking cases such as the young landlord who in his presence stubbed out his cigarette on the nape of his coachman's neck as if he were an object and not a human being. The writer conducted interviews and visited a family of manorial workers. When he entered the house the young peasant woman who was at home alone began to undress as she used to doing when one of the "masters" appeared to ask for favors. She had assumed from his urban clothing that he was one of them.

My own position as a member of a minority oppressed and discriminated in the previous years, generated natural feelings of solidarity in me. These were reinforced during my university years when I made friends with several classmates coming from those strata of society. Based on those experiences I welcomed the promised social changes.

When I returned to Hungary, a radical land reform, initiated by the communists and realized by the communist agricultural minister of the transitory coalition government, Imre Nagy, (later the hero of the 1956 revolution) destroyed the dominant big estate and parceled out the land for the peasants. De-Nazification proceedings led to the trial and imprisonment of

27,000 war criminals and a purge removing 75,000 government employees who enthusiastically or only too sheepishly served the Fascist regime. Tens of thousands of citizens of German origin, officially those who joined Hitler's *Volksbund* organization, were expelled from the country. Unfortunately the entire process was tainted by personal vengeance and closing old family feuds. Nationalization of mines, banks, and major companies followed, at first in a gradual manner after 1945. Then in the spring of 1948 all firms that employed more than 100 workers were nationalized in a single move. In 1949, a second wave nationalized small businesses employing more than 10 employees. Between 1948 and 1951, about another 300,000 private businesses, mostly shops were strangled and closed.

Nationalization after the war, although far less radical than in Hungary, was not an East European phenomenon. It was widespread throughout Europe, equally characterizing the policy of the Labor government in Britain and de Gaulle's France. In postwar Germany half of the economy was in government hands, and neighboring Austria nationalized the bulk of its industry. At that time in my life I could not evaluate this trend from an economic point of view. Nationalization looked to me like social justice. One must not forget that this program has characterized utopian dreaming throughout the entire history of mankind: Plato and Thomas More, Rousseau and Marx all shared the idea that private property is the origin of all kinds of sins. Plato's "Republic" and More's "Utopia" describe strongly egalitarian societies, without private property. On More's island, each community builds hospitals and other welfare institutions. The program of the communists was no different. Education and health care soon became free and I was able to enroll at the University without paying a cent. Otherwise it would not have been possible. In 1949 I had a minor operation and we did not have to pay for that either.

Above all the communists were strongly anti-nationalist. I had learned to hate all kinds of nationalism bitterly. Internationalism offered a world for me without discrimination and hatred. The communists who shared my fate in Dachau had made a good impression on me, and I also felt admiration for the Soviet Union as its army marched from Moscow to Berlin defeating the bitterest German resistance. Soviet soldiers spent more than four years in the front lines and they had lost, as we learned by then, some 20 million people. They had carried the heaviest burden of the anti-Hitler war. Now, since the

Soviet archives opened, we have figures on the Soviet death-toll far exceeding even than that number. The British historian Hugh Seton Watson noted about those years in his 1952 book on Eastern Europe that the Soviet Union enjoyed the highest prestige throughout Europe at that time.

Altogether, postwar Hungary promised me a historical renewal and strong safeguards against the revival of Fascism and the restoration of the past. It offered a correction of the aberrations of prewar capitalism as we knew it. How very interesting that in 1993, after the collapse of communism, Pope John Paul II, the socially sensitive Polish Pope, in a statement for the Italian newspaper, *La Stampa,* expressed a somewhat similar view to what my father and I felt that time. The Pope declared: "Several severe social and human problems of Europe and the world are rooted in the aberrations of capitalism. Communism was a response to irresponsible capitalism." (La Stampa, 1993, November 2) Like many intellectuals and young people in Hungary as well as in Italy, France, Czechoslovakia, and other countries, my father enthusiastically joined the Communist Party in 1945. Soon after, at the age of sixteen, I followed in his footsteps.

Having written that, I must note that Joe, my son-in-law called my attention to the memoirs of Marcel Reich-Ranicki. During the Hitler era he was deported from Berlin to the Warsaw ghetto, was liberated in Poland at the end of the war, and remained there. Later he moved back to Germany and became literary reviewer of the major German paper *Die Zeit*. He described his motivation to join the Communist Party in 1945 excellently. Let me quote:

> I joined the Communist Party of Poland. No one forced me to do so, no one even suggested it to me… Now, shortly after 1945, [the communists] were exceedingly attractive, indeed, they had something captivating to offer me, as they had to many intellectuals, not only in Poland, but also in France, Italy and other West European countries…I was fascinated by the chance of participating in a worldwide, universal movement, a movement of which countless people expected the solution of the great problems of mankind. I believed that I had at last found what I had long needed: a refuge… There was, so it seemed to me, the only one way to accomplish the long overdue rearrangement of society… That was especially true for Poland. (Reich-Ranicki, 2001, 228)

My feelings for Hungary were more than similar.

We remained blind to several disturbing developments. We did not watch closely, for example, nor did we notice or care in the intense political competition that former ordinary Arrow Cross members were also recruited by the communists, including workers who had joined the Hungarian National Socialist Party, which emerged as the strongest political party in Hungary in the 1939 elections. The communists welcomed them to increase their power base. We took at face value that an "anti-Republic conspiracy" in early 1947 with the participation of leading Smallholders Party politicians wanted to turn back the wheel of history, as the official reports stated, and did not realize that their trial was the opening of lawlessness and despotism. We did not know about the Stalinist purges in the 1930s, or those after the war. It was too early to separate empty promises from real actions. I too took the promise of building a new Hungary at face value.

The atmosphere of our family changed after the war and the death visited on us. Both my parents threw themselves into politics. My father spoke two or three times a week at political gatherings. Our Jewish religious routine was abandoned. In my early childhood, without being deeply religious we celebrated the Jewish holy days and went to synagogue on those occasions. My brother already declared himself an atheist during the war years. Now, after the death of my brother, my father also denied the existence of God. My grandmother, alone in the family, quietly continued to light the candles for herself on Friday evenings. Religion disappeared from our life.

The war and Auschwitz had a polarizing impact on the Jewry in Hungary. Some became Zionists and left for Palestine. More departed to the West and became professionals or went into business. Some of these became even more Zionist in America than the ones who settled in Israel. Between 1945 and 1948 about 160,000 of the 260,000 Holocaust survivors left Hungary. In Poland and Romania there was a similar trend.

The bulk of those who remained wanted to forget about being Jewish. Communism became a crucial vehicle for traveling to this non-religious world, which declared itself internationalist and anti-nationalist. It offered a road towards integration into a society that no longer recorded ethnicity and religion in Hungary. Knowingly or not, many Jews who joined the Communist Party were motivated for this reason. I knew several families who after the war never told their children that they were Jewish. I even witnessed certain painful conflicts in some of my friends' families when children came home from school and made anti-Semitic remarks they learned from schoolmates, or accidentally discovered their background from old documents hidden in drawers. Although I never lied about it, Jewishness, except those few months after the war when I joined a Zionist organization, became a non-issue for me. I rarely talked about my war experiences. In other words, I belonged to those who wanted to forget. It was buried in me, nevertheless, not at all forgotten. There was a kind of blocking psychological barrier, rather typical at that time.

Recently I have thought about that psychological barrier. I tried to understand why for an entire decade I never mentioned my Dachau story to my good German friend, Roland Schönfeld, although we met in Munich several times. When at last I talked about it, just the two of us sitting in the Hofbräuhaus, the famous Munich beer-house that always reminded me of Hitler an the Nazis, whose preferred meeting places were these kind of beer houses, he was shocked. True, he never told me his story of having been a child-soldier in the last months of the war either. Strangely enough, both of us had some common feeling about that period and history. In my case, it is bizarre to feel some kind of shame.

My inner and not thoroughly clarified feelings became more understandable for me in connection with the international scandal generated by the memoirs of Günther Grass, the outstanding German writer whose works and moral standing I love and admire, when he, at almost 80, confessed for the first time that he had been recruited into the *Waffen SS* at the age of 17. As he explained, "What I had accepted with the stupid pride of youth I wanted to conceal after the war out of a recurrent sense of shame. But the burden remained, and no one could alleviate it." (Grass, 2007, 110–1) From the very beginning, I understood him and did not change my view of him and my admiration. Of course, my story was rather different, but my feeling not much at all. Heinous humiliation and compliance with evil have left behind the feeling of shame. Only recently did I realize that I was not alone with this feeling. A Hungarian Jewish writer, Ivan Nagel, who was hiding in Hungary to escape while Grass was in SS uniform, noted:

> I myself had no reason to feel shame—after all, I was one of the persecuted –nevertheless for 55 years I could not speak about it. I understand

Günther Grass, who is able to talk about his shame, his disgrace only now. Life is not… [a] finished manuscript that you can publish at any time. (New York Times, 2007, July 8)

Interestingly enough, in my case it changed, my psychological blockage was nearly eliminated during my Ford Fellowship year in New York in the mid-1960s. The city's multi-cultural atmosphere and its Jewish districts in lower Manhattan and Brooklyn where people were proud to belong to their community eliminated that built-in hurdle. Talking with a new Yugoslav friend, another Ford grantee, as we began talking about ourselves by way of introduction I "naturally" mentioned my Jewish background. This was repeated many years later when I became friends with Kati, who was to be my second wife.

Since the new regime offered healing we were happy to believe that its new world would eliminate painful social problems and open a new chapter in our lives. Very soon, however, we hit the hard wall of reality. In those years, everything was subordinated to war preparations. In the spring of 1948, the Berlin crisis raised the specter of World War III. The Soviet Union, in retaliation for the West German currency reform, closed the road from the Western occupation zones to West Berlin. Berlin was located in the Soviet occupation zone, but itself was divided into Western and Soviet occupation zones and according to the agreement, the two million inhabitants of West Berlin were supplied from the Western occupational zone by train and by truck. This became impossible after the Soviet blockade and the American army responded by airlifting fuel, food and everything else to Berlin. The American airlift was fraught with the danger of escalation which even an accidental military incident might trigger. Three years after the end of history's most devastating war, we were frightened by the possibility of a new one. It was unbelievable, and retrospectively practically impossible, but we were unable to exclude the reality of the danger, and lived in the shadow of horror that a new war might erupt. Although, this was avoided in Europe, we suffered from excessive military preparation which absorbed most of the feeble resources of the country.

The Stalinist early 1950s reintroduced fear and hatred, but besides its general ugly features and numberless uprooted victims, the dictatorship also hit our family hard. My enthusiastic father, who did not stop delivering lectures and providing other services for the cause, had been appointed director of a small nationalized paper factory in 1948, a major task since the factory was severely damaged in an air raid in 1944. Although he did an excellent job of rebuilding and increasing output, one day in 1952, without any explanation, he was dismissed and was unable to get another job for a year. He sought justice but nobody listened to his complaints. He had no income, and had to sell the old piano, the only asset we had. Fortunately, during my second year at the University I was employed as Department librarian, and earned some money, and mother took an evening job at a theater as dresser. My father in his early fifties had to sit at home hopelessly. Although he learned some new skills, including accounting, and began to work again, the injustice and humiliation of this experience soon undermined his health leading serious circulation problems, diabetes, and eventually the amputation of one of his legs.

Like the bulk of the population, we lived in poverty. There were shortages of everything, which led in 1951 to the reintroduction of wartime rationing of basic food items. Meat disappeared from shops and in the University's cafeteria we ate turnips for cattle. After the war, I inherited my father's leather coat, a terribly shabby old piece what he wore during the 1930s, and then in labor battalion service, moreover, he used as coat and blanket in the Mauthausen concentration camp. Later, as a great advancement, I bought a green loden coat, but because of total lack of choice, almost every man on the street had the same type of coat from the same material, cut and even color, as if we were in uniform.

In that situation everything, even small and insignificant goods gained high value. Let me illustrate that with two memorable episodes. A friend of mine told me a story about an overcoat he was able to buy during a postwar visit to Sweden. It was winter, and in his beautiful, newly bought coat, he went to an appointment at the Swedish Academy of Science. He entered to the building from the street to a foyer. The door was not locked, and the waiting room was unguarded, but he was asked to hang his coat on a hook on the wall and go to another room with his host. With his East European reflexes he was unable to leave his valuable coat unguarded in an unlocked, empty room so he declared that he was cold and preferred to keep his coat on. The room was well heated, and after a while the host suggested that he remove his coat, but he insisted on keeping it on. The Swedish host unsuspectingly noted: "how interesting. I had a Polish visitor yesterday, and he was also so sensitive to cold that kept his overcoat on."

In the mid-1980s one of my good Hungarian colleagues asked me: 'when you stay at a hotel abroad, do you collect the soap, shampoo and ballpoint pens before you leave the hotel as I do? It is a shame and I do not need them at all, but cannot get rid of that habit I developed during my first visits in the West.' I had exactly the same experience and feeling. I remember how glad I was when sitting at the breakfast table at a fine hotel with West German friends in Munich and after having finished eating, the wife of my friend collected the untouched small jars of strawberry and apricot jams and put them into her purse. This habit is probably more human and widespread than I thought.

We were very poor and had no savings. To illustrate the situation let me mention that after the defeat of the 1956 revolution and the crippling strikes that followed for months afterwards, a panic of a new inflation pushed people to spend their saved money. We also decided to spend what we had, but all we could buy on that money was two shirts.

In that poor environment one of the most intolerable institutions introduced was the co-tenancy in the cities: the city council placed a second family into larger apartments, and the families had to share apartments with strangers. Since our apartment had three rooms, and after my grandmother's death there were just the three of us, we were in imminent danger of having another family moved into one of our rooms. This did not happen because of my marriage in January 1953: to have or to rent an apartment was out of the question, so we moved into one of the rooms in my parents' apartment, to remain there for eight years without hope of having a place of our own.

After the worst years, however, we regained hope: on June 28, 1953, the Central Committee of the Communist Party made a resolution condemning the serious "mistakes" of the previous period and even named the top party leaders who were responsible. As a result Mátyás Rákosi, who was both party chief and prime minister of the government, resigned at least his government position, which was taken over by Imre Nagy. We learned about four decades later when the secret documents were published that the top Hungarian leadership was ordered to go to Moscow, met the Soviet Politburo and was ordered to make these changes.

The program of the new government revitalized us. I hoped and believed that our life would radically improve. All of this happened exactly in the same summer when I was appointed assistant professor at the Department of Economic History of what had already been renamed Karl Marx University of Economics. In the coming years we gradually learned about the terrible crimes that had been committed and experienced the first promising steps of the Nagy government to correct the policy. The disastrous collectivization policy was halted and the peasants were allowed to leave the forcefully created collective farms. The industrialization policy that served war preparation was condemned and somewhat changed. Consumer goods appeared in shops. The hostile political rhetoric and the permanent search for "enemies" were muted and hope returned. We felt that making a new start was possible.

At the Department of Economic History where I had begun teaching we organized a session on the deformation of historiography in Stalinist Hungary. I addressed the modern period, as associate professor Pál Sándor on the historiography of earlier centuries. Together we published a study on this topic, my first printed publication, in the summer 1953 issue of *Századok*, the journal of the Hungarian Historical Association.

Nevertheless, in March 1955 the brief honeymoon of improvements and revival ended. Infighting led to the victory of Rákosi and the removal of Imre Nagy from power. That negative change was again directed by Moscow. Malenkov, the mentor of Nagy, was removed, and Khrushchev struck a tactical alliance with the hard-line old guard led by Molotov. Now we know the protocol of that 1955 meeting in Moscow of the Hungarian and Soviet leaders and the changed position of the Soviet Politburo, which again sided with Rákosi and harshly criticized Nagy. A large portion of the former true believers, young extreme left-wing communists, intellectuals, and writers who wanted to change the world after the war grew alienated from the regime and rejected the return to Stalinism. Some former Stalinists, deeply chastened, became the strongest opponents of Stalinism and the reemergence of Rákosi. Three extremely troubled years followed, which led to the revolution of 1956.

The 1956 Revolution in My Life

During the two decades in my formative years, from the late 1930s to the late 1950s, I witnessed four regime changes in Hungary. This experience in itself was a major history lesson for me. The conservative-authoritarian Horthy regime, a close ally of Hitler up to then, was replaced on October 15, 1944, by the murderous Arrow Cross Hungarian Nazi regime of Ferenc Szálasi. After the liberation of the country a transitory quasi-democratic, multi-party system emerged, with two multi-party parliamentary elections in 1945 and 1947. Although the Communist Party gained only 17 and 22 percent of the votes respectively, its role, relying on the presence of the Soviet army and the Soviet-led Allied Control Commission, headed for a while by Marshal Voroshilov, the right-hand man of Stalin, was much stronger.

Between the summer of 1947 and the summer of 1948, when the emerging cold war became manifest, Mátyás Rákosi, who followed the orders of Stalin, established a strict Stalinist regime and hermetically closed the country with mine fields, barbed wire fences, watch towers, and a border guard ready to kill. The countryside was flooded by the terror of collectivization, and we were taught "not to eat the chicken but wait for the golden egg of a coming faultless and prosperous future."

We were totally cut off from the West. Publication of Western books, a strong tradition in Hungarian cultural life, ceased. In 1949 altogether three foreign books were published in the country: the selected works of Lenin, Stalin's book on Leninism, and a volume of Pushkin's poems. Modern art was absent from art exhibitions. From 1951, the time of the second National Art Exhibition on, only "socialist realist" propaganda works were allowed to be exhibited. Real human behavior, including kissing disappeared from Hungarian films until its revival in 1953. Terror flooded the country, the economy was destroyed and cultural life was deserted.

After the death of Stalin in March 1953, and during the "thaw" that followed, the regime lost its strength and most of its previously enthusiastic young intellectual believers, including myself. On this ground a growing dissatisfaction led to the 1956 revolution. It was a full-scale, classic revolution combined with a fight for independence against the Soviet army, a revolution that became a central experience in my life. Learning the truth about the faked show trials, ruthless killings and lies was shocking. The show trials, nevertheless, were only the top of the iceberg of terror: we learned that in a country of 10 million inhabitants, 1.5 million people were arrested, half a million tried and imprisoned, and 40,000 were interned by the police without any court procedure.

The unveiled facts about the disastrous economic policies and war preparations made clear that the severe shortages, lack of meat, fruit, vegetable, clothing, and housing—I did not have an apartment until the age of 30, when I was already married and had my first child—was not an unavoidable destiny but man-made and a consequence of criminal acts. Stalinism degraded our life to near-poverty level. It was symptomatic that I did not see banana, orange, lemon and real chocolate from my childhood until the childhood of my children. The best years of my life were tarnished.

I participated enthusiastically in the politically overheated, agitated sessions of the *Petőfi Circle*, a newly established popular forum of anti-Stalinism, which organized sessions on such central questions as agricultural policy in the fifties, history writing, the situation of literature and journalism under Stalinism. Most of them were held at my university in the largest auditoriums. Former leading true believers such as writers Gyula Háy and Tibor Déry, Géza Losonczy, a former top party intellectual and journalist, Zoltán Vas, imprisoned for 16 years along with Rákosi in the Horthy era and top economic planner of the Party after the war, and several former young disappointed Stalinists turned into the most passionate and convincing critics of the system. We learned more and more about the total deformation of the regime.

Imre Nagy's government between 1953 and 1955 and his struggle against the Stalinist Rákosi leadership offered promise and hope for the entire population, and very personal hope for me: Imre Nagy was one of my professors and later my colleague at the University of Economics. He personally saved my job when a layoff eliminated four assistant professorial positions at our Department of Economic History of altogether six positions. In March 1955, however, when Rákosi again became triumphant Nagy was removed and expelled from the Party. It was a new shock.

In this situation, ripe for upheaval, the reestablishment of Stalinism was impossible in Hungary. In early 1956, we learned of the secret session of the Twentieth Party Congress in Moscow where Nikita Khrushchev unmasked the crimes of Stalin. With tens of thousands of people I attended the reburial of László Rajk, the victim of the first full-scale and widest publicized, Hungarian show-trial in Budapest in 1949. It was a dramatic event, although the situation was confusing: in the postwar years, before his trial and execution, Rajk was the powerful and ruthless strongman of the Party, Minister of Interior and Police and second in command. The absurdity of the moment was best expressed when Professor Sándor Szalai, an old Social Democrat and the founder of Hungarian sociology, who also participated at the reburial shouted to one of his friends above our heads: "If poor Laci (Rajk) was alive, he would order to shoot into this crowd!"

Stories of Rákosi's orders to torture and kill people became known: among others, the Szűcs brothers' horror story. One of them, a high official of the secret police, was put in boiling oil. In the summer and early fall of 1956, the news of the Poznań workers' uprising and the revolt of the party intelligentsia in Poland mobilized the reformist party intelligentsia and youth in Hungary too. The rehabilitation of Władislaw Gomulka, the former Secretary General of the Communist Party and formerly a victim of Stalinism because of his support for an independent (non-Soviet) "Polish road to Socialism," served as a model for Hungarian anti-Stalinist reform communists, who sought major changes under the leadership of Imre Nagy.

In mid-October 1956, all Budapest universities burned in high political fever and held round-the-clock meetings. Demands for change were in the air. The *Petőfi Circle* began organizing a major public demonstration, the first one in a decade in Hungary. On October 22 students and faculty attended the continuous meetings at the University separately discussing the demonstration planned for next day and a declaration of demands. The Polytechnic University circulated the resolution of the student body, which became the basis for the debate. The most important points of the demands were as follows: formation of a new Hungarian government under the leadership of Imre Nagy; the immediate withdrawal of the Soviet troops from Hungary; free multi-party elections; worker autonomy in factories; freedom of the press; revision of all the previous trials and amnesty for political prisoners; and replacement of the Soviet-type coat-of-arms with the 1848 Hungarian emblem.

The presiding rector (chancellor) of the university, Béla Fogarasi, left the faculty meeting in protest against the "extreme demands." Several of us advocated joining the students, and I was selected by the faculty to present this decision to the students' meeting. I announced it to an auditorium packed with students: "We are going with you!" On the morning of the revolution the leading daily, *Szabad Nép* published a report on the university meetings. "The student meeting began in the early afternoon at the University of Economics," reported the daily "Meetings with such a burning and enthusiastic atmosphere have not been held here in recent years... Ivan Berend, on behalf of the faculty, spoke about the need for personal changes, the need for the dismissal of those who are blocking the road to renewal." (*Szabad Nép*, 1956, October 23)

On that historic day my name appeared in a newspaper for the first time. However, even that brief news report reflected that I misunderstood the character of the "deformation" of the regime by thinking that the terrible crimes were the consequence of a felonious leadership, the Rákosi Gang. I did not realize the real cause was the uncontrolled structure of power. It took time before I fully understood the real origins of the problems.

After several tense hours when the Minister of Interior banned, then allowed, and then banned and allowed the demonstration again, I marched along with about 200,000 university students through the Buda side of the city. As a symbolic expression of solidarity with the Polish upheaval, we were stopping at the statue of Joseph Bem, the Polish general, who was also a hero of the 1848 Hungarian Revolution. "Long live the courageous!" shouted people who welcomed our march through the city. During this demonstration, the Stalinist coat of arms, modeled on the Soviets', was

The 1956 Revolution in Budapest: a destroyed Soviet armored vehicle in my street.

cut from the center of the red-white-green national banner. This flag with a hole in the middle would become the symbol of the revolution.

We crossed Margaret Bridge to Kossuth Square in front of the Parliament, singing, shouting, demanding that Imre Nagy be returned to power. I remained on the square for several hours. It was already dark when, at last, Imre Nagy appeared on a balcony and addressed the crowd. He apparently did not fully understand the situation, was quite confused, and addressed the crowd first as "dear comrades." He was booed, changed words instantly to "dear friends" and in a few minutes' speech asked for patience. I walked home.

The next morning we learned that late in the evening and during the night armed uprising had erupted in the city, and Soviet troops were intervening. Public transportation stopped, and I walked to the university. A revolutionary university battalion was established and I immediately joined. We received guns and I walked home that evening with a submachine gun on my shoulder. My Akácfa Street became quite renowned in the first days of the revolution. In one of the first symbolic actions, the crowd demolished the huge statue of Stalin. While his boots remained on the pedestal the heavy bronze statue was dragged for miles to the corner of my street where hundreds of people worked for days to disintegrate it and keep a piece as a memorabilia.

Throughout those days I crossed the downtown area twice a day, back and forth between my home and the university. The scenery was dramatic. Trams and buses were overturned, cobblestones broken up and piled to make barricades. Dead bodies were everywhere. Soviet tanks and armored vehicles rattled all over the city and fired randomly. Several times I had to duck into doorways for safety. Burned-out Soviet tanks and burned Soviet soldiers remained behind. The world learned the term: Molotov cocktail. At the crossing of Rákóczi Boulevard and Múzeum Ring I saw a pile of smashed bloody human flesh—a group of fighters trampled down by a tank. People were everywhere. Agitated groups pointed to a roof from where a secret policeman opened fire on the crowd. At another corner a small group of people savagely beat a man after somebody recognized him as member of the hated AVO, the secret police. Some of the AVO officials were already lynched and hanged on sycamore trees.

The bloodiest episode took place on October 30 at Köztársaság tér (Square of the Republic) when the mob, searching for secret tunnels and torture chambers, attacked the Budapest headquarters of the Communist Party and killed several people, including young soldiers who were recruited into the armed forces of the secret police. Some were shot dead, others hanged on trees. Somebody cut out the heart of one of the hanged men.

Although I continued going to the University every day with my gun, I did not use it and did not participate in the fighting. A revolution is more beautiful in history books than on the streets. Imre Nagy's government could not gain the upper hand and became increasingly isolated. Although Nagy and his government accepted the most radical demands after the first uncertain days, the extremist groups did not accept him. Every day Radio Free Europe urged the fighters not to accept Nagy—saying that he was just another Communist. Demagogues at the street corners depressed me. The radicalization and escalation of fighting discouraged me because, as I had already thought, it could not produce results. I always bought several of the newspapers that flooded the streets in those days. On November 2, I read an article by the populist writer László Németh, who had been silenced for a decade after the war and worked as a teacher in the countryside. He returned to the capital and in the weekly of the Writers' Union, *Irodalmi Ujság* (Literary Journal) warned about the danger of bloody revenge and the revival of the prewar political guard ready to "make a counterrevolution from the revolution and transform 1956 to the 1920s,"—the years of—as they were called—the "white terror." I read this article with great interest and shared concern. (Németh, 1956)

(Fifty years later Charles Gati tried in his *Failed Illusions* an excellent analytical book to answer the question "why did the 1956 revolt fail?" He built rightly on the well-known and obvious part of the answer, the overwhelmingly superior military might of the Soviet Union and the inaction of the West, but added the "lack of effective leadership and the weakness of the Nagy government," citing the "unwise" radicalism and maximalist demands of the insurgents: "Their misjudgments contributed to the revolution's downfall." Romantic nationalism, Gati added, haunted both the fighters and the government of the country, which had a "political culture that those who bravely fight for hopeless causes and lose deserve more admiration than those who opportunistically seek, and obtain, small gains." (Gati, 2006, 19))

We may not expect self-limitation from a revolution and faultless leadership in a life-and-death struggle. However, that was exactly what I felt that time: radicalism and lack of leadership may lead to tragedy. In a certain sense, I was wrong, because 1956, in its defeat, became victorious precisely because of its uncompromising radicalism. Internationally, in the long run, it played a major role in undermining the regime. In the short run it fatally wounded Western communism and also became a watershed in the history of Hungarian state socialism: even after the bloody defeat and retaliation against the revolution it was impossible to continue as before. The ground for major reforms and a better life for the population were prepared.

After the second Soviet military intervention on November 4, 1956, which defeated the revolution, we sat down with György Ránki, my closest friend and co-author, to discuss the possibility of leaving the country. Tens of thousands of people, with some of my close friends among them, did so. It was a major dilemma, one of the biggest in my life. The wrong decision might destroy our life. The country's situation looked hopeless. The regime was restored but the overwhelming majority of the population was hostile to it. Waves of strikes dragged on. Tens of thousands were arrested. What next? In the first twenty-six years of my life too many horrible events had already happened. It would be better to go. On the other hand, we wondered what could we do as refugees in the West? Find work in a shop, an office, or a factory?

We were confused. Our main consideration was our profession. We finished collecting the archival material for our second book, and—as it turned out later—mistakenly thought that we could not continue working as historians abroad. Our daughters were two years old, and that was another concern. My father was also strongly against our possible leaving and in the end, we decided to stay.

In my personal life, the experience of the failed radical revolution pushed me towards realistic, possible reforms and acceptance of unavoidable compromise. The goal of democratic socialism, or as it was phrased twelve years later in Prague, "socialism with a human face," which is based on democratic institutions and law, recognizes human rights, eliminates censorship, introduces an efficient mixed economy with both state and private ownership, and market incentives, I thought, had a chance after the manifestation of the failure of Stalinism.

At the time reformers like me believed in the possibility of reforming the system. Certain important steps had already been taken in Yugoslavia and Poland where collectivization was replaced by private farming, the closed society was opened, and travel was made possible. The need for a radical change in policy, including economic policy, was in the air.

After the second Soviet intervention on November 4, 1956, Khrushchev decided not to reinstall the totally discredited Rákosi–Gerő leadership. After some hesitation he asked János Kádár to form the government. Kádár had been a blue-collar worker before the war who joined the illegal Communist Party in 1931. Before the end of the war, he became the home leader of the small illegal party. He hadn't lived in emigration in the Soviet Union, and was not Jewish, unlike the entire "Muscovite" Stalinist leadership. After the war he became part of the top postwar communist leadership and, as minister of interior, played a certain role in the show trial of Rajk in 1949. In less than two years, however, he also became victim of Stalinist lawlessness. Released from prison before the revolution, he collaborated with Imre Nagy, was member of the revolutionary government and welcomed the "glorious revolution." This background made him an excellent candidate to lead the reestablished communist power in Hungary. Actually the Yugoslav leader, Josip Broz Tito convinced Khrushchev to select him over the preferred Hungarian communists who were in Soviet emigration.

Kádár accepted this role and although followed the Soviet *ukaz* and launched a bloody retaliation, his past history, pragmatic character and wider elbow room after 1956 enabled him to condemn Stalinism and the Rákosi regime and speak about a dramatically renewed socialism. A simple, uneducated, but smart and shrewd man, he used his background and new style to gain credibility and later even popularity.

The Kádár government, which under Soviet military shield took over the country after November 4, 1956, immediately, in the same month, appointed a reform committee to prepare the new economic model for the country. A few of my former professors became members. The plan that was put on the desk of Kádár in April, 1957, recommended the reestablishment of a quasi market system. Firms would be motivated by profits, instead of a compulsory central plan. The reform model, however, was shelved because the regime was rapidly consolidating. In the mid-1960s, however, Kádár had to return to reforms, and wide-spread preparatory work began.

My work from the early 1960s on focused on post-World War II economic tribulations and policy mistakes, and my scholarly research advocated reform. I wanted to show that the road Hungary followed after 1948 was seriously wrong in many respects. In those years the Party maintained an official view on the 1950s, which was repeated in various Party documents. The Party's leading economist, István Friss, a member of the Central Committee and head of the Institute of Economics, published a study in which he argued that the economic policies of the 1950s were basically correct. The misstep occurred only in 1951 when the first five-year plan was corrected and the targeted industrialization goals were significantly increased. Although the increase was necessary, the Rákosi–Gerő group set unrealistically high economic goals which precipitated the crisis. This evaluation implied that Stalinist economic policy was all right and that Hungary should follow the same path, but at a more moderate pace.

My 1964 study on the mistaken concept of forced industrialization (I will return to its content later) was harshly attacked by István Friss and made my thin book a political sensation. Another study on the harmfulness of the system of centralized planning, however, which I published in Belgium as well, and presented later at the 1970 Congress of the International Economic History Association, sparked off such a discussion that one of the founders of the association, the British scholar Michael Postan, found this to be (with strong exaggeration) the best paper at the Congress. I became, as he sad, his "pinup boy." It is noteworthy that this congress was held during the celebration of the hundredth anniversary of Lenin's birth in Leningrad, the birthplace of the Bolshevik Revolution.

I continued to write and publish critical analyses and presented one at the tenth anniversary of the 1968 New Economic Mechanism reform in Hungary, which had begun changing the Soviet type of economic system by introducing important market elements and eliminating compulsory planning. Market prices began to appear and companies employed the profit motive. A private business element was inserted into collective farm practice. Moreover, official statements made it clear that the introduced reforms were only the first stage and after five years further steps would be taken towards an efficient economic system.

Instead of further steps, however, the transformation stopped, and at the end of 1972 a strong left-wing counteroffensive began denying its results. The reform was blamed as responsible for the revival of capitalism and petit-bourgeois attitudes, as a system that prefers peasant interests and harms the workers. At the tenth anniversary of the introduction of the reform in 1978, deep silence signaled the changed atmosphere. The reform was not mentioned in public. I urged its continuation.

Soon after that, I presented the story, based on archive materials, of the Soviet-led, hard-line attack against the Hungarian reform model in the early 1970s. In dozens of publications, including university textbooks on the period, I rejected using the official pejorative terminology, "counterrevolution," to describe the 1956 uprising. My research and publications led to various invitations to serve on reform committees and advisory bodies assisting the reforms.

Several decades later the revolution returned to me in a dramatic way. Already president of the Hungarian Academy of Sciences, in 1988, I was appointed chair of two important committees. One of them, initiated by Party reformers, was a committee of historians who analyzed the postwar historical road that led to the crisis of the country. I tried to exploit this opportunity by asking for a meeting and interview with János Kádár, who at that time had already retired from active politics but still held the rank of honorary "president" of the Party. I spent more than two hours with him and asked all the important questions connected with his role in 1956, when he, convinced by Soviet leaders, disappeared from Budapest, deserted Imre Nagy's government, in which he had a leading role, by traveling secretly to Moscow and accepting the job of reintroducing the socialist system after the Soviet military invasion. Unfortunately, I did not get a straight answer from him, but only a rambling, incoherent litany instead which brooked no interruption. I thought he simply did not want to answer, but a few months later it became clear that he had lost his mind.

It happened at a Central Committee meeting in April 1989, when the already retired Kádár left hospital to make a surprise appearance. He launched into a chaotic speech, the last in his life. The sentences had neither beginning nor end. Phrases about his and his wife's illness and events that happened thirty years before were entangled in a meaningless monologue. His talk was recorded and published in the early 1990s. Let me quote a part from it from Ivan Sanders' translation:

> I have an illness, very similar to my wife's- weight loss... My wife... underwent major stomach surgery while I was in prison...My problem is... the reason I am so forgetful, though most often I know what I want... and I am losing weight, too...You'll hear me say strange things today. What is my responsibility? Not what I said but what a Westerner was saying in the presence of Soviet tanks. He said that the Danube flows too swiftly... All my life, whenever possible, I have spoken freely, without notes... All this in spite of the fact that I am a simple man, I had little schooling-four years of prewar elementary school and four years of prewar middle school...That's where my responsibility comes in. Whatever you may say from now on, whatever that will be, I will not mind. They can shoot me for all I care. I am fully aware of my own responsibility now, and I will never name names... Frankly, I can't think of anyone to whom I feel answerable right now... After a nine-day stay in the hospital and other checkups, begging your pardon, I appeared here... three weeks before the operation was to take place, the motor nerves in my hand got paralyzed. I had no way of knowing

of course how long microsurgery involving one's hand would take... I had become a scapegoat in the biblical sense... I bear the responsibility because *I* committed a grave error...Day and night my brain turns over feverishly... And to economize a little, my lunch need not be delivered to my home... My most important objective by far at that time was to get to Szolnok in safety...Regardless of who I was surrounded by...I assumed responsibility, I really did, for the safety of those who sought refuge at the embassy. But I was as naive as can be; I assumed the responsibility because I thought that my request that two of those people issue a statement... Now then, historically, I, too, see everything differently. ...these two men's request was that they be free to depart and return to their homes, I couldn't meet their request...You know very well what this means for people to whom the legality of a government is important... I hadn't called a single holder of power counter-revolutionary. Not even *him*... the Yugoslav Ambassador told me... he received authorization to try to persuade these two persons... He told me later: I've tried for three days straight to make them change their minds, without any success... You can approve any evaluation of my conduct that you like. But I know that when I was again free to move about, there were two newspapers published in Szolnok... my life and many other people's lives depended on my saying what I had to say... the main charge against me was that I was a Soviet agent. But I was not a Soviet agent... I can prove it to you. The next charge was that I ended up in Soviet territory-how could that be? I still don't know...the doctor told me that the one thing he will not allow me to do is speak if there is a recording device anywhere nearby, because I may stumble over words, fluff my lines, so, forgive me for saying it, but I don't know what I should do... How long have I been talking... But at the 22nd Congress-that dreadful toast of Khrushchev's lasted an hour and a half, in which he tried to explain why they were forced to resort to unlawful means and kill Beria... But the point I'm trying to make is that the doctor said I cannot hold forth anymore on important matters... As for the other thing, that started on the 28th, when unarmed people, on the bases of their clothes or complexion, were murdered as in a pogrom. And these people were killed well before Imre Nagy and his associates... from a distance of thirty years, yes, I feel sorry for all of them...

I will answer, in turn, the most burning questions-whatever seems pressing now and what torments me still. Answers to why I haven't spoken. (Sanders, 2006, 111–23)

All these fragments of sentences may be decoded, and are connected with his takeover after the 1956 revolution. He was taken to the Soviet Union on November 2, 1956, after Yuri Andropov Soviet Ambassador in Budapest invited Ferenc Münich and Kádár to the Embassy. They were then "asked" to get into a Soviet car, taken to the Soviet military airport in Tököl, and with a stop where they were joined by Leonid Brezhnev, flown to Moscow. The next day Kádár met with Soviet leaders but remained in the dark about his status. Was he a guest or a prisoner? The Soviet Politburo agreed only in November 3, the day before the second military offensive, to ask him to form the government which would officially reside in the Hungarian provincial city of Szolnok. One of the "two men" he alluded to was Imre Nagy, who asked asylum at the Yugoslav Embassy after the second Soviet invasion, and wanted to "go home." Kádár and the Yugoslav Ambassador agreed to this, but Kádár required Nagy's "announcement" of resignation from the premiership to create the legal base for his own government. When Nagy rejected that, Kádár decided to kill him without "legal basis."

Hearing this long and confused speech made my stomach turn. I went home and could not eat my dinner. Kádár's deeply hidden thoughts erupted in a confused and illogical way. I thought such a thing could only happen in a Shakespearean drama. I heard that in the ensuing days Kádár packed a small bag which he placed next to the front door in case he was arrested. He ordered his wife to lie behind the door to block the police. Guilt haunted and tortured him. He suffered nightmares and died in July 1989, the day the Hungarian Supreme Court started the process to acquit Imre Nagy.

In my report, which I wrote towards the end of 1988, I broke the taboo and for the first time in Hungary in thirty years, I publicly rejected the regime's official evaluation of the 1956 uprising as "counter-revolution," and characterized it instead as a genuine popular uprising and fight for independence.

John P.C. Matthews, who joined Radio Free Europe in 1951 and later became the head of its European operation, published a monumental book, *Explosion. The Hungarian Revolution in 1956*. The nearly 700 page long volume discussed the role of my report in a chapter on "Reemergence." Let me quote a few sentences from his evaluation and his long quotations from the report:

> The historical subcommittee under Ivan Berend comes up with a ninety-page report...it tells the truth about Imre Nagy's decision to declare neutrality and withdraw from the Warsaw Pact... The report tells the truth about Kádár, as well... "After November 4, Hungary still had to align its policy with the Soviet political line... from the 1960s up to the middle of the 1980s a practically post-Stalinist policy gained the upper hand, so there was no chance for any radical transformation... The uprising that was called a revolution... soon came to be called... the unfortunate October events, but later... a counter-revolution..." Most important, the report tells the truth about the Revolution itself. "The extremely powerful mass demonstration of October 23 took the place as a response to apparently ineffective old solutions... to be followed the same evening by the 'critique of arms' replacing the 'arms of critique,' which eventually led to an overall national uprising against the ruling regime. The university students... were soon joined by huge masses of workers in the last week of October. This was demonstrated by their participation in the fight as well as the organization of a united and long-lasting political strike..." At some point Pozsgay decides to reveal to the Hungarian people the major finding in the Berend report: what has been referred to for thirty-two years as a counterrevolution has been found by experts to have been a true national uprising and revolution all along. The news electrifies the nation. (Matthews, 2007, 592–5)

My report was debated at the January 29, 1989 meeting of a four-member ad hoc committee. Imre Pozsgay, Minister of State and a leading reformer of the Party that time, participated in the meeting, but left early. When I reached home in the late afternoon I heard on the radio that in a public statement, he had announced the rehabilitation of 1956. This ignited a political explosion. In March, the entire report was published in 300,000 copies in a special issue of the monthly journal of *Társadalmi Szemle,* (Societal Review) sold out in hours and was reprinted. I gave interviews and on one occasion was invited to speak on TV together with the daughter of

Imre Nagy. This re-evaluation of 1956 contributed to the de-legitimization of the regime that had destroyed the revolution.

Characteristically enough, on February 1989, the Party's Central Committee discussed this issue, and at the same meeting the body came to vote for holding free, multi-party elections within a year.

The government also asked me in 1988 to chair another committee to work out an economic plan for a transition to a market and privatized economy. The document, which was prepared and also published in the same year, established the economic policy of the new government of Miklós Németh. I was also appointed Chair of the advisory body of the government and became part of the Hungarian *refolution,* as Timothy Garton Ash calls it, a reform-revolution, which paved the way for a peaceful transformation.

My Universities

This title imitates the title of a novel by the Russian writer Maxim Gorky, who considered his life as his universities. This was not exactly my case. I spent four years at two major universities of Budapest, the University of Economics, and the Eötvös Lóránd University between 1949 and 1953. I defended my doctoral dissertation in Economics (in 1957), then became "candidate" (the equivalent of Ph.D.) in 1958, and doctor (similar to the French and German second, or habilitation degree) of history in 1962 at the Hungarian Academy of Sciences.

In a real sense, however, my universities began earlier and ended much later.

The most important period of learning in my life was the last four years of high school, the eight-year long gymnasium of German type. Because of my poor grades in elementary school it was not easy for me to be accepted. In June, 1941, I went with my mother to a kind of interview at the Jewish Gymnasium in the 14th district of Budapest. This was run by the Jewish community and in 1941 I would not have been accepted by other schools. A loudspeaker at the corner of *Városliget,* a large park one block from the school, announced to pedestrians that Germany had attacked the Soviet Union on June 22, and an hour later the director of the school, a famous linguist, informed us that I was rejected. It was a disappointing day. However, my mother did not give up, and in the end, partly because my brother was already an excellent student at the same school, she arranged my accep-

The Jewish Gymnasium, my high school in Budapest, where I studied between 1941 and 1948. This school and some of its teachers influenced my entire life. It was there, at the age of 16, that I decided to become a historian.

tance. Although I continued to be a poor student until the end of the war, this very school became my first "university" after the war.

The German type of gymnasium is an outstanding educational institution. It is well known, that one of them, the Lutheran (Evangélikus) Gymnasium in Budapest, years before, produced an extraordinary group of students. One of them was Neumann János, later known as John von Neumann, who helped building the ENIAC, the first giant computer, and was one of the founders of game theory, which changed modern economics. Four others from the school, including Neumann's classmate Jenő (Eugene) Wigner, American atomic physicist from the 1930s, became Nobel laureates, mostly thanks to one legendary math teacher László Rátz.

The Jewish Gymnasium was also exceptional, and had an additional advantage during my time there. For several exceptional scholars, who could not get university jobs in the institutionalized anti-Semitic regime of Horthy's Hungary, which in certain periods either limited the number of Jewish students or totally banned them from universities, Jewish professors were not employed. The Jewish Gymnasium was virtually the only forum where they could teach. Actually, many of my gymnasium teachers became university professors a few years after the war.

As a consequence, I met two excellent young scholars, who were my literature and history teachers. Miklós Szabolcsi, ten years our senior, opened the world of literature for me. He was not a regular high school teacher, and never taught parts of the curriculum he considered to be boring or took grading seriously. He behaved as a fatherly friend and adviser who made us passionate readers by his deep analyses of poems and novels. He was always ready to discuss our readings. I went to the National Library, and during those years read one or two books per week, classic works by Balzac, Proust, Goethe, Thomas Mann, Hemingway, Sinclair Lewis, Steinbeck, Andre Gide, Tolstoy, Dostoyevsky, Gorky, and many others. In our school newspaper, *A Diák* (The Student), edited and written by a handful of us, I wrote a review of Jean-Paul Sartre's new book about anti-Semitism, which in 1947 had just been translated and published in Hungary. One summer when I had to remain at home in bed for two weeks with tonsillitis I read all of the dramas of Shakespeare.

Every week I bought cheap tickets to one of the theaters. The newly established *Művész Színház* (Art Theater) performed the best contemporary plays and I did not miss one. When the National Theater performed *Hamlet* several times in a row with three different actors in the title role, I went to see all of the performances. The high cultural atmosphere in our class directed me to the Budapest Opera. It was an outstanding institution with superb singers who were not allowed to travel, although some of them had sung in the Metropolitan Opera before. The musical director and conductor was Otto Klemperer (and I was happy to see his bust half a century later in the lobby of the Los Angeles Music Center where he also conducted). I queued before the ticket office every weekend when it opened to buy the cheapest tickets for the whole week and got acquainted with the world of opera. In 1947–48 in a single season I heard Mussorgsky's *Boris Godunov* eight times. (In 2006 we drove two and a half hours from Los Angeles to San Diego, where Boris Godunov was performed. I still remembered the names of the Hungarian singers and even the Hungarian lyrics of the opera—since all of the operas were performed in Hungarian.)

Zsigmond Pál Pach, my history teacher from the age of twelve, influenced me the most. He was only eleven years older than me, but he had an old scholar's manner and embodied the highest possible requirements. His history classes, as I later realized, were more university lectures than high school classes. History was a revelation to me: I felt that I was beginning to understand the world. For our generation history was not simply one subject among others, but life itself. Those years were heavily loaded by history and I was keen to study.

At the age of sixteen, in the sixth year of the gymnasium, I decided to participate in the annual national high-school history competition. Every year the educational authorities advertised this competition, picked a central topic and every high school student was eligible to participate. The requirement was to write a research paper, which was evaluated by a committee. In 1946, the central topic was the 1848 Revolution in Hungary. In the sixth year, we had not yet covered that period; it was part of the eighth-year curriculum. I did not mention my plan to my teacher, but went to the National Library, read and read, and attended public scholarly lectures and debates on the topic, which was possible since the centenary celebration of the 1848 revolution was already on the horizon. To present my paper was an adventure, and—what a great surprise!—I received third place at the national competition the only sixth-year student among eighth-year students.

Next year I participated again and this time came in second. The head of the Budapest School District invited me to his office and encouraged me to study history at the University and become a historian. More important, my gymnasium teacher, Pach, was appointed next year to the reorganized, independent University of Economics (a former Economic School of the Technical University) as head of the Economic History Department. His appointment determined my destiny: I decided to enroll in that university in order to study with him. In my eighth year at the gymnasium, I was already taking part in a university seminar in his Department.

In the fall of 1949, my university studies began. Next year we moved in the new university building facing on the River Danube in Budapest, originally the country's Chief Customs Office House before being remodeled for the University. One cannot imagine a worse period for higher education than the years between 1949 and 1953. When I first attended a lecture class, the country had just been shocked by the news of the arrest and trial of László Rajk, one of the top communist leaders. This was the first show trial with contrived accusations and confessions to be broadcast on

The Budapest University of Economics, where I studied, became professor and rector.

radio. Rajk and his co-defendants confessed to all the unbelievable accusations including treason and a plan to kill Rákosi and other leading communists. They told of a conspiracy directed by the Yugoslav leaders Tito and Ranković aimed at undermining the socialist regime in Hungary. As we learned much later, they were first tortured and then, with sudden change of tactics, approached as honest communists and asked to provide a major service to the cause of unmasking Tito, who had rejected Soviet patronage. Tired and hopeless, these true believers were ready to do this service believing the false promise that after the trial they would be resettled in the Soviet Union, even rewarded by living with their families under different names. Of course, they had not understood anything and were hanged. Rajk's last words under the gallows were "Long live Stalin!"

When all the lies, false accusations, and crimes of the show trials came to the surface Rajk was reburied with full honors in 1956, on a gloomy, rainy and windy day in the unofficial national cemetery (*Kerepesi temető*), where the personalities of history are laid to rest. Later I felt surprised that the revolution did not start on that day.

I have to confess that in 1949 I believed all of those impossible lies. I just could not imagine that somebody would confess to such crimes if innocent. I was certainly not alone, and at only nineteen years of age, had never even heard of the Stalinist show trials of the 1930s. With many others, I was also grateful to the Soviet Union for defeating Hitler and eliminating the murderous Horthy and Arrow Cross regimes. I learned the truth much later, partly from a few survivors of the trials, partly from official condemnations of Stalinism, and mostly, and much later, from well documented books based on archival documents. However, I still wonder how I could have believed in those lies.

(A quarter of a century later, in the early 1980s when I was a fellow at the Woodrow Wilson International Center for Scholars in Washington D.C., the Arena Stage, one of the leading theaters of the city, and its Director, Zelda Fichandler staged a drama by István Örkény, an outstanding Hungarian playwright, about the show trials. It was based on the Rajk trial. The actors had a very hard time understanding this irrational history, why the accused confessed to everything when they were innocent. The playwright was a close friend of mine, and his widow visited Washington and suggested to Zelda that she invite me into the preparation. Zelda invited me to the rehearsals to coach the ensemble. The irrationality of these events was never as clear to me as at that time.)

The Rajk trial signaled the dawn of a new high Stalinist era in Hungary, an era that determined life and university studies in a devastating fashion. Purges followed one another. People disappeared, including several members of the communist leadership, members of the Politburo. Sándor Zöld, Minister of Interior after the Rajk trial, killed his entire family and himself when one night in the early 1950s the secret police knocked on his door. Those years were a time of an economic disaster: goods disappeared from shops and real wages decreased by 20 percent. War-time rationing was reintroduced.

And this situation and atmosphere characterized the entire period until I finished my studies at the university. As I prepared my final examinations, the news was announced that Lavrentiy Beria, Stalin's cruel henchman, had been executed in the Soviet Union. The declaration of a "new course" by Malenkov and Khrushchev precipitated the "thaw," as the following years were characterized by the Soviet writer Ilya Ehrenburg. High Stalinism gradually began to melt.

In other words, I studied at the university between two executions and during one of the worst periods of Hungarian and Central and East European history. Education was over-politicized, entirely ideological, and mostly primitive. We hardly read scholarly readings or even received information about them, but prepared for exams from a single textbook in each subject. Some were translated Soviet text books. Once, preparing for modern European history examination, I computed the numbers for the declining real wages and living standard in interwar Poland. It declined by 20 percent in the early 1920s, and another 40 percent in the early 1930s, and by the end, according to the figures of the translated Soviet textbook, the Polish workers' wages had declined by more than 100 percent and become negative figures. Ridiculous. All previous and foreign scholarship was excluded. In the first year we had twelve subjects, lectures every day until far into the afternoon. Everything was mandatory with no possibility to choose.

Additionally, during my university years we had to participate in military reserve training and spend one month between the school years in two summers in military training, and three months after graduation. The military exercises always targeted Yugoslavia, in preparation for a possible attack by Tito's army. Political officers delivered extremely primitive lectures to us, irritating the entire student battalion. Once, for example, a young lieutenant quoted something from Stalin, and hilariously misstated his name: instead of I.V. (Iosip Vissarionovich) Stalin, he called him "first and fifth" Stalin. Fortunately, I was never again called up and did not have any contact with the army after 1956.

The atmosphere at the university was frightening as well. Some of my colleagues were openly humiliated at meetings, and disciplinary punishments endangered further studies. One of my closest friends, Miklós Szuhay, became one of the victims. His offense was to return from summer vacation in his North Hungarian village and openly talk about the horror of the elimination of the well-to-do peasantry. In 1948, following the Soviet pattern, collectivization of agriculture began. Private farmers, many of whom had only just received a parcel of land after World War II, were forced into collective farms. Police force was often used to break resistance: farmers who refused to join were beaten and even imprisoned. Stalin's infamous "de-kulakization," the elimination of "kulaks," well-to-do farmers who were declared to be class enemies, accompanied the entire process. The official propaganda trumpeted the great success of collectivization and peasant enthusiasm for the system. In reality, in spite of the brutal terror, only one third of the landed peasants joined and the bulk of them resisted. Half of the animal stock was slaughtered. Telling the truth was treated as criminal scaremongering.

The accusation was thus dramatic and dangerous, but we could not resist smiling when we heard the first sentence of the denunciation: "Szuhay originates from the nobility." The name of his village was Alsó-szuha; half of the population of that village also took their family names from the place, with "y" ending indeed showing some noble origins. But nobility had been abolished in Hungary in 1848, more than a century before. Furthermore it was so very commonplace that a huge part of that poor village nobility had lost their land even before that and become peasant-nobles who cultivated small parcels alone. That was the case with our colleague whose family owned only three hectares of land.

To illustrate the atmosphere with another example I recall a strange episode from my freshman year: the entire freshman class of 250 students sat in an auditorium for a lecture by a professor in accounting. Like all the others, he introduced his topic by listing quotations of Lenin and Stalin about the importance of accounting. When he mentioned the name of Stalin the first time, a group of students began a standing ovation. "Long live Stalin!" Everybody had to stand up and shout.

In 1952–53, a new danger frightened us. Copying the Soviet show trial against the "murderers in white," the infamous doctor's plot, similar cases were under preparation in the satellite countries. The bloodiest was arranged in Czechoslovakia, the "anti-Zionist" Slansky trial. Another one was prepared in Romania, and Rákosi "unveiled" a Hungarian Zionist plot. In Moscow, Jewish Kremlin medical doctors were accused of killing top communist leaders. The goal was to initiate, as it was officially called, an anti-Zionist, in reality anti-Jewish campaign to channel dissatisfaction into the traditional Russian anti-Semitic stream. Arrests and the preparation of a similar show trial began in Budapest. Besides the top level arrests, small local purges began: at my University, two professors were accused of Zionist crimes, human trafficking into Israel, and purged. The small economic research unit they led was closed.

I was in my early twenties and wanted to learn to become an economic historian. I cannot say that there was no opportunity for that. In the generally not demanding and low level of university teaching, I met with a few excellent professors, who followed classical university requirements. First of all Zsigmond Pál Pach a great scholar of early modern Central Europe. He represented the best classic German scholarly tradition, was a master of its methods and possessed tremendous knowledge. His works had hundreds of footnotes covering sources and literature in several languages. He analyzed sources, quoted the most important literature on the topic, and presented various views on debated questions. He had a broad knowledge of languages, including excellent Latin. In his case, it was not a dead language: once, many years later, I have even heard a joking toast he delivered in Latin at a dinner party after an international conference. He was a devoted Marxist and in his classes, already at high-school, and then even more so at the university, he gave a convincing Marxist interpretation to history, which not only impressed, but also persuaded me to use this framework as a key to understanding history. I learned much from him and without his influence and assistance I certainly could not have become an acceptable historian. At the university I also studied economics and read Karl Marx's works. In that environment, and for a young economic historian, it was natural to follow this school of thought. Marxist interpretation of history elevated Hungarian history writing by confronting traditional nationalist mythologizing. New branches of historiography which had hardly existed before, such as social and economic history, were introduced. The sturdy Hungarian school of economic history became internationally known and praised. It was not only an East European phenomenon. Marxism had a huge influence on history writing all over the world after the war, including France, Italy, Britain, and even far away Japan, where postwar historiography was dominated by a Marxist approach.

Here I have to mention the most important part of my university education. Professor Pach, who was also appointed deputy director of the Institute of History of the Hungarian Academy of Sciences, organized a research team to work on nineteenth and twentieth century Hungarian economic history. Though a freshman, I was recruited to that research group and was sent to the National Archive. I worked entire summer vacations collecting sources from the ministerial archives and later, newly opened bank and industrial company archives. I began learning the profession. Originally we students were hired only for collecting materials while a few older historians from the Institute were designated to use them and write the studies. Soon, however, it was clear hat this kind of collaborative research didn't work, and after two years the working group was dissolved. Fortunately, I worked with my high-school schoolmate and closest friend, György Ránki, who had also enrolled in the University of Economics, and we studied together at those times. He was also part of that research group.

When the plan of the collaborative work was dropped, we had already collected masses of archival material most of which was unknown since it was found in the previously private and closed company archives. It was almost natural that we begin organizing the sources, and we decided to write a book together on pre-World War I Hungarian industry. We sat together at the desk and discussed each sentence and by the time we had finished our undergraduate studies, our first draft of a book was ready. That was the best experience and learning possibility we could have. In 1955, two years after receiving the B.A. degree, our first book appeared. It was a pretty poor work, strongly politicized and bearing all the marks of the age, but it was excellently researched, full of rich, original archive materials and calculations.

Whether classical or contemporary, Western economics were excluded from our university studies. At least I read *Das Kapital* and several other works of Karl Marx and learned to think logically from our economics professor, Tamás Nagy. I liked political economy, and Professor Nagy tried to convince me to join the Economics Department after graduation, but I had my plan to become an economic historian.

During those university years I learned to love statistics and statistical methods. The classes of György Péter, my professor of statistics and head of the Hungarian Statistical Office, had a lasting impact on me. I still remember his introductory lecture when he, among others, explained that statistics always work with average figures, which do not exist in real life. He illustrated this with the following example: one man sits in a restaurant next to the window and eats two wiener-schnitzels. A hungry beggar walks outside, next to the window. In the statistics it appears that we have one wiener-schnitzel per head. (Kati, my wife, often says jokingly that my favorite readings are still statistical reports, and there is some truth to that.) Professor Péter had a tragic life. He spent nine years in prison as a communist during the Horthy regime, and would be later imprisoned again by his "own" regime where he committed suicide in his cell.

Most of all, I learned how to work hard. I learned a lifestyle of work. Nevertheless, that poor university education had several negative consequences. There were huge gaps to fill later, and certain tasks which one should complete at the university, such as methodical reading of classic and contemporary economic and sociological theories. It is difficult or partly even impossible to make up properly for the vast body of previous scholarship once you have finished university when your own research and teaching agenda loom large.

"My universities," fortunately, were not accomplished at the universities. The most important factor of my further education was the opening of the country and free access to modern, Western scholarship. This would not have happened without the major political changes ignited by the 1956 revolution and realized by a much milder Kádár regime after 1960. The sixties in Hungary offered a higher education in politics and economics for me. I learned about the major obstacles to radical change, but the possibility of gradual reforms and transformation, let alone major lessons in economics. In those years I bumped into zillions of practical economic problems that I wanted to understand. Those years, indeed, definitely belonged to my universities.

Changes did not happen immediately. The retributions following the 1956 revolution were bloody. Thousands of people were imprisoned or interned, about four hundred executed. But János Kádár, a true communist believer but also a pragmatist, who took over the country after Soviet invasion of the November 4, 1956, realized that his regime could not return to the early 1950s. As Talleyrand once wittily put it, you can do several things with bayonets except sit on them.

Kádár, who actually took over the Party leadership during the revolution, and was a member of the Imre Nagy government, in an emotional radio statement on November 1 1956 praised the revolution as our "glorious democratic people's uprising." In the months after the second Soviet intervention when Kádár formed the government, official communications referred to 1956 as the "national tragedy," and "unfortunate October events," without labeling them.

Kádár promised radical changes: one of the first decrees of his government declared the acceptance of workers' self-management, an institution that was established by the revolution, and led to strikes against his government over several months. The government declaration stated: "All the activities of the state-owned companies will be directed by Workers' Councils." He also accepted the Nagy government's measure of abolishing the hated "compulsory delivery" system that prescribed in physical terms the amount of farm produce to be delivered to the state. Since it was a law, the peasants had to deliver regardless of the "prices" paid by the state which were actually lower than the costs of production. This system crippled the peasantry and the food supply. A few months later, Kádár's party published its agricultural program. It abandoned forced collectivization and focused on agricultural development. Collective farms, the program stated, would become voluntary organizations and could take on various forms, including a collective farm as an umbrella organization for private farm units. Collectivization, indeed, was not continued until the end of 1958. In his famous speech in 1961 Kádár declared that "those who are not against us are with us," replacing the old Stalinist slogan that expressed the opposite.

Kádár's tightrope walk after 1956 was skillful, although the task he attempted to achieve was unsolvable: to separate his regime from the hated Stalinism of his predecessor, stressing the need for change and reform yet maintaining continuity and following the "Marxist-Leninist," in reality Stalinist, principles and value system. The official evaluation of the revolution, nevertheless, soon changed. Instead of the neutral "unfortunate October events," it was labeled a bloody "counter-revolution, aimed at restoration of the Horthy regime," organized by "traitors" around Imre Nagy, launched by fascist elements, the mob, and assisted by the "imperialist powers." Official documents repeatedly asserted that it took place at a time when the "healthy revolutionary forces were already on the best way towards a democratic renewal of socialism." The condemnation of the revolution provided the legitimization of the Kádár regime.

Nevertheless, the amnesty in the early 1960s freed political prisoners, traveling abroad became possible, and the economic situation began to improve. The way Kádár cut the Gordian knot was through pragmatic but cautiously veiled reforms. From the mid-1960s on, the Kádár regime slowed industrialization and promoted agriculture. By the middle of the decade food shortages disappeared. Consumer goods became available and the government became more consumer-oriented. To reach these goals important market elements were built in to the economic system. Five-year planning, although officially remaining in place, was not a compulsory prescription for companies. Previously fixed, non-market prices at least partly were replaced by market prices. The regime followed the Soviet order to collectivize agriculture but allowed a market orientation and a hidden private agricultural activity under the umbrella of collective farming. Living standards improved. After 1958, real wages increased by 2-4 percent per year. People in poverty decreased to 15 percent of the population. The terrible housing situation began improving: from the revolution until 1970 the number of apartments in Budapest increased from 470,000 to 630,000. Mechanization of households began: in 1960, only 1-3 percent of the population had household appliances, but by 1967 half of all households had washing machines. When TV broadcasting began in 1958 there were only 16,000 TV sets in the country. Within a decade their number increased to 1.2 million and more than one-third of the population watched the programs. In the same period, the number of car owners increased from one percent to twenty percent of the population. A general health care system was introduced. In 1967, one million people, ten percent of the entire population, traveled abroad.

By introducing the only consumer-oriented society in the Soviet Bloc the Kádár regime became acceptable to the population. The nickname "goulash-communism" reflected this. This phenomenon fit into the analysis of Max Weber, the German founder of modern sociology: "It often happened," he stated, "that a regime, which was forced on a country by a minority later became considered legitimate even by those who opposed it at the beginning." (Weber, 1978, 37) A poll at Kádár's death in 1989 reflected the population's view: 75 percent maintained that one of the greatest political figures of Hungary had passed away. The Guardian reported in the summer of 1999, ten years after his death and in the middle of a relatively successful transformation, that according to the latest poll, Hungarians still viewed him as "the most positive personality of this century." This view was expressed again by a poll around 2006 when Kádár gained an elegant third place among the best historical figures of the country's entire thousand year long history.

The Kádár regime, isolated and boycotted by the West, was gradually accepted. An agreement was signed with the Vatican, and religion was no longer persecuted. Hungary joined the United Nations, and in 1964, Ralph Bunche, the American deputy secretary general of the United Nations made an official visit to Budapest. (I could not imagine at that time that in a quarter of a century I would have my office in a building named after him at UCLA, his alma mater.)

Under the name of the New Economic Mechanism, the Soviet type of central planning was virtually eliminated in 1968. Even though a distinct Hungarian economic model had emerged different from the Soviet centrally-planned economy, Kádár always denied the existence of a Hungarian model.

In this changed environment a major shock pushed me towards a new path of study. In 1960, the XIth International Historical Congress was held in Stockholm. Financed by the Academy of Sciences I was allowed to participate with Pach, Ránki and other Hungarian historians. This was the first time in my life that I participated in an international congress, met with Western scholars, and heard their discussions. Our Western colleagues were experienced: international congresses already had a half century existence. Two postwar congresses in 1950 and 1955 already revitalized the institution. Everything, however, was new for me and my colleagues.

An entire plenary session was devoted to the debate of Walt W. Rostow's recently published book, *The Stages of Economic Growth: A Non-Communist Manifesto*. I did not hear about this work before and the sharp debate with his active participation was highly impressive. Most of the participants rejected Rostow's linear growth stage theory, which differentiated five stages from traditional economy, via a "take-off" towards sustained economic growth and high consumption.

I realized with a shock that I knew nothing. It was also a shock that the lingua franca of the Congress was English, a language I did not speak. Although frightened and trembling, I made my first brief comment in one of the sessions in German. I realized I needed to learn English to be able to read the huge part of the scholarly literature that I did not know. The next year I enrolled in the evening course of the Eötvös Loránd University's English Department. After my graduation I received a British Council grant and went to Britain for a month in 1965.

This trip was a great experience—my first stay in the West for a longer time, and alone. The host institution provided an excellent, rich program and a good opportunity to practice my freshly learned English. I visited London University, and the London School of Economics, and the city became one of my favorite places. The two Marks and Spencer's shops on Oxford Street were the best places to shop. These shops were already known in Hungary. In one of his shows a comedian in the popular political cabaret said that Marks and Spencer were more popular among Hungarians than Marx and Engels. (From the mid-sixties on, the cabaret's political function in Kádár's Hungary proved the difference compared to the Stalinist fifties. Critical political jokes were allowed. Kádár with his wife often sat in the first row, laughing and applauding.)

During my stay in Britain, Sir Winston Churchill died and was buried. He was a legendary figure and the savior of Britain. I learned at that time, however, about his "percentage agreement" with Stalin in October 1944 when he cynically offered, and Stalin accepted, the future division of spheres of interest. Churchill aimed for a free hand in Greece to maintain Mediterranean dominance, offering as compensation most parts of Central and Eastern Europe to Stalin.

I also visited Glasgow University, Oxford, and Cambridge, and met several outstanding economic historians. The beauty and elegance of this world was in extremely sharp contrast with my own drab world in Hungary, and it overwhelmed me. History was present everywhere. Look up—behind that window Newton had his study! These universities have been teaching since medieval times and embody continuity, stability, and a splendid isolation from the turmoil of the world. The red brick buildings from the period of Henry VIII, the beauty of English Gothic architecture in the Chapel of Kings' College were the frame of a university life unknown to me. I was invited to high-table dinners at Jesus and All Souls' colleges. The living tradition, elegance and wealth amazed me. I had never seen anything like it and it all looked like a faraway dream-world.

(I would have been more than surprised if had looked into my future when this outlandish world would be "natural" for me as visiting fellow to some of these colleges, Honorary Doctor of Glasgow University, and most of all, the father of a Cambridge professor, my younger daughter, whom I often visit at their home next to River Cam.)

My "second University" was granted by the Ford Foundation, which offered full year grants at American universities from the mid-1960s on to Hungarian scientists and scholars. My friend, György Ránki, went with the first group, and insisted that I should go too. From 1966, I spent almost a full academic year at Columbia University. This was when I read "everything" I had missed during those original university years. One of the great experiences was the open-stack system of the American academic libraries. I had never seen this splendid system before. I would spend long days among the shelves, have a coffee and a roll for lunch, and go back to read. It seemed like heaven, the best time to read everything possible on the economic history of Central and Eastern Europe. It was a revelation to read the best works on the real history of the Soviet Union.

(Looking back I see that Columbia University became intertwined with to the destiny of my family. Besides thinking about it as my second alma mater, it became the real alma mater of both of my daughters, who after graduating from universities in Budapest, studied at Columbia, and received their Ph.D.s there: Zsuzsa in sociology and Nora in medieval history.)

Living in New York was equally exciting and also offered new knowledge about the world. New York was an enormous living organism the like of which I had never seen before. Walking in the streets and experiencing the diversity of its various parts was kind of an education itself. I was impressed by the New York museums. Besides the Metropolitan, Guggenheim, Frick, the Cloisters, and others, the greatest impact on me was made by the Museum of Modern Art. I had conservative views on modern painting, actually halting at the impressionists. The MOMA with its chronological presentation of modern art made understandable the development of art trends, and introduced me to a pleasure in modern art which has stayed with me since. I also had a chance to see a major one-man Salvador Dali exhibition at Columbus Circle, which impressed me strongly.

For roughly half an hour twice a day I would walk on Broadway between my hotel and Columbia University. Once I read a flyer about a midterm election campaign event with Robert Kennedy, who was helping the campaign of a congressional candidate. It was exciting news. The assassination of his brother was a terrible shock for us even in Hungary. In the morning of November 23, 1963, my daughter Zsuzsa was nine years old and getting ready for school when the radio announced the news. She started crying. Three years later, I waited at a corner on Broadway, a designated place for one of the campaign stops, to see Robert Kennedy in person. He arrived and addressed the gathered crowd. Afterwards I was able shake his hands. It was a happy feeling and has remained a happy memory.

That Ford Fellowship year in the United States was a rich offering. I received several invitations from American colleagues, and at the end of my stay I made a two-and-a-half month lecture tour, stopping at twenty-two universities around the United States, traveling by Greyhound bus and sometimes by plane. I met several colleagues and made new friendships, some of which turned out to be life-long. At the beginning of my tour I wrote out all the lectures I was to deliver, but they were followed by at least an hour-long question-and-answer period. I started answering questions without notes, and still recall the triumphant feeling when in Bloomington, Indiana where a colleague and friend of mine invited me to his class and I delivered my first lecture in English without a written text.

When I returned to New York I made a balance sheet of my visits. I was deeply impressed by the beauty and high standard of intellectual life of the campuses I visited and I jokingly noted that I would be happy to work at all of those universities except two: Harvard and UCLA. I had good experiences almost everywhere. When I arrived somebody was waiting for me, or my program was deposited at the hotel desk. The next morning somebody picked me up and took me to the location of the lecture where almost always a good crowd participated in my talk. After my talk, I was invited to homes of colleagues. But at Harvard no one waited for me. There was no letter at the hotel, and in the course of two days I was unable to contact anybody. In the end, I went back to New York without meeting anyone there. UCLA was a different kind of disappointment. During my three-day visit I never understood where I was in a chaotic city. I could not even get a picture of how the city was put together. How could one live in such a place? (It never occurred to me in January 1967 that twenty-five years later I would be teaching precisely in that city, and at that university.)

The opportunity to travel opened new professional possibilities for me. My horizons broadened, contributing to my further education, as other invitations followed, and I regularly participated in international history and economic history conferences and congresses. The most important of these were three visiting fellowships at Oxford University: at St. Anthony's College in 1972, and again in 1973, where I participated in a major project on modern Central and East European economic history; and in 1980 at the elegant All Souls College where I spent half a year. All Souls is not a teaching college but a kind of advanced studies institute with permanent, life-time fellows, only males at that time. A few years later it was a sensation when the first female fellow was elected.

Every afternoon we had high tea, and in the evening fellows dinner, when we had to wear tuxedo. Dinner was served by butlers in white gloves. The food was better than at the best restaurants. Dessert, fruits, and dessert wines were served in a separate room, and sometimes, on festive occasions, included a hundred-year old Madeira from the wine cellars of the college. It was a great experience but also a challenge: according to British college tradition, one often was supposed to lay down his knife and fork and talk with one's neighbors during the meal. I was almost unable to adjust to this custom because in my childhood all I heard was: "never talk while eating!" I finished eating quietly while the others' plates were still almost untouched. It was equally uncomfortable that my colleagues used knife and fork even for apples and banana. This looked artificial to me.

The great historian, A.J.P. Taylor once described to me his early college memories. After a heavy meal and excessive drinking, he said, he drove home, opened the car door but could get out only by falling. I could easily imagine that situation. Nevertheless, it was a very useful time to work undisturbed on a project. My fourteen-year old younger daughter, Nora was with me, and attended school there.

All Souls was often visited by high-power politicians. The newly elected Prime Minister Margaret Thatcher dined once with the fellows. One of her cabinet members was a fellow of the College. Another time Prince Charles arrived. All the fellows were waiting in the courtyard, and the Warden introduced us one by one, saying when they came to me: "Our visiting fellow from Hungary…" but having no time to mention my name because Prince Charles looked at me and asked: "Professor Berend from Karl Marx University of Economics?" I was more than surprised and impolitely asked him: "how do you know?" He smiled and answered: "I prepared in the car," and asked about the situation in Hungary, compared to Yugoslavia which he had visited and knew.

Those and several other visits, grants which made possible relatively longer stays at American universities and research institutes were my endless universities until I reached my early 50s. (I did not think about it then, but in retrospect, without these additional "university years" I would not have been able to build a successful career as a historian, and open a new chapter in my life in 1990 by teaching and continuing my research work and publications 6,000 miles away from home on a different continent, in a different country and culture, in a very different city and a different university system, at the University of California in Los Angeles. The best, most balanced and pleasant, sunny time of my life would certainly never happen without those illuminating fellowships and visits.)

Those invitations, visits, and lectures, although I did not realize it immediately, had another important side effect: they strengthened my position and provided me with better safeguards in Hungary. During the often sharp confrontations of the 1980s, György Aczél an insider of the Kádár leadership, kindly suggested ways to strengthen my international standing as protection against potential political dangers.

A Widening World, Learning by Traveling

"My universities" after 1960, as described above, were directly connected with the transformation and opening of Hungary. The new situation seemed unnatural to me, because the country had been closed since 1947–48. The borders were physically sealed off by means of barbed wire fences, mine fields, and watch towers. After my forced travel to Dachau in 1944, I could not leave the country again until 1958, when, on an Academy of Sciences grant, I was allowed go to East Germany for a month. I stayed in East Berlin. The Berlin Wall did not yet exist, and I could visit West Berlin by *U-bahn* or *S-bahn*, the efficient underground and speed-train systems. I often did so, and the difference was amazing. The eastern half of the city was still in ruins and cleaned empty lots. The famous boulevard *Unter den Linden* was surrounded by empty façades and bombed and burned buildings, and except for the newly built *Stalinalle*, one saw hardly any new buildings at all. West Berlin, however, had become a flourishing city with packed department stores. The only ruin I saw there was the bombed-out church on *Kurfürstendam*, preserved as a war monument. Nevertheless, this trip to a peculiarly partitioned city was not yet an eye-opening experience for me. West Berlin, in the middle of East Germany, might have been, and in certain sense was, a kind of shop-window. But I did not think that I had seen "The West."

The real shock, however, came a few years later: after 1961, Hungarian citizens, with some restrictions, were allowed to get passports and make tourist trips to the West. This was a part of the new policy of the Kádár regime, and it met with euphoric welcome, especially among intellectuals and professionals. Tourist trips to Italy, France, and other places became trendy; friends often came together to watch slides and photos made during these tours.

I can prove the truth of Mark Twain's remark that "travel is fatal to prejudice, bigotry and narrow-mindedness." The regular visits to the West exposed several official lies and narrow-minded views. Among others it became astonishingly clear that the highly touted growth advantage of the planned economy was simply not true. Western Europe, by the time I became acquainted with it, was a rapidly growing, highly prosperous world. Governments launched successful housing programs and built millions of apartments. The road system was incomparable. It took about the same amount of time for a Hungarian train to cover the modest 40 kilometer distance between Budapest and the small town of Vác in the 1960s as it did in 1846, when the train was inaugurated as the first railway line in Hungary, eventually the first part of the line that was to connect Budapest with Vienna. But in 1976 I experienced the 200-kilometer-per-hour speed on the Shinkanzen train in Japan during my first visit there. The West shifted into fifth gear with full employment and a four percent growth per annum. This was not due alone to the historical advantage that the West inherited, but also the result of the efficient postwar modernization policy, and the capability of the system.

The opening of Hungary went hand in hand with the arrival of automobiles. Until the 1960s, private cars hardly existed in Hungary. In 1965, only one person in a hundred had a car, by 1988, 18 per 100 people. The regime opened towards consumerism to pacify the population, and after decades of extremely poor conditions, an enthusiastic society welcomed this change as a sign of a new world. Looking back at those years, we remained quite poor, but we did not feel that way. Just the opposite: as I reconstruct my feelings, I thought that things were getting better day by day, although in fact only a relatively narrow layer of the society, the intelligentsia and professionals could afford luxuries.

Those years became a turning point in my life. By 1961, with the help of the University, I was able to buy an apartment of my own, the first one in my life. Zsuzsa was six years old, and we moved into the 600-square-foot apartment with a feeling of extreme luxury. I had become associate professor, and my wife was a high-school teacher. In 1962, we also bought a Czech-made Skoda Octavia car. That was the first year when, having triumphantly received my passport, I could go to Rome! Then, as on my previous trip to Stockholm, we took the train, but on all later trips, I had already the confidence to drive by car. The Hungarian currency was not convertible, but the National Bank provided $75 for a tourist trip that you could buy, and if you went by car, some additional money for gasoline. We packed some non-perishable food because we planned to stay for two weeks, and could not afford restaurants. The cost of living in the early 1960s, of course, was still very cheap. Even in the mid-sixties, when I spent a year in New York as a Ford Fellow, from my minimal grant I paid only $23 for a week for a miniature, 21' by 9' hotel room on the West side of Manhattan, within walking distance of Columbia University. It even had a kitchenette.

But during these trips we stayed at terrible hotels. In Vienna it was impossible to sleep in the cheap hotel, because of the renewed offensives of bedbugs. We paid only $5–6 per night for those hotel rooms even in Paris. At that time tourist guides were published in the United States with the title "Europe on Five Dollars a Day." Nevertheless, $75 per a person for two weeks was dreadfully little. Even a good Italian ice-cream seemed to be a luxury, and we could not afford a bus or a tram. But who cared? We walked and walked, eager to see everything, and we visited every church and museum possible. And we traveled every year, until regulations tightened again, and hard currency became available less often, every third year only.

Those tourist trips to Italy, France, Greece, Austria, Germany, Egypt, the Dalmatian seashore, and several other places offered endless pleasure. Some of those trips enriched me with unique and entertaining experiences. In 1964, for example, I received an invitation from the St. Johanns Club, Vienna to give a lecture on the Hungarian reform. I was informed that they also invited Ota Šik, the "father" of the Czechoslovak economic reform. I accepted the invitation although I had never heard about that club before. It turned out that the institution was an exclusive club of the Austrian aristocracy. Among the participants I met with several people, some my age, but whose surnames matched those of the highest political and landowning families from the history of the Habsburg Empire. There were princes and counts, descendants of members of the inner circle of the court, family members of former prime ministers and leading military personnel, such as Cerni, Schwarzenberg, Festetich, and even a Habsburg.

I delivered the lecture, answered dozens of questions and talked with several participants, especially because after my talk, they invited me to the closing ball of their meeting that same evening. I was told that it was a white tie event, but they encouraged me to come in the dark gray suit I was wearing. The ball was a shocking surprise to me: men I had talked with about Hungarian economic problems were dressed in tails bedecked with various kinds of medals and decorations, the women in full evening dresses. It looked a grand operetta by Franz Lehar but it was real, a social enclosure from the previous century.

Those trips also strengthened my belief in human creativity and taught me to admire human achievement. In this respect three trips made an equally great impact on me: the monumental ruins of ancient Mycenae on the Peloponnesian peninsula; the amazing Aztec Sun and Moon pyramids in Teotihuacan, Mexico; and, in a surprisingly similar way, Manhattan in New York. All of them, although in different ways and thousands years away from each other, demonstrated the greatness of human knowledge and creativity.

These first trips had a much greater importance on my life than visiting the Uffizi museum, the Vatican, the Louvre, Versailles, the Acropolis, or Greenwich Village. We stepped out into the open air from the closed society we had lived in before. A closed society, as Karl Popper characterized it, was not only physically cut off from the other parts of the world, but also lacked true information and used the arts as a propaganda weapon. During the early 1950s, as a consequence, I believed that Soviet agriculture was the most advanced in the world because in the newsreels I saw harvesting combines in Ukraine, which I had never seen before, and knew nothing about the West for comparison. One could not get a foreign daily newspaper, and libraries also had to close sections where "dangerous" works were located. Our information was based on the official one-sided and often false radio-broadcasts and what we learned from the official newspapers. Now we suddenly experienced and learned the truth about the West.

On one of my Western trips I bought George Orwell's *1984*. Another time I read *Darkness at Noon* by Arthur Koestler, a former compatriot.

Reading these was a revelation. During my Ford scholar year in New York, I read everything about the creation of the Soviet economic model and the historic debates in the 1920s. It was totally new to me, and I was able to publish a summary of it in *Valóság* (Reality), an influential social science periodical in Hungary. I saved some money from my grant in New York, and subscribed to Time Magazine, which came by mail to Budapest regularly for two years. Traveling was an eye-opening exercise, a school stocked with fresh information.

My trips, both the tourist excursions or "official" visits based on conference invitations and grants, were enlightening, and the people I met and talked with even more so. My 1982–83 year in Washington, D.C., with a grant from the Woodrow Wilson International Center for Scholars, access to the Library of Congress, weekly debates and discussions in the wonderful "castle" building on the Mall with well-known politicians and Jim Billington, then director of the Center and later Librarian of Congress, crowned my Western experiences. Unlike the debates during most of my other visits, these were not restricted to my professional field but covered a huge variety of cultural, political, and contemporary issues. American politics and problems of various countries broadened my horizon, for example, a discussion on Chile with fellows of the Center who had emigrated after the Pinochet coup. I realized that the broad spectrum enriched my approach to the historical issues I was preoccupied with. That year also gave me firsthand information on the Polish Solidarity movement via Tadeusz Kowalik, one of Lech Wałęsa's advisers, who was also a fellow, for a second year there because it became impossible for him to go home to Warsaw after Martial Law was introduced in 1981. We have been close friends ever since that time.

During these trips, mostly through scholarly-tourism to Egypt, Iraq, and India I also saw some Third World countries and gained understanding of important historical and political questions: What are the causes of backwardness and are there cultural factors in it? What might be the way out? Simplistic, over-politicized answers did not satisfy me any longer.

Hungary's narrow world with its lies and one-sided information, the political thinking and ideology that penetrated our lives gradually lost influence, and I began to understand the world, the different countries, the wide variety of views and arguments. The socialist "achievements," which

I had found truly convincing before, became relative and limited. Although I preserved my social sensitivity and the longing for social justice I had developed during and after the war, I now realized that there are multiple roads towards achieving it. Moreover, I realized that the effectiveness of the one I welcomed after the war and later experienced in Hungary fell behind West European practice.

Two or three visits to Sweden and Denmark taught me about the Western welfare state, especially since I had both friends and relatives there. One of my former colleagues from the university, another former friend and colleague of my wife, and one of my cousins, left Hungary in 1956 and settled in Stockholm. I met them several times and our talks opened a window for me to see and understand that world. At the time of my visits, the "Swedish model" was discovered in the scholarly and political literature in the West as well. Although its practice was present for decades, it was only then that the Swedish or Scandinavian social model became a major topic of economic discourse.

I had long talks with Italian "Euro-communist" historians, once in the middle of Rome on the wonderful square of *Campo di Fiori*, a lively market in the morning but a pleasant restaurant row in the afternoon and evening. Sitting there and eating seafood for the first time in my life while discussing political and philosophical issues made it clear that Eastern communism was manifold mistaken. These experiences played an important role in my political education, in the process of what I call "social-democratization" of my standpoints. My eyes opened to the conclusion that Western social democracy and the welfare state embodied and more efficiently realized the values I appreciated, and served the most efficiently the combined goals of social justice and economic prosperity, catching up with the most advanced countries. I just realized from my scholarly research that the Scandinavian countries, which were hardly more developed economically than Central Europe around 1870, accomplished the most impressive growth and reached the per capita income level of the West by the 1960s.

If Western visits made socialist achievements seem relative and petty, like most Hungarians in those days, nevertheless, I was proud of the progress we had achieved in Hungary compared to other Soviet Bloc countries. I felt it possible to advance further and further on the road to reform. Various visits to neighboring countries strengthened that belief.

Traveling to neighboring state socialist countries was impossible in the 1950s. Even the eastern borders of the country were hermetically sealed. The situation changed, of course, after 1956, and I made many trips to all these countries. These visits were exciting and offered interesting comparisons, also showing that Western views were often over-simplified when they saw the entire region as all the same, a uniform red-spot on the map. A few episodes made deep impressions on me.

My first visit to Yugoslavia in 1968 impressed me deeply. Here was a different kind of socialism from what I knew. I felt I was in the West. The shops were full of goods and the Slovenian capital Ljubljana looked like a Western city. The Dalmatian coast and the Istria peninsula were a tourist paradise. Although the situation strongly improved in Hungary during those years I felt that we were still decades behind.

But my visit to Belgrade in late 1989 showed a dramatically different situation. A devastating hyper-inflation of more than one thousand percent that year had ruined the economy, and I got a taste of the steeply rising tide of nationalism when visited the Serbian Academy, the hotbed of Serb nationalism at that time. While Yugoslavia was an envied model for me in the sixties, it became clear that serious drama would follow in the early nineties. I was not surprised, but felt a deep sorrow when the multiethnic country exploded and declined into bloody civil war in 1991.

My visit to Poland in 1976 remains memorable because of the huge difference in the economic situation compared to Hungary. It was summer, and I was invited to dinner at the home of the Rector of Kraków University. The Rector's wife proudly noted before the dinner that she was extremely fortunate because she had been able to buy meat and some fresh tomatoes in the black market. The state of food supplies in Poland was desperate. Although Gomulka rejected the forced collectivization of agriculture after 1956, the government nevertheless applied all the restrictive Soviet-type policy measures against agriculture, including the compulsory delivery quota system and a non-market, artificial price level. This killed all incentives for the peasants, and millions of farmers were not interested, or were unable to, produce for the market, in a marked contrast to Hungary where food shortages were unknown from the mid-sixties on, and the reform made collectivized agriculture market-oriented and quite prosperous.

This visit enriched me also with my first personal experience of Polish noble gallantry as an everyday habit. Although non-existent in the United States, the old Central and Eastern European custom, at least in earlier decades, had been for men to kiss the hands of women when introduced. Poland, however, was more extreme in this respect than any other country. During our visit, the University of Kraków had a celebration and the Rector gave a reception on that occasion. We were invited. The Rector stood at the entrance, welcomed the arriving guests, and when we arrived he kissed the hand not only of my wife, but also of my daughter—who was only seven years old. It was the first time in her life that such a thing happened to her.

Romania's conditions were always among the worst. Three of my visits between the early 1960s and January 1990 gave me broad information about the country. My first two-week visit in 1961 educated me about the infamous Romanian communist-nationalism. After arriving in Bucharest I asked the office of the Ministry of Education to send me for a short visit to Cluj-Kolozsvár, the capital of Transylvania. They refused to do so, but I insisted, and in the end I was allowed to visit that strongly Hungarian-inhabited city. I was received by the Institute of History, and invited to lecture, but told that I must speak in Romanian. Because I did not speak that language, they suggested that I write the text in one of the world' major languages for them to translate it into Romanian. Somebody would read the Romanian translation after my short introduction. As I already knew, most of the members of the Institute were Hungarian. Only one man in the audience was ethnic Romanian, but he was as fluent in Hungarian as most of his generation. It did not matter; my lecture was read in Romanian.

During that visit, I was invited by a known Hungarian intellectual to a dinner at his home in Cluj-Kolozsvár. We had already been served the main course and started eating a lamb chop when the wife apologized. "Today, I was unable to get meat at the shop." I did not understand, but she explained: to Romanians lamb was meat, but not to Hungarians to whom meat meant pork. In the early 1960s, though the two communities, Romanian and Hungarian, with almost equal share in the city's population, lived next to each other, had contacts, even intermarriages, they still had their own different customs and separate social lives.

On a visit to the mid 1970s to Bucharest I went one evening to the theater from my hotel. Crossing the street at a spot without traffic lights,

I was stopped by a policeman. The only document I had was my Hungarian passport. He put it into his pocket and refused to return it. I had heard a lot about petty corruption in Romania; moreover, on the previous day in the Romanian National Museum I had seen and admired the famous nineteenth-century painting "Going to the office," of Nicolae Grigorescu. It showed a man with a piece of paper in his left hand, some kind of application, and a goose under his right arm. I did what I had never done or even tried in my life before: I passed a banknote to the policeman. Its value was equivalent to a dollar or two. He gave me my passport back immediately, and let me go to the theater in time.

I was also invited to a meeting which was opened by Nicolae Ceauşescu, the notorious party boss. As a guest and member of a Hungarian educational delegation, I was seated in the first row, and observed the dictator closely. He looked like a man lacking self-confidence. He stuck to his written speech, and did not look up at the audience even once. He bore the marks of a rigid and obstinate personality. I was not surprised by the events of December 1989 in Bucharest, including the bizarre televised "trial" and execution of the Ceauşescu couple that I watched in my Budapest apartment.

My third visit was connected with those events. I arrived to a ruined Bucharest in January 1990, two weeks after the revolution that swept the Ceauşescu regime away. The burned-out buildings signaled the bloody confrontation between rioting people and the heavily armed Securitate, the police army, the only armed revolution in Central and Eastern Europe in 1989. All the other regimes had collapsed virtually peacefully. I delivered gifts from the Hungarian Academy, a huge collection of books, since the Bucharest library was burned down, and the promise that we would finance three Romanian scholars' participation at the Leuven International Economic History Congress that year. Romania was starting its transformation from far behind, and the European Union strongly criticized the widespread corruption, demanding strong actions against it. Success would be not easy.

Traveling continued to be one of the most important universities in my life. Trips to China in 1986 and 2003 offered extremely personal impressions of a masterful project in economic transformation and modernization. On the first trip, beside Beijing and Canton, I visited villages and one of the special economic zones, Shenzhen, where privatization and marketization began and Japanese companies established subsidiaries after the terrible setbacks of Chairman Mao's "people's blast-furnaces" in backyards and the devastating Great Cultural Revolution.

The second trip took us along the Silk Road. I experienced the impressive results of the reforms that had started at the time of my first visit two decades before. I was immensely impressed by Shanghai with its visibly exceptional dynamic modernization, but also struck by the sharp difference between such ultra-modern cities and the nearly medieval villages. Progress, nevertheless, was striking, and it strongly influenced my view and work on Central and East European post-communist transformation. China followed a rather different path from that of the countries of Central and East Europe. The political structures did not change, but behind the shield of authoritarian power, China was methodically building up a competitive capitalist economy. The transformation and introduction of market economy began in agriculture, which was the dominant sector of the Chinese economy. The regime did not rush to privatize state-owned companies, but opened the door to the establishing of private ones and encouraged foreign investments, creating a competitive private sector. All this transformed the economy without the serious transitory decline that characterized Central and Eastern Europe, and generated an unparalleled growth rate of around 10 percent a year. I admired the smart gradualism and exceptional success of Chinese transformation.

The success of the Chinese reform was especially interesting for me, because its beginning was closely connected to the Hungarian economic reform. In 1978, a large Chinese delegation arrived in Budapest and, among other places, visited my university. I arrived at my office from another meeting a few minutes late, and the delegation was already there. I will never forget the picture: in the waiting room of the rector's office there stood a coat rack; it was winter, and the rack was full of completely identical gray overcoats. All of Chinese had the same coat just like we had in Hungary in the 1950s. I entered my room to welcome the Chinese economists but could not resist asking the question: how would they figure out whose coat was who's after the meeting? They came to learn, but soon surpassed the "teachers."

Also through my travels across Mexico, including the medieval atmosphere of the Chiapas region's native villages, I understood the problem of backwardness even better.

Those experiences illuminated the central role of social and cultural factors in life and their impact on economic performance. On a Sunday morning we were allowed to visit the Catholic church of one the Chiapas villages. The church was full of people, sitting on the ground in big groups. No priest was around, but they performed a religious ritual themselves. A middle aged lady swung a chicken around her son's head and body, and then killed the chicken. Pagan animal sacrifice inside a Catholic church clearly signaled the survival of old tribal cultural traditions.

I learned the most about Third World countries and the possibility of breaking out of backwardness during our recent three week visit to Indochina. Thailand, Laos, and Cambodia, especially the last two, are parts of the least developed world. The countryside remained frozen in the pre-industrial age. Poverty was extremely visible. The saddest experience was our visit from *Siem Reap* to the enormous *Tonle Sap* lake, the second biggest in the world, where nearly three and half million, mostly Vietnamese immigrants live in boats, floating "houses," in deep misery without the barest elements of modern civilization. In that region the average income of the population is half a dollar per day. Our boat was approached by several small boats. In one of them a woman was rowing and nursing her baby. Five or six year old children jumped over to our boat and tried selling bananas. Selling and begging were combined. Illiteracy is dominant in Cambodia, and corruption penetrates every sphere of life. I talked to a former teacher who left the school, partly because teacher's salaries in Cambodia offer an income of less than one dollar a day. He mentioned that the students' families, living in deep poverty, are being forced in different ways to pay teachers some extra cents and they collect about $4 per day from a class.

At the end of the trip we arrived in Singapore, nearer to the Equator than the other countries we visited before and with a similar history of colonial status. Actually in the early nineteenth century when the Brits colonized the small island, there were altogether one-thousand fishermen who lived there. When the Brits established a commercial outpost, Chinese immigrants began to perform the physical work. Singapore established its independent state in 1965. The government introduced a paternalistic kind of enlightened absolutism with modern healthcare, and high level education. Nowadays, the country has 4.3 million inhabitants, mostly Chinese, and 44 percent of the college-age generation is enrolled in higher education. Strong state intervention penetrates every sphere of life and the economy. Singapore created a highly developed, clean paradise. Living standards reached 70 percent of those in America. There is excellent, modern housing, no garbage on the streets and no corruption in the country. In the taxi, a posted English warning informs you that it is a criminal act for the driver to ask for more than the officially established fee. They built up high tech industries, moreover, a post-industrial economy where 70 percent of the population is working in services and exports high tech services. All of these things were accomplished within forty years.

The sharp contrast between Cambodia and Laos on the one side and Singapore on the other, countries in the same region, under the same climate, and a similar colonial background, clearly demonstrate the role of the human and educational factors in modern social and economic transformation.

Although in a very different way, it was also galvanizing to see the rapid development of Sicily in the late 1990s. This traditionally backward region of Italy, the "south of the south," which before had a lower economic level than Eastern Europe, had made striking progress. The beautifully reconstructed and renovated medieval churches and other buildings put the role of the European Union's assistance on exhibit. The EU's fingerprint was everywhere.

On the other hand, I gained a rather different impression from my visit to Greece in the late 1990s. The Greek islands were beautiful, but infrastructure did not work. Even in my childhood I did not see anything like the Mykonos port police's crank telephone. Schedules for the boat lines among the islands were not available, and in Athens garbage was not collected. Waiters often cheated in restaurants. I began to understand the interesting and unique exception of Greece. This was the only country accepted from the Mediterranean periphery into the European Union a half decade before Spain and Portugal. But unlike those two countries, let alone Ireland, Greece that was not industrialized before, was unable to use the opportunity, could not compete and develop closer ties to the West, and suffered a relative decline compared to the faster growing old member countries of the Union.

In the International Community of Historians; Friends all Over the World

The exciting and inspiring XIth International History Congress in Stockholm in 1960 organized by the International Committee of Historical Sciences, and the political changes in Hungary opened a gate for me to integrate into the community of historians. This Congress turned out to be the cradle of a new scholarly organization, the International Economic History Association. Fernand Braudel and Michael Postan, the two doyens of economic history, founded this independent institution that held its first meeting there and continued to meet somewhere in the world every three or four years from then on. I never missed a congress of either of these two organizations, and became a permanent speaker and organizer of sessions between 1965 and 1994.

Both the international history congresses every five years and the economic history congresses became natural scholarly environments in my life. Their importance for my work was extraordinary. They opened the window of international scholarship, gave new inspiration, and contributed to publication possibilities in the West.

To illustrate their importance, let me mention the International Economic History Congress held in Munich in 1965, which inspired György Ránki and myself to turn towards comparative history. Until that time we had conducted archival research, publishing a few books on Hungarian economic history. However, when Eric Hobsbawm organized a session and invited us to present a paper on comparative Central and East European labor history at this Congress, our study proved to be a breakthrough that changed our careers. First of all we realized how inspiring and interesting the comparative approach was, and how much deeper and better the understanding of history that it afforded. From Munich we went to Vienna to participate in the International History Congress. We had just returned to Budapest in a mood of euphoria, when the telephone rang and Professor Shepherd Clough of Columbia University was on the line. He had arrived in Budapest from Vienna and wanted to meet us. Sitting on the terrace of the famous downtown Gerbaud coffeehouse, Clough invited Ránki and me to write a comparative economic history of Central and Eastern Europe in the 19th and 20th centuries for Columbia University Press. That was difficult task and a real challenge, but we accepted instantly without hesitation.

At almost the same time Professor Walter Minchinton of Exeter University, England, also came from international meetings to visit Budapest, and asked us to write a book on modern Hungarian economic history for the series National Economic Histories, which he had begun editing for David & Charles and Barnes & Noble. That was much easier for us: we could use all the research and publications from the beginning of our career. Both books came out in the United States and Britain in 1974, and were almost immediately translated and published in Italy and Japan.

The opportunity opened up for us both to become integrated into the international world of scholarship, and we made it turn into reality. We were both hard workers who regularly did 12–14 hour workdays and delivered the manuscripts on time. The key factor of our rapid integration, however, was the advantageous political situation. Though these were the years of the Cold War, they were also a period of efforts to decrease East–West tension and confrontation after the Kennedy–Khrushchev meeting, and especially after the 1963 agreement. In the scholarly world, attempts were made to increase regular exchanges. Nevertheless, most of the Soviet Bloc countries remained closed off. Our colleagues from most of the neighboring countries were isolated, cut off from the international community. Some historians who were allowed to appear at international forums had to perform ideological services consisting of ideological attacks against the West.

Karl Dietrich Erdmann, President of the International Committee of Historical Sciences between 1975 and 1980, wrote a book on the history of the Committee and its international congresses. He maintained that between 1960 and 1985, politics and an Eastern "ideological offensive" dominated the meetings. After the Stockholm Congress, a Western participant complained about the "non-scientific, if not anti-scientific debates which are not encouraging for the organizers of future congresses." Another complained about ideological Eastern, most of all East German and Soviet attacks that "tyrannized the Stockholm Congress." Erdman noted the fear that historical congresses "could degenerate into public spectacles." (Erdman, 2005, 247–9)

After the San Francisco Congress in 1975, a Soviet journal proudly announced: "The activities of the scholars of the socialist countries transformed the congress into a platform for the propaganda of Marxist historical understanding." The Bucharest Congress in 1980 was used to propagate Romanian communist-nationalism and historical myths by celebrating the "2,050th anniversary" of the "foundation of the first centralized, independent Dacian state," which was considered to be the foundation of Romania. The traditional nationalist "Daco-Roman continuity" myth became the official historical explanation in communist Romania. According to that the Roman invaders in the second and third centuries blended with the Dacians in Transylvania and created the Romanian nation. Bulgaria, in a similar way, joined to celebrate the 1,300th anniversary of their state formation. I witnessed these ideological confrontations and stupid propaganda campaigns with shame.

Scholarly collaboration between East and West in this over-politicized environment was almost impossible. Only the Poles and the Hungarians were the exception. We could travel freely, had become up to date on modern scholarship in our fields, spoke foreign languages, and concentrated on scholarly work. Whenever a Western institution or scholar looked for Eastern contacts and collaboration, Poles and Hungarians were the obvious partners. Polish and Hungarian historiography at its best reached a high international standard and was widely acknowledged and published in Western journals. Historians from these countries participated in international projects and were invited as visiting professors by Western universities. At the XVIIIth International Congress of History in Montreal in 1995, a three-member panel conducted a televised discussion of the usefulness of research and history writing. One of the members of the panel, the Norwegian Professor Ida Bloom, generalized that historiography in postwar communist countries merely served the political directives of the party and government. The panel's British member, Professor Theo Barker of the London School of Economics, and the retiring president of the International Committee of Historical Sciences, sharply rejected that stereotype referring to the scholarly results of Hungarian historiography which he knew well.

It was crucially important to keep the international associations and congresses alive. Furthermore, the International Economic History Association and congresses were organizations of cooperation and scholarly forums, not ideological battlefields. My former professor, Zsigmond Pál Pach, as a clear expression of this recognition, was elected President of the International Economic History Association at its Edinburgh Congress in 1978, and the next congress was held in Budapest in 1982. My friend György Ránki became First Vice President of the other historical organization, the International Committee of Historical Sciences and would have become the President of the Committee at the next election in 1990 had he lived. These were great honors and also reflected our situation in the international scholarly arena. I became member of the Executive Committee of the International Economic History Association in 1982, and later, in 1986, vice president.

With longer visits to various countries and regular participation in international scholarly forums, I enlarged my circle of friends, an equally important part of my life. Friendships have always been important to me, and I have been surrounded by friends since childhood. I was the type who made more friends than enemies. I think I also had the instinct to recognize friends in people I met. In most cases if I felt some natural empathy and connection at the first acquaintance, I did not change my mind. First impressions played an important role in my human contacts. I always had a hard time revising an opinion I formed on a first meeting. On the other hand, sometimes a bad first impression later changed from further intellectual contacts. As it turned out, in most cases I had to return to my first impression because it was better than the intellectually crafted second one. Altogether I was always interested in people, and if I liked somebody I became a good friend.

To illustrate, let me mention two episodes from my twenties. At university I became a close friend of Feri Hecht, who had been a factory worker before, and I helped him to get ready for exams. After graduation he joined the Hungarian secret police. During the 1956 revolution, members of that institution were hunted and often lynched. On one of those October days Feri, dressed as a regular police sergeant, dropped by my home to ask for help. He worried about his wife and young son, and also about the belongings in their apartment. I immediately went over to their apartment and accompanied his wife, Ilonka, and the child to our place. She packed belongings in two baggages, I took two of his overcoats and we walked back with the heavy load to our apartment. They stayed at our apartment for several days until they found relatives to take them in.

A few weeks later, after the second Soviet invasion defeated the revolution on November 4, as in an absurd drama I got a call from Vera, the wife of another good friend, István Eörsi, a poet I also knew from university, a close friend who actively participated in the revolution and was arrested after the defeat. She worried about a possible search of their home and, wanting to save certain books, asked me for help. I went there in the evening and made two trips, taking books in suitcases to my home, where they remained for some years. I must note that although my friendship with Eörsi continued after his return from prison in the early 1960s, later, after he was divorced and, more important, became a courageous dissident while I was elevated to the establishment's elite, he grew alienated from me.

I take friendship seriously, but my diplomatic nature and my natural inclination to avoid confrontation also helps keep friends, even if in certain spheres of life our views grow sharply different. If I see basic values in somebody's character, I easily may shelve my reservations about secondary issues such as certain weaknesses or political differences. What do I mean about basic values? Let me explain it by one characteristic example. I considered one of my colleagues and friends to be a superb historian, extremely smart and also a warm, likable, loyal man and friend. On the other hand he was an arch-conservative on several social and political issues. I strongly opposed his positions, but I felt that his personal integrity was paramount. By an unspoken gentlemen's agreement, we avoided discussing issues that divided us. Each of us knew we would not convince the other on issues that divided us but we were able to remain good friends. Several friendships from high school and university years have accompanied me to the present.

These characteristics have led to friendships everywhere, including the international scholarly community. Colleagues whom I met during my stay in a country or at a conference often became and remained personal friends. I have, for example, close friends in Japan. The origins of our friendship go back to the 1970s when a dozen young Japanese historians arrived in Budapest for post-doctoral studies. They spent one or two years there, some of them working with me. Shingo Minamizuka and his wife Naoko were among them. We established a lifelong friendship and collaboration. I admired his diligence and talent, including his self-taught and fluent Hungarian. Small wonder that he became a leading historian, and later Dean and Vice President of Chiba University and director of a World History Institute in Tokyo.

My friendship with Barry Supple began in Oxford during my stay at All Souls College. He invited me to lunch in Nuffield College, where he was reader of economic history, and I totally forgot about the appointment. He called me: what happened? I told the truth and went over when he insisted. I immediately felt a close connection and we remained good friends. It happened 27 years ago. Meanwhile he became Professor of Economic History at Cambridge and Master of St. Catherine's College while I moved to the United States. We have visited each other in Budapest, Cambridge, and Los Angeles. Our meetings are not frequent, but the connection remains strong, and unchanged.

Herman Van der Wee, one of the best Belgian economic historians, and his wife Monique also became life-long friends. Herman taught at the Catholic University of Leuven, and we worked together in various ways, partly in the International Economic History Association, of which he became president, but also preparing conferences and presenting papers at same sessions. We visited each other several times and he made a real difference as a "tourist guide" with a deep knowledge of each historic building in Leuven and Bruges.

Among other close friends from different countries, I must mention Eric Hobsbawm, who has had a tremendous impact on me, inspiring me to write complex histories that combine economic, social, cultural, and political factors as they influence each other. His series of *The Age of Revolution, The Age of Capital, The Age of Empire*, and *The Age of Extremes* became a model for me. My series, an informal trilogy on the nineteenth and twentieth century history of Central and Eastern Europe, followed this pattern. I do not have to say how happy I was when Dan Chirot of the University

With Eric Hobsbawm (left), in his garden in London.

of Washington in his 'blurb' on the back of my *Decades of Crisis*, the middle part of my series, stated: "Like Eric Hobsbawm's masterful histories of economic, social, and cultural change in Europe, Berend's book covers a vast variety of changes, and convincingly shows that they were all related."

It was much more than a symbolic gesture for me that Hobsbawm participated in the conference at UCLA to celebrate my 75th birthday, and that we set at the table with him and his wife Marlene at his 90th birthday celebration in London. The festivity was called, paraphrasing the title of his famous book, "Towards an Extreme Age." For the occasion, his son and daughter sang a song that ended in the following way: "The greatest cause/ He'd ever seen/ Towards equality/ For human beings/ Although he's ageing'/ He's still engagin'/ Now Eric's ninety."

The international scholarly community has a huge importance in my life. When I made my first brief contribution at the Stockholm Congress in 1960, I had to run back to my hotel and check words in the German dictionary. A series of conferences in Copenhagen, Munich, Vienna, Edinburgh, Leuven, Moscow, Bucharest, Bloomington, Madrid, Milan, Oslo, Sydney and others, sometimes connected with pre-conferences, taught me the routine and self confidence to be an active participant and also strengthened my identity in the international community.

It was not always undisturbed. Though I was so proud of the Hungarian passport which enabled me to travel as a "European," it turned out to be an intimidating document. Entering a Western country was often a painful and humiliating procedure. Everybody else went through quickly but we were special cases and subject to careful checking. I felt humiliated, discriminated on the basis of citizenship. This experience brought back the affront I suffered before and during the war which I so wanted to forget.

During the 1960s, another unpleasant fact made me feel like a second-class citizen: I traveled to meetings with no hard currency. If I received an official invitation, I became eligible to go, sometimes with travel and accommodation expenses covered by the institution that invited me, sometimes by the Hungarian Academy of Sciences, but restrictions prevented me from obtaining hard currency for the trip. At various professional meetings, in the close company of a dozen colleagues I would try to escape from the buffet during the break because I could not afford an espresso, and I would try to avoid invitations because I would not be able to reciprocate. Once, however, I could not escape in time. I participated at the Bureau meeting of the International Economic History Association in *Poggio a Caiano*, Italy, and Rondo Cameron of Emory University insisted on inviting me. I had to confess to my shame that I had no cash and could not return his kindness. For a while I did not feel equal in these communities. Gradually this feeling disappeared.

The possibility of traveling never became a natural occurrence. For quite a while, because of all the political uncertainty, I had the uneasy feeling that the current trip could easily be my last. Uncertainty accompanied all of us all the time because everything was a "gift" from above and not a legally institutionalized right. Since most of the Soviet Bloc countries did not open their borders for travel, I expected my ability to travel to disappear from one day to the next. This did not happen. I lectured all over the world and felt privileged. In Beijing I lectured at a research institute and in Jerusalem at the Hebrew University. I lectured in Barcelona, delivered the Santory-

Toyota lecture at the London School of Economics, and made remarks at a conference in Baghdad.

One of the most unforgettable lecture trips took me to Japan in 1976. With a month-long *Gakushin* grant I went to Tokyo, visited other cities, and lectured every weekday at a different university. Each talk was planned for three hours, and at the end there were dozens of questions. Some who attended had Xerox copies of pages from my books, and their questions would begin: "In 1974 you wrote the following," to be followed by a question, based on the quotation. It was an unusual way of asking questions, but extremely impressive and clearly expressive of the hard-working Japanese character.

In 1990, the International Committee of Historical Sciences elected me First Vice President at its Madrid Congress. Thus I was Vice President of both of the history and economic history associations and in 1995, the XVIIIth International Historical Congress in Montreal elected me president of the International Committee. My first, anxious steps into the international scholarly arena at the 1960 XIth International Congress in Stockholm were still a vivid memory. Thirty-five years had passed, and all that had happened in between and led to Montreal seemed like a miracle. On the inside I still felt like the "Easterner," an outsider not quite equal in the international community, but happy to take part and learn from others. My "Stockholm feelings" recurred for many years. Such a mindset is hard to shake. Then began an exciting five years of preparation for the XIXth Congress in Oslo in 2000.

The Oslo Congress was an emotional event and memorable in my life for several reasons. First of all, I became enriched with a unique euphoric experience as a father: I sat in the last row in one of the auditoriums, where my medievalist daughter and colleague, Nora made her debut in the international arena of historians. After the long sessions, Nora and I spent evenings of endless conversation over dinner with great friends the Hobsbawms and Villaris.

As President of the International Committee, I had the privilege to address my one thousand fellow historians from all over the world, and say goodbye to my troubled and wonderful twentieth century. For the opening session of the Congress I organized a panel with superb historians from France, Germany and India. For my introduction, I spoke as a historian whose main source was, besides historical and statistical facts, the seventy years of his own life. Let me quote in a shortened form my farewell to the concluding century:

Was it, as Sir Isaiah Berlin expressed it, the most horrible century of Western history? Eric Hobsbawm's monumental world history characterizes the twentieth century as the *Age of Extremes,* "a quarter of a century of a 'Golden Age' between two, equally long periods of catastrophes, decomposition and crisis." Mark Mazover gave the provocative title, *Dark Continent*, to his book on Europe's twentieth century, which "brought new levels of violence into European life, militarizing society…killing millions of people with the help of modern bureaucracies and technologies."

No doubt, human history has not known more well-organized and efficient regimes of extermination, ethnic cleansing, and world wars of mass destruction than the various dictatorial regimes and major wars of the twentieth century. During World War I, sixty-five million people were mobilized, nearly one-third of them were wounded and crippled, eight million people died. The statistics of World War II are even more shocking: in one single battle of Stalingrad one million people died, and on the small territory of the Auschwitz concentration camp, 1.5 million were slaughtered. Altogether more than forty million people perished.

The number of victims in this century is even larger as a consequence of bloody civil wars in Russia, Spain, Yugoslavia, Guatemala, Rwanda, the tarnished dictatorships of Hitler, Stalin, Mao, Pinochet, Mobutu, naming only a few, and the so-called "local wars" of the second half of the century in Korea, Africa, and Vietnam—where, alone, four million people were murdered.

Every word that has been said about the horror of the twentieth century is true. However, as an historian and eyewitness who was imprisoned in Hungary and experienced Hitler's concentration camps, who lived in a country of extreme historical storms and who has been a contemporary of three revolutions and five regime changes, I also look back to this concluding century as an age of unparalleled progress and human advance. I look back to the century, as Charles Dickens looked back to the bloody ending of the eighteenth century in the first paragraph of his *A Tale of Two Cities* in 1859: "It was the best of times, it was the worst of times, it was the age of wisdom. It was the age of foolishness, it was the epoch of belief, it was the epoch of incredulity, it was the season of Light, it was the season of Darkness, it was the spring of hope, it was the winter of despair."

It is the same for our extreme twentieth century. In the economic arena, the twentieth century was a period of unparalleled increase in the goods and services available, for eating, clothing, and accommodation, but also for education, culture, and entertainment. The economy increased sevenfold in Asia, sixfold in the West, fourfold in Latin America and Central and Eastern Europe, and it doubled in Africa during the 20th century. One of the most spectacular consequences, together with the achievements of science and medicine, was a new demographic revolution: the population of the world increased threefold during this single century, and the average life expectancy at birth increased from 24 to 60 years in India, from 32 to 60 years in Russia, and from 47 to 76–78 in Germany, France, the United States, and Japan.

People, in other words, live two to three times longer than before. They are also much more educated: the average years an individual spends in various stages of education increased from seven to fourteen years in the advanced West and in Central and Eastern Europe. In Asia, the number of years spent in school increased from two to nine.

Knowledge became the most decisive economic factor in an emerging or growing post-industrial society. The so-called communication and service revolutions of the last third of the century, comparable only to the British Industrial Revolution two hundred years before, created a new technological base for communication and services, for the economy more generally, and also for entertainment and education. In the technologically most advanced countries, 50 to 60 percent of the population is connected to a worldwide network. Their present seems to be the future of most of the others.

A tremendous increase in output led to a trade explosion never seen before: world exports increased nearly thirty fold, connecting each region and country more closely to the other parts of the world. Such ferocious trade went hand in hand with a dramatic change in the division of labor within the world economic system. At the beginning of the century, two-thirds of the world trade consisted of unprocessed goods. Nowadays, processed industrial products have become dominant: three-quarters of the trade among the industrially advanced Western countries consists of processed industrial products, but 60 percent of the exports of developing countries are also manufacturing products. The new structure of world trade helps the industrial progress of developing countries.

On the other hand, the gap between the rich core and the semi- and unsuccessful peripheries of the world system has consistently broadened during the twentieth century: the inter-country income spread was 10:1 at the beginning, 26:1 in mid-century, and 40:1 at the end of the century. The poorest 20 percent of the world's population receives only 1.3 percent of the global income and has a 0.9 percent rate of participation in world trade. While some areas are catching up with the West, others are lagging more and more behind.

As the most spectacular development in Europe a miraculous progress of integration progressed during the second half of the century. The foundation of the European Common Market in 1957 laid the ground of the ever-enlarging European Union with a single market, a Central Bank and a common currency, and assists the catching-up process of its less industrialized members. Ireland, long a backward periphery of England, reached the German educational level and surpassed the British income level. A Europe of hostility and war is becoming a continent of cooperation and integration.

The twentieth century, which experienced several murderous and failed regimes, has also seen a most promising innovation: the welfare state. So the century of bloody world wars and dictatorships has also humanized market capitalism, reinterpreted human rights to include the right to work, health care and education, and created a more equal society. The existence of the welfare state during the last third of the century, in the period of globalization, nevertheless, was challenged and many of its achievements were sacrificed for a more efficient and competitive economy, freed from the "burden" of welfare expenditure. We are, indeed, still living in the best of times and the worst of times, in the season of Light and the season of Darkness.

Experiencing and Writing History: a Special Friend, Books and Debates

One evening in 1967, at a dinner party following my lecture at London University, a colleague and friend introduced me to another English colleague mentioning that I had published five books. Before shaking my hand, this sharp-tongued Englishman stated: "How interesting. I recently met a Polish historian who also published several books. The salaries in Eastern Europe are seemingly so low that people are running to publish a lot." Salaries were undoubtedly low, but one could not make money by publishing scholarly books either. For me research and writing was my life, my hobby, and my best entertainment.

I started writing history because from childhood I had been touched by history and inhaled it in my everyday life. History was not a subject but life itself, penetrating into the private and everyday life of Central and Eastern Europe. That I began my life as a victim of history probably influenced me later to develop an activist attitude toward trying to influence history. My reaction was not conscious and deliberate. Actually, it did not influence my work from the beginning, but developed gradually. At first I aimed at a better understanding of history. I wanted to understand the country I lived in and the area my home country belonged to. I sought to understand and present the history of this peripheral country and area, whose troubled past and social fabric was significantly different from the lucky advanced countries of Europe, and I turned to contemporary history because the history of the countries was strongly distorted by backwardness, foreign domination, and social hatred. I realized the importance of comparative history because that was the only solid base for understanding the unique characteristics of the given region.

Historiography became inseparable from my life. Many young people experience a crisis over which direction to go, what profession to choose. I have never been in that kind of predicament. My life seemed just to happen to me. I decided to become a historian unusually early, soon after I was sixteen years old. During the 1950s and 1960s, from the age of twenty on, I spent a great part of my time in archives. It was the most fortunate period for this research since the modern period of Hungary's economic development had not been a research agenda. It was not only *terra incognita* but the archives containing the sources had just been opened. The archives of banks and companies had been kept private until the nationalization, but made public after 1950. The situation was chaotic without hard and fast rules. For a while researchers were allowed to conduct research in those archives. Much later, somewhat stricter rules were enacted, but a well-established archival law was long in coming to Hungary.

I was lucky to start my research work with my friend, György (Gyuri) Ránki. We helped each other through several difficulties. Gyuri was a wonderful friend. We had become schoolmates in 1946 when he returned from a sanatorium in Sweden where he spent a year recovering from the disease he contracted in Auschwitz. Our lives were surprisingly similar even before we knew each other. We were born in the same year in the same city, and both of us were deported to Nazi Germany, though the Jews of Budapest were typically not deported, especially at the age of fourteen. Both of us survived the concentration camps. We studied at the same high school, went on together to the same University, prepared together for exams and, both of us deciding to be economic historians, we started to work together. While students at the university we even married on the same day in January 1953. Our first children, both girls, and both named Zsuzsa, were born in the same year. We worked together for many years, even when Gyuri had a second, part-time job in the 1980s at Indiana University in Bloomington and we were 6,000 miles apart.

There were, however, "disturbing" differences in our lives, too: he divorced and had only one child, while I had a second daughter from the same marriage. Later, nevertheless, these differences also disappeared: my marriage

With colleagues and György Ránki (far right). Second from left is Gyula Juhász..

went wrong too, and I also divorced, though only after his death. At that time the second difference evaporated as well: his biggest secret came to the surface—that he had a secret second child by his girlfriend. His death at the age of fifty-eight was shocking for me. I cried bitterly during my farewell at his grave. Because of all of the similarities in our lives, his death seemed to be a signal about the possible end of my life as well. I am writing these lines, however, nearly twenty years after Gyuri's early death. Our lives, at the end, because I survived him by decades, became very different and in 2008, I delivered the Memorial Lecture at the 20th anniversary of his death at the Hungarian Academy of Sciences.

Gyuri was an extremely gifted scholar. He was much better at languages than I was; read and spoke several, including English, German, Italian, French, Russian, and Swedish. In a funny way, he created a kind of uniform pronunciation, and spoke all these languages with the same thick Hungarian accent. He was also a fast worker who never got tired. We inspired and complemented each other and made an effective team. We sat next to each other in the archives, and then at my desk at the university when we wrote. I always did the writing because I was better at that, although, during the first years we discussed our writings sentence by sentence. In later years, we sometimes went to a resort of the Academy of Sciences in the *Mátra* Mountains where we wrote several chapters of our co-authored books from early morning to late evening without disturbance. Before lunch we would go out for a fast walk down the mountain to another village located 900 feet below; in an hour we came back and continued working after the meal.

In the first period of our joint work we published a series of studies and books on the Hungarian economic development that included the impact of the Dual Monarchy. In our first book, published in 1955, we still took for granted that the lack of national independence had been harmful and blocked Hungary's road to modernization. But in a study in the mid-1960s we challenged the traditional view and rejected the traditional nationalist explanation of failures which, according to the Hungarian historiography, were always caused by outside factors and forces. In the sixties we were challenging the "colonization," or Austrian "imperialism," thesis, a traditional dogma held both by nationalist and Marxist Hungarian historiography before and after the war. We proved that the impact of the Dual Monarchy was positive. An advanced transportation system was built, which became sixth in Europe before World War I according to density (length of rails per unit of land and number of population). The banking sector profited even more from the existence of the Monarchy, generating an important capital inflow, which, according to our calculations, covered about 40 percent of investments. However, we also discussed the consequences of a "dependent development" without using the term.

In three books we described and analyzed the economic and industrial development of Hungary between 1900 and 1945, and in a fourth, German–Hungarian economic relations during Hitler's rule. We worked in Hungarian and German archives, some of them just becoming accessible for researchers. The documents of major Hungarian banks, for example, were not even in the archives yet, but still in the city's old bank buildings and cellars where they had been stored during the war and the bombings. We took sandwiches with us and worked entire days down there. One day in the cellar our sandwiches were eaten by rats. We wrote our notes on post-card sized pieces of paper and made calculations on paper by hand. Xerox machines and even calculators did not exist. We felt we were part of an interesting discovery since we were the first to read those documents.

Previous historiography in Hungary neglected and excluded twentieth century history as "not yet history."

This work to present the first historical analysis on interwar Hungary was exciting since after four hundred years in the Habsburg Empire, the country not only became independent in 1918, but also lost two-thirds of its previous territory. Adjusting to the new situation was difficult, and the country, wanting to create a base of independence, turned to economic nationalism by cutting its strong ties with Austria, building high tariff walls against imports, and attempting to replace them with domestic production. It was most successful in consumer goods industries such as textile, leather, paper, etc., which increased the level of industrialization in an overwhelmingly agricultural country. Nevertheless, the leading agricultural sector lost its markets because of the tariff wars that erupted in those years. Output decreased and the countryside was in deep poverty. The newly emerging industrial sectors were technologically backward, operating with used machinery bought in England. More important, the developing sectors in Hungary already became declining internationally.

In sharp contrast to the prewar period, foreign investments arrived in Hungary for only a few years during the second half of the 1920s, but inflow stopped during and after the Great Depression, which hit Hungary hard. Analyzing the statistics we realized the extreme rigidity of the country's economic behavior. Before World War I, Hungary delivered 25 percent of the world's wheat-flour export, and the grain economy, based on the huge markets of the Habsburg Empire, was the leading sector. This market collapsed and the grain prices fell, but the grain economy remained dominant, and the country sank into a deep economic crisis. Especially when we compared the Hungarian situation with the flexible Danish agricultural adjustment to new market conditions and requirements we understood the role of cultural-educational backwardness. Until the early 1870s Denmark, Hungary and Romania were all grain producing and exporting countries. After 1873, American and overseas grain imports precipitated a crisis in Europe, where costs of production were higher. Danish farmers, thanks to better training and organization, such as special agricultural Sunday schools, formed cooperatives for milk production and food processing. Within five years, they were able to replace grain production with animal husbandry. Moreover, when the German market stopped buying

Danish live pigs, the farmers turned towards the English "breakfast table," and exported processed bacon, butter and other dairy products. Within ten years, the Danish farmers successfully realigned production, while the uneducated Hungarian and Romanian peasants tried to compensate for falling grain prices by producing more of the same product, pushing prices further down and precipitating a decline into poverty. The role of cultural factors in economic performance was overwhelming.

This situation also taught us to discuss the relationship between the economy and politics. The permanent agricultural crisis in this agrarian country pushed Hungary right into the arms of Hitler. Nazi Germany, gearing for war and a war economy, offered its markets, and was ready to pay higher than world-market prices for agricultural products. In early 1934 Germany signed a trade agreement with Hungary and soon became the country's main trade partner. Hungary became economically dependent on and even subordinated to Hitler. This became a factor, together with the revisionist policies of the Horthy regime aimed at restoring its former borders, in Hungary's shift towards the far right. In 1939 Hungary joined the "Anti-Comintern Pact," the alliance with Hitler which, in the end, led to participation in the war, made the country a battlefield for half a year and brought about the tragic devastation of Hungary.

Beside publishing books on interwar Hungary jointly, Ránki and I also published our own monographs on the various problems of the immediate post-World War II reconstruction period in 1962 and 1963. These works offered a natural base for one of our first books in English in the National Economic Histories series published in Britain, *Hungary: A Century of Economic Development* (1974). The book covered the history of modern Hungarian economy, including a last, seventy page long chapter on the postwar socialist transformation. In 1982, it was followed by *The Hungarian Economy in the Twentieth Century*, our next book of 316 pages, also published in Britain.

Here I must return to our changing views. Although the Marxist approach to history remained influential in our interpretations, it gradually lost its role as an omnipotent key as we became more mature historians. First of all, our personal experiences of history suggested that violent revolutionary actions are not the best way to change historical trends positively. The numerous revolutionary regime changes I witnessed, from either the Right or the Left, ended disastrously. On the other hand, post-

World War II Western Europe provided a different example: positive social and economic changes were realized through parliamentary reform. During my university years I read much about "social democratic revisionism," but later, after I became acquainted with the writings of Eduard Bernstein, Karl Kautsky, and Rudolf Hilferding, I realized that these main theoreticians of the German Social Democratic Party around the turn of the twentieth century were the ones who created the basis of modern, twentieth-century social democracy for advanced countries and prophesized the success of reforms that became the forerunners of the regulated market system and the welfare state.

Based on evidence we found in archives and saw throughout the world, and from our own basic statistical calculations, we began to develop our own views. We revised several elements of the theoretical framework that we could no longer accept. Soon we dropped the oversimplified, essentially vulgar Marxist approach, which was widespread in Central and Eastern Europe, and as we began to study modern economics, and read contemporary Western works, we started to understand the various arguments and approaches of modern historiography. We could no longer accept the traditional Marxist view of imperialism, which indiscriminately condemned foreign investment in less developed countries as an exploitative tap on domestic resources. The facts clearly showed the fallacy of the exploitation concept, according to which all the advantages originating from economic contact between peripheral and advanced countries were accumulated in the core countries and all the disadvantages in the peripheries.

The opposite, liberal Ricardian concept of comparative advantage, which suggests that this contact is not a zero-sum game, and both parties profit from it necessarily, was also proved wrong when confronted with the evidence. What we realized in researching the industrialization process in the European periphery differed radically from both assumptions. Numerous cases prove that for backward countries the outcome of such an economic relationship might be either disastrous or advantageous. The outcome is not predetermined but depends on the *domestic* situation of each country, on whether they have the "social capability" to profit from the connections and generate spin-off effects.

In this respect, I have to mention my great experience as a visiting professor at Berkeley where I regularly attended the joint Berkeley-Stanford economic history seminar led by Moses Abramowitz, who introduced the concept of social capability in his path-breaking work. Reading Alexander Gerschenkron, Joseph Schumpeter and Alfred Chandler, Ránki and I realized and understood the importance of government policy, entrepreneurship, and management in economic development.

Last but not least, we also rejected the rigid concept of a superstructure that only "reflects the base" and is determined by economic factors alone. When I made an attempt to write a comprehensive history on interwar Central and Eastern Europe in two consecutive editions in the 1980s, economic, social, political and cultural history gained equal place in it. I tried to present the interrelationship and mutual "determination" among all of these spheres, instead of presenting the cultural arena as a reflection of the economic base, or a determined superstructure.

Studying modernization attempts of relatively backward countries I realized that the most important factors influencing economic performance are not only, or even mostly, economic but social and cultural, rooted in social traditions and attitudes, and sometimes arriving from outside. For example the cultural influences and ideas, coming with romantic nationalism from the West to early nineteenth century Central and Eastern Europe ignited attempts at economic modernization. On the other hand, relative economic backwardness did not lead to cultural backwardness but contributed to the emergence of a world-class literature and modern avant-garde art in Russia, an artistic movement whose strong mission was to attack obsolete social institutions and ignite modern transformation in Russia and Central Europe at the beginning of the twentieth century.

Nevertheless, several important elements of my thinking are still influenced by the Marxist approach to history, though in many ways this influence is more Keynesian. I admire and have been influenced by Karl Polanyi and Joseph Stiglitz as well. Anyway, I remain immune to neo-liberal economics that idealizes the market and rejects any kind of intervention from outside, and to postmodern arguments that deny the possibility of understanding what really happened. Hegelian dialectic, used by Marx, explaining turns in history, also had a permanent impact on me. Although I am not a determinist, I still believe in the important impact of the economy on other spheres of life, and I also believe that in spite of the rise of the middle class, the class interpretation of society still has its importance. Although

I understand that in the United States, class differentiation, due to special historical circumstances, is strongly interwoven with problems of race that still remain an important factor in politics, I do not agree with the one-sided racial interpretation of societal problems either. They are strongly embedded in class relations, the discrepancy between poor and rich, which generate huge gaps in education, cultural and behavioral patterns.

A few years after our 1974 book on the modern economic history of Hungary came out in Britain, a new British Ambassador arrived in Budapest. Gyuri and I were invited to the Ambassador's residence for dinner. Ambassador Wilson had shown us our book before dinner and remarked: "your book was recommended to me when I was getting ready for this new post. When I read it I was unable to decide whether the Hungarian authors were living in the West or in Hungary." That was excellent news: we had dropped a biased approach and reached a more balanced interpretation.

A new turning point in our professional career occurred in the mid-1960s when we turned to comparative economic history. At that time, Hungary had started to open up and we could work abroad in American and British libraries. Together we published several studies and four books on this broader, comparative topic.

From the late 1960s we began working on our *Economic Development of East-Central Europe in the 19th and 20th Centuries* for Columbia University Press. The book came out in New York in 1974. The central methodological dilemma was how to cover the eight countries of the region. In the historiography of that period comparative approaches were rare. If a work discussed several countries separate chapters were usually given to each. In reality, they were not comparative histories but compendia of independent studies. We decided to use a rarely implemented comparative method. Instead of discussing countries such as Poland and Czechoslovakia, or sub-regions such as Central Europe and the Balkans, we decided to build a topical structure to compare agricultural, industrial, and trade performance, and tariff and industrialization policies across the board.

This method definitely helped reveal national peculiarities. General trends and even regional and sub-regional characteristic became clear. In several instances features which in the national historiography were interpreted as uniquely Polish, Hungarian, or Yugoslav, showed themselves to be quite uniform in Central and Eastern Europe. It was a revelation to us regarding Hungarian economic development as well: we realized that we were wrong in our previous work, when we blamed the country's debt problem in the 1920s entirely on mistaken governmental policy. All the countries of the region applied similar policies and we realized that all of those newly established independent countries were cornered without real options in the given European economic situation. The illuminating outcome of the comparison inspired us to write a study on comparative methodology, which was published in the memorial Festschrift of Fernand Braudel in Paris.

In the early 1970s, Michael Kaser, a leading expert of communist economy at Oxford University, invited both of us to join an international team working on a major three-volume project, *The Economic History of Eastern Europe 1919–1975*. Our single-authored studies, Ránki's on the role of state, mine on the comparative interwar agricultural performance of the countries of the region, became parts of the enterprise.

The good taste of comparative history gave us the incentive to initiate a new project: an even broader comparative study, our *The European Periphery and Industrialization, 1780–1914*, published in a joint French–British series in 1982. In this work, which I considered to be the best of our joint publications, we covered and compared the Scandinavian region, the Mediterranean countries, and Central and Eastern Europe, and we analyzed the different industrialization attempts and the various factors that influenced success or led to failure. Our approach was complex and included cultural and educational as well as political, infrastructural, and economic factors such as export possibilities and the role of capital inflow. It was a great feeling when fifteen years later, one of the most talented young Swiss economic historians, Thomas David, told me that he became an economic historian because he had read this book.

The last volume that Gyuri and I published together was an *Economic History of Nineteenth Century Europe*, which appeared in Hungarian at the end of 1987. Since we had analyzed the peripheral regions of Europe in our previous work, here we turned to the comparative history of the entire continent. Here too, the innovation compared to the existing economic histories of nineteenth-century Europe, was the rejection of country-by-country discussion in separate chapters. We tried instead to develop subregions which were somewhat similar. We had a chapter on the Balkans, the Mediterranean countries, the Scandinavian countries, and the smaller West European countries, since basic similarities existed in those regions. Still, we stopped half-way, and Austria-Hungary was discussed as an independent and almost self-sufficient unit. Britain, France, Germany, and Russia were also discussed in separate chapters.

A new and interesting interrelationship, however, became evident from this approach: the industrialization of Austria and the Czech lands gave a tremendous incentive to the agricultural parts of the Habsburg Monarchy and generated a belated agricultural revolution to exploit the huge market of the industrialized provinces. The interrelationship among the various parts of the Monarchy also led to a more advanced infrastructure in the backward areas than in countries of similar economic level. Banking and credit systems, for example, reached a higher level of development than that of the economy itself. An extensive railroad construction boom also brought about a more highly developed transportation system in the relatively backward countries and provinces. For example, Hungary surpassed several more advanced West European countries in this respect. Even the more backward parts of the Monarchy such as Bosnia-Herzegovina profited from the huge capital investments and the creation of a mining industry. Bosnia was backward within Austria-Hungary, but more developed than its neighboring independent Balkan countries. Altogether almost all of the provinces, even the relative laggards gained from the complex internal relationship.

When this book came out we jokingly noted that, unlike in the previous third of a century, we did not have our next joint project in our minds. A few months later, in the spring of 1988, my closest friend and co-author of ten books died at the age of fifty-eight. I had known about his illness. Actually I accompanied him to the doctor when it was discovered, but it was still unbelievable. Only a few weeks before, at the end of 1987, we traveled together to a conference in Israel. We changed planes and had to stay overnight in Munich. As always, we shared a hotel room. Around Christmas, we also went together to the Mátra Mountain and made our usual walks. When he was hospitalized in late February, I was scheduled to go to India but before the trip, I went to see him in the hospital. He was a bit better and assured me "you can go without worrying; I will wait for you." He did not. While I was in India, he died. I learned about his will from a disordered note he made in his date-book in the hospital: "I ask Ivan to finish my incomplete manuscripts, but I don't want him to say farewell at my funeral because it would be too heavy a burden for him emotionally." I, indeed, finished his unfinished manuscripts, among them a fine economic history of World War II, but nevertheless said farewell at his coffin. He was right; I had to stop a few times when emotions overwhelmed me.

Twenty years later, unfortunately already alone, I returned to nineteenth century European economy, and began working on an economic history of the continent without national boundaries. Europe, though divided into nation states often hostile and fighting each other, emerged as an economic unit where various regions influenced each other via trade, investment and railroad construction as well as through economic ideas and joint institutions that made national borders much less important. Moreover, except a few countries, national borders dramatically changed during the nineteenth century: united Italy and Germany were established and huge multi-ethnic empires were dissolute. Regional differences such as between south and north Italy, western and eastern Germany, central and eastern France, were often sharper within a nation state than between nations.

At a commemorative session at the twentieth anniversary of Gyuri Ránki's death, the Hungarian Academy of Sciences in Budapest organized a Memorial lecture and asked me to speak. I have chosen an unusual genre for my talk. I "told" Gyuri what kind of new ideas and debates emerged after our last joint work had been published, and after his death, about nineteenth century European economic history; what kind of new challenges dominated economic history writings during the first three postwar decades. I finished with the following sentence: "Probably these were the most important points to mention. I stop here though there are still a lot to say. My dear Gyuri, we can endlessly discuss them when we meet again."

During all those years, we became integrated into the international community of economic historians and published studies in various foreign journals: the Annales in Paris, the Journal of European Economic History in Rome, the Viennese monthly, Europäische Rundschau, the London-based Journal of Contemporary History, and Texas Rice University's Austrian Yearbook, and others. We contributed to the Austrian volume on the history of Habsburg Austria-Hungary. Gyuri Ránki and I were asked to send studies to various *Festschriften*, including commemorative volumes for Fernand Braudel of France, Kristof Glaman of Denmark, Federigo Melis of Italy, Hermann Kellenbenz of Germany, and Eric Hobsbawm of Britain.

Although our interests were the same in our joint work, gradually both of us developed separate areas of research as well. Gyuri was attracted to diplomatic history and published broadly in that field, while I turned to contemporary economic problems of state socialist Hungary and published several studies and books on that topic. I met with these topics first "accidentally" during my research on postwar Hungarian reconstruction. After the 1956 revolution, I had access to the archives of the Communist Party and government of the 1940s and 1950s. General rules did not exist for using these archives. Decisions were made one by one, and the researcher did not know which parts of the archive would be opened to him, or, more importantly, which parts would remain closed.

After the publication of our first three books together, in 1960, at age thirty, György Ránki and I were awarded the highest scholarly honor in Hungary, the Kossuth Prize. As a consequence, I was elected Secretary General of the Hungarian Historical Association, a hundred-year-old institution of great prestige. That was the time when I applied for and received permission to do research in that archive. That was how the non-*Rechtsstaat* (non-constitutional state), but nevertheless somewhat liberal state socialist country worked. Although my research period was the years between 1944 and 1948, in several files I found valuable, often shocking material on the early 1950s. I made endless notes and after publishing my book on postwar reconstruction, I began working on a new study: the preparation and concept of the first Hungarian Five-Year Plan, the central economic document of Stalinist economic policy in Hungary.

If the discovery of exciting archival materials was somewhat accidental, my interest in that period and questions was genuine. We were only a few years past 1956 and the dramatic renunciation of Stalinism, including its entire program of forced, militarily motivated industrialization. The regime of János Kádár immediately announced a new era, including a new economic policy, and established a reform committee as early as the end of 1956. A program for eliminating central planning by introducing market prices and profit motivation in the economy was presented by the Committee in April 1957, but it was not even discussed by the government forum and dropped. Meanwhile the Kádár regime was consolidated and Soviet control blocked the road for such a radical change. Kádár did not want to provoke the Soviets.

The need for change, nevertheless, was pressing. The economy was bankrupt and the standard of living low. Long-term stability was strongly dependent on economic success and rising living conditions. This was evident, and I saw the need to return to reform and change the economic system. What went wrong and why? What happened in the economy in the 1950s? I wanted to understand and make it known to others. I had an exaggerated belief in the importance of my research. In retrospect, I think it was exaggerated in two senses: partly because of my naïve belief that history could be influenced by discovered truth and published facts. I also felt that I had a kind of mission to write about the recent past and make contemporary history part of Hungarian historiography. I still think it was important to modernize history writing, and that my efforts had a certain impact there, even as I gradually learned about the limits of influence of history writing. I certainly was too self-centered and emotional to evaluate the meaning of my own work. Let me confess that I am always moved when I watch the *Man of La Mancha* on stage or screen. I identify with Don Quixote's exaggerated belief in his lunatic but moral mission.

When my book on post-war Hungarian economic reconstruction came out in 1962, I was ready with a small new book on the introduction of Stalinist economic policy in Hungary. I presented the manuscript to the same publishing house, which concentrated on economics and law, and had published two of my previous books. The director, a former colleague of mine from the University, wanted to talk to me. She did not agree with major parts of the manuscript, hesitated, waited for a whole year, and then decided to publish it, except for a few pages which were omitted. The publisher also added an unusual preface maintaining that the content of the book expresses my views and my views alone, and that several controversial statements and conclusions might be wrong and corrected later. They "justified" the publication saying that thorough debates were needed to analyze the history and economic history of Hungary's socialist transformation, and that my work discovered and "courageously debated" part of the undiscovered history of the country.

This 135 pages study discussed, as its title reflects, the *Economic Policy at the Beginning of the First Five-Year Plan, 1948-1950.* The first Five-Year Plan between 1950 and1954 was the realization of Stalinist economic policy in Hungary. The overambitious and mistaken concept led to failure, starvation and required revision of the plan, as early as 1953. I dug out the facts and reasons for failure and sharply criticized the entire economic program.

It was an indictment of Stalinist economic policy, and foreshadowed the critique of the very essence of central planning. I showed that the permanent increase of plan-targets that aimed the forced industrialization of the possible fastest way, regardless the cost, the technological modernity, and efficiency. What emerged was an economy of waste. According to my calculations, one-fifth of the entire production was lost in the form of useless, low-quality and damaged products and frozen, incomplete investment projects that the government was unable to finish.

In the archives there were invaluable documents on the role of military considerations. One exciting example was the construction of the Budapest subway system. The original plan was to build an under-the-surface network with open-trench methods. The plan was changed, and the government started building deep tunnels, using Soviet machines to establish a road system under the Danube for tanks, and a system of bomb shelters for the city's population. Backing the idea for this project were both the experience of the war and the destruction all major Danube bridges in Budapest, and the London practice of using the metro tunnels as shelters. After heavy investments, nevertheless, the government was unable to continue construction that had to be stopped in 1953.

The central idea underlying the first Hungarian Five-Year Plan was military preparation. Having discovered these documents, I asked for an interview with Ernő Gerő, second in command in the Stalinist period and responsible for the economy. After Rákosi was removed from Party leadership, Gerő replaced him as Secretary General in 1956. He was himself removed during the revolution and left the country, but after a short stay in the Soviet Union, he returned to Budapest and lived as a pensioner, in isolation, making his living from translations. I was surprised, but he was ready to see me. He was the first to inform me of the telephone call from Stalin in 1948 concerning the unavoidability of World War III in three to four years. Clearly he revealed this in self-defense, but much later other evidence corroborated the truth of the story. One of my UCLA students, while doing research for an excellent book on Ana Pauker, the top Romanian communist leader, also came across the same information—the Romanian Party leadership had received it in a similar way from Moscow.

When I enthusiastically worked on that project, in 1961, I received a surprise invitation from Endre Sík, Minister of Foreign Affairs, to see him in his office. I could not imagine the reason but appeared at the given date. He and his deputy received me and explained that the international situation of Hungary had changed significantly. The "Hungarian affair," the condemnation and exclusion of Kádár's Hungary at the United Nations was taken off the agenda, and the country was accepted by the international community. Foreign Minister Sík said that the country needed highly educated top-level diplomats, and offered me a position in the country's diplomatic service. I expressed my appreciation for the offer but explained my absolute commitment to research and teaching history and politely declined the offer. I was in the middle of an exciting project, and felt it was my mission to continue.

I continued my research on contemporary economic problems and published several studies on that topic. Hungary was in an interesting position. In most Soviet Bloc countries the publication of my studies would have been impossible. It was not a coincidence that though several of my books co-authored with Gyuri, or my own books and studies were published in Western countries, none of them were translated and published in the Soviet Union. Only two or three of our articles appeared in any of the Soviet Bloc countries. The first of our translated book was published only after the regime change in the 1990s in Croatia, and another one is coming out now in Serbia.

The Kádár regime, rooted in the defeat of the 1956 revolution, strongly wanted to appease the rebellious population and gain some popular recognition and support. This is what was behind the unique consumer orientation and also the de-politization of society, ending the forced indoctrination of people, and also giving more freedom to travel, speak, and publish. The Kádár leadership sought both to stay the course and to disconnect itself from the Stalinist past of Mátyás Rákosi. This situation continually created new possibilities to speak up, giving the impression that change was not out of the question. The regime's stop-go reform process of liberalization generated hope and hopelessness at the same time but always inspired me to advocate further economic reforms. It also provided a certain elbow room for research and publication. Unlike the situation in a rigid Stalinist regime, it was now also possible to publish critical analyses on the recent past in post-1956 Hungary.

When the major economic reform, the New Economic Mechanism, as it was called, began in the mid-1960s, I was invited by the preparatory committee to present an analytical paper on the mistakes in past economic policy. This work, on important policy correction attempts, was extremely attractive for me, both from the professional and the political point of view. It validated the importance of my research as important for understanding historical processes. A further element of vanity in my enthusiasm was obvious: I was in my early thirties, still at the start of my career and the members of the Committee that prepared the economic reform belonged to the real intellectual economics elite. Included were some of my former professors, György Péter (statistics) and Tamás Nagy (political economy). Some other members such as István Friss, on the other hand, harshly criticized my small book about the first Five-Year Plan for political reasons. It was a good feeling to be invited to take part in that work. Another political factor is also clear: I believed in the importance and possibility of change. As a genuine optimist by nature, I also believed in success, although I always had to realize that the reform at best remained, as I once called it in a talk, the most radical half-measure. It surpassed that level only during the second half of the 1980s.

Besides, changes were never guaranteed to continue in Central and Eastern Europe. The country was so dependent on Soviet political trends and subject to pressure. When in 1968 the major reform did break through in Hungary and promised more freedom and a more flexible and efficient economic system, it contributed to the formation of a strongly reform-oriented group of state socialist countries. Besides Yugoslavia, Poland, and Hungary, Czechoslovakia also joined the reformers. Soviet intolerance and steadfast opposition to change, nevertheless, led to the Soviet-led military invasion against the Prague Spring in Czechoslovakia in the summer of that year. One Sunday morning the telephone rang and a friend asked me, "Have you heard the news?" No, I had not. The armies of the Warsaw Pact countries, including Hungary, had invaded Czechoslovakia! I was shocked, and looked out upon the empty Sunday morning street from the window with tears in my eyes. I remember that I felt, probably for the first time in twelve years, or for first time in my life that I was wrong to remain in Hungary in 1956.

Interestingly enough, I almost never regret anything that I did or did not do in my life. What happens—happens. It is strange for a historian, but I do not like to look back on my life. There is no sense to ruminate about anything that belongs to my past. I prefer to concentrate on the present and look forward. As it happened, I soon returned to this mode of thought. However, bad times came first.

On August 31, 1972, a frightening article was published in Moscow's Pravda about the Hungarian economic reform, the "difficulties of the Hungarian search for new ways," and "forecast" that "the next plenary session of the Central Committee of the Hungarian Socialist Workers Party will soon convene… [already] preparatory work is directed at a thorough analysis of the economic reform… Such measures are being elaborated which will increase the role of central planning and state control." That openly forecast the return to Soviet-type central planning, and significantly strengthened the hard-liners in Hungary. They initiated a major campaign against rising income differentiation and "petty bourgeois attitudes." As one article in the Party's daily declared: "One of the commonest of mistakes is to place qualification and professional talent in the first place and assign political preparedness and suitability a second and third place in the selection of managers" (*Népszabadság*, 1975, January 8). Another article reported the "workers' view" that "our intelligentsia is overvalued both financially and morally." The Party's monthly journal published articles about "protests in the name of socialist values against… bourgeois and petty bourgeois tendencies manifest in consumption." (Társadalmi Szemle, 1975, 42)

Three months later the Party's Central Committee indeed brought a resolution. The top reformist politicians were dismissed and, as I described this process in my 1988 book on the history of reforms in a chapter entitled "The reform comes to halt and reversal," the country, during the 1970s, began returning to the traditional Soviet-type of economic system that existed before the reform.

This uncertainty and permanent struggle for change strongly influenced the agenda for my research. My own research projects targeted central problems of post-1956 economic history in Hungary. New doors were opened for research and debate. The 1973 Oil Crisis and the dramatic changes in the world economy from that time on shook state socialist Eastern Europe and undermined its relative stability. All the temporary advantages—fast economic growth, full employment, and slowly rising living standards—were endangered. In Hungary, economic growth slowed from 3.6 percent per annum to 1.6 percent. Because of the dramatic rises in the price of oil and imported goods, foreign trade deficits accumulated while the country could not increase the prices of its second- and third-rate quality export products accordingly. Low quality and technologically obsolete products had to be sold at lower prices. The "terms of trade," which is the relation of a country's export and import prices, declined by 30 percent, and led to the accumulation of an enormous trade deficit.

The regime, however, wanted to continue to base political stability on consumer orientation and tried to maintain living standards. In order to achieve that, the country sought and received loans from "petrodollars," the immense surplus income of oil-producing countries because of the oil-price explosion. In a few years, more than 20 billion dollars in debt accumulated and was mostly consumed. Altogether four billion dollars were invested in the economy, but not enough to adjust to new economic challenges. Repayment was based on new credits, but rising interest rates made repayment more and more difficult.

The new situation drove the Party and the government back towards reform. The regime's rigid and inefficient economic system endangered political stability: the country had to go further in creating a more responsive economy with more market and entrepreneurial incentives. While in the early 1970s, marketization was curbed and the reform measures introduced in the mid- and late 1960s were partly eliminated, after 1979–80 Hungary returned to market reforms. A wave of concealed privatization began, as state-owned companies, shops and restaurants were rented out to private persons. The Soviet type of banking system with a single national bank in the center was changed and commercial banking was also established. Western-type value-added taxation was also introduced and the price system neared that of market economies. Most of these reform measures were introduced during the 1980s with an accelerating speed; following continued debates and struggles between the conservatives and the reformers.

The changing environment opened new possibilities for the reform-oriented intelligentsia. Discussing Hungary's economic performance and analyzing the reasons for failures, and understanding why policy changes were not realized gained more importance than ever. The possibility for change and the peaceful reorientation and rebuilding the economic system to adjust to the world economy and its requirements gained momentum. It was important to document and analyze what had happened in the Hungarian economy and, even more important, to explain that what was rejected was based on ideological and political considerations. And that was the main reason the country missed the crucial opportunities to adjust to the world economy. Failures, missteps in post-war Hungarian policy, and political struggles influenced my historical research. I had the goal to unveil hidden facts and unrealized but clearly needed policy changes. In other words, my research was motivated by my involvement in policy-making. The country was not closed any longer, but very few people closely followed Western development and debates. Provincialism excluded important information about the world.

I continued my research on contemporary Hungarian economic problems of the decades from the 1950s to the 1980s, and published two more books on these topics. The first, *Gazdasági útkeresés—1956–1965,* (Search for Economic Renewal—1956–1965) in 1983, discussed the post-1956 reorientation of economic policy, its partial success and eventual basic failure. I documented recognition of the need to replace *import-substitution policy*, which characterized Hungary and the entire region of Central and Eastern Europe since World War I, and continued during the Soviet type of drive to industrialization. The essence of that policy was protectionism, excluding foreign imports as much as possible and replacing them with domestic production. This kind of economic policy, although definitely serving industrial development and even relatively fast economic growth, killed outside competition and incentives for technological modernization. Import-substitution, which economically isolates a country, in other words, was counterproductive in the long run. I argued for an export-driven orientation, which forces countries to compete with others and to adjust to modern technology.

The reorientation of economic policy also required a change from the traditional *extensive* development policy, which characterized Central and

Eastern Europe for almost the entire twentieth century. Unlike *intensive* development strategy based on technological renewal by innovation, extensive development was assisted by forced capital accumulation and investment together with high labor input, but using the existing technological knowledge.

In our earlier research Ránki and I calculated that capital accumulation—that part of the national income that was saved—was only 6 to 8 percent in the region. Soviet-type industrialization policies after World War II increased capital accumulation to 25–30 percent by limited consumption and exploiting of the peasantry, forcing them to deliver their products to the state, which paid prices, which were much lower than world market prices. I coined the term for this policy "forced accumulation of capital." This made it possible for the state to make huge investments into industry and created millions of new jobs by recruiting millions of new workers, i.e., combine investments with labor input. Industrial employment increased by five to six percent per year until the 1960s. This policy was the essence of postwar economic development in Hungary as well as in the neighboring countries. Unfortunately, in spite of rapid economic growth, this path of development prevented the economy from developing and adopting new technological innovations, made it inflexible, and stunted its competitiveness.

The title of the last chapter of the book expresses the conclusion of this work: "Results and Failures of the Decade of Economic Reorientation and the Need for Radical Reform." Hungarian economists recognized the need to change import substitution and extensive development and the government announced such a policy reorientation, but failed to bring it about. Radical reform was needed to change the failed policy.

Five years later in 1988, as I mentioned before, I published a book on the history of *The Hungarian Economic Reforms, 1953–1988*. It was translated and came out in Cambridge two years later. Based on thorough archival research I documented the gradual progress of the reform, its stop-and-go history. It expanded on the previous book in documenting the failed major reform attempts after 1956, when the clear recognition of the need to turn to market orientation was dropped for political reasons. The Kádár government, as I mentioned before, appointed a committee in November 1956 to work out a new economic system. Characteristic of the time, the co-chair of the committee was a leading non-party economist, previously a minister in the postwar Smallholder Party government, who had been marginalized during the 1950s. By the time the report and recommendations were finished in the spring of 1957, the regime, surprisingly soon, had politically became stabilized and did not even discuss the issue, and the Soviet type of economy was preserved.

Within a decade, however, the importance of a change became evident again. The shelved reform proposal was revitalized. A new committee was formed and in the mid-sixties the new reform plan was accepted and introduced. The first results were promising and originally two more radical reform steps were planned in five years to continue the process. This did not happen. As early as the end of 1972 vicious ideological attacks were launched against the reform. I meticulously discussed the renewed attacks against what was called New Economic Mechanism and the success of the reform steps of the late 1960s, which had been halted and partly destroyed in the early-mid-1970s.

A new Party resolution accused the reform of revitalizing capitalist elements and petty-bourgeois attitudes harmful to the working class. A re-centralization and gradual quiet return to the Soviet type of planning began. It obstructed a timely and appropriate reaction to the 1973 crisis. A few years later in at the end of the decade, the regime had to return to further reforms. Discussing and publishing this history had a practical importance in the given situation. It was, of course, connected with the pressing need to respond the challenge of the emerging and deepening economic crisis. Scholarly works and popular articles on the failures and mistaken policy are able to have an important impact on both public opinion and the reform camp and, via all of these, on the political demand for corrections and reforms. Meanwhile, during the 1970s and '80s I also attempted to "translate" the scholarly findings into policy recommendations via the advisory bodies and reform committees I participated in.

At that time I was named to several advisory bodies because of my post as Rector of the University of Economics and my status as a researcher of post-war Hungarian economic history. I was able to discuss the historical roots of Hungarian economic trends and compare them with international developments. This was needed in the work of those committees. A special cultural tradition of the country significantly increased the impact of historical studies. Historiography has a special meaning in Hungary. Current issues were often discussed in a historical context. Like philosophy in Germany, history was a way of thinking about politics and social issues in Hungary. The strong historical orientation goes back to early nineteenth century romantic historicism: the myth of a glorious past became the source of strength to cope with contemporary problems. History explained failures. Everything that went wrong in Hungarian history was explained as the consequence of the Ottoman conquest and its 150-year-long occupation of the middle part of the country, the 400-year-long Habsburg rule, or the Trianon peace treaty after World War I that mutilated the country. In other words, everything was explained as the result of outside factors. Historians, as a consequence, often became involved in contemporary political debates. My case was no different.

In 1990, my professional career reached a turning point. I accepted an invitation from the University of California in Los Angeles and joined the History Department. My motivation requires a detailed explanation and I will return to it. At this point I am going to discuss only its impact on my professional activities. I began teaching nineteenth- and twentieth-century history of Central and Eastern Europe and modern European economic history. There I could continue my work without interruption and establish a second career in the United States. The only difference was that from that time on I read, lectured, and wrote in English.

Writing in English was a significant challenge. In Hungary my style was praised for its elegance and sophistication. But Hungarian is a non-Indo-European language, entirely different from English in structure, and like German, it equates elegant style with long, often half a page long, complex sentences. They are actually two or three sentences combined, sometimes even a fourth added between dashes. English is just the opposite. It also concentrates more on facts, using one adjective to characterize something, instead of two or three decorative synonyms as in Hungarian. Even the construction of texts differs in the two languages: Hungarian requires introductions dealing with historical or other issues; English is to the point. If you do not announce in the first paragraph what you want to say, you are lost. It was painful to adjust and the "end result" was never satisfactory. I write as I can and not as I would like to, but now at last as fast as in my mother tongue. According to my wife, however, this is part of the problem, but I need that rhythm for writing.

Teaching, however, did not require this kind of adjustment. Teaching, I believe, is a combination of at least three elements: knowledge of the subject, ability to explain complex and sometimes complicated issues in an understandable and, as much as possible, simple way, and, what is equally important, the expression of the personality, which is always connected with a kind of acting. Anyway, I have never felt constrained teaching in English. It also deserves mention that I love teaching, and that students often remark on my enthusiasm for my work in their evaluations. It is not easy to explain my attraction to teaching. The environment of students must be one of the elements. It is hardly possible to imagine a more attractive task than trying to influence young people's way of thinking. My own experience of a few teachers who had a lifelong influence on me may also be a factor. When I was at the beginning of my career, students often thought that I was also a student. Later on I felt refreshed and inspired to be surrounded by young people whose goal was to learn and to establish a foundation for their lives. I always liked them. I also enjoy explaining historical trends. I like the logic of lecturing and it happened many times that I recognized new interrelations, new explanations of certain historical events during class lectures. It was and is a permanent intellectual inspiration, an excellent state of mind and an important factor in research.

The years in Los Angeles and at UCLA have turned out to be the most harmonious and fruitful part of my professional and personal life. When I try to explain the reasons, a few factors are evident. On the personal side, after a decade of trouble in my first marriage I had a happy second marriage in a new environment, which was very propitious for a new start. My professional life during my last years in Hungary was extremely interesting but over-heated and hectic. Not without reason is "may you live in interesting times" said to be a curse in Chinese. I had had enough of public life. Although I enjoyed it, I had also grown weary of it. The conflicts and disappointment at the end (which I will describe later) certainly also played a role in that, but I found an easy way back to the undisturbed, quiet life of research and teaching. That was my real world. I even had a strange hunger to do it because of the pressure of the previous decade when I had only my stays in Oxford and Washington, summers, weekends, and the very early morning and late evening hours to work on research projects that I never wished to be separated from.

I have known a few Hungarian and American colleagues who became academic administrators for a few years and never found their way back to research and teaching. I jokingly asked one of them, who had returned to Stanford University after several years of work at the Ford Foundation and extensive travel to Europe, "how was going back to the periphery?" He answered seriously: "like going back to the periphery." Actually he did not remain there for long. It was lucky that I always forced myself to continue my scholarly work even when I was burdened by academic administrative tasks. However, I did it because that was my best "entertainment." All in all, I fully enjoyed returning to full-time teaching and research.

A third element also contributed to my satisfaction. I felt the impact of a unique historical experience: a peaceful regime change in which I was not a bystander watching from the sidelines but an active participant. It definitely helped me understand history better. I consciously wanted to exploit that accumulated experience in my work.

Also worthy of mention were my dramatically and positively changed working conditions. Never before in my life did I have at hand all of the statistics and other kinds of studies available for my work in one place. UCLA's research library offered that possibility. In Hungary I had to go to different libraries and in most cases continue the research abroad to collect all the sources. Here, in the worst case, I must to wait a few days to get the missing work from another library, including the "mother of all libraries," the Library of Congress. It makes a significant difference, not only in terms of time spent, but also in keeping up-to-date with the literature.

It sounds probably a bit odd, but personal comfort in accommodation is also a factor. In Hungary, I never had a study at home. The largest apartment I lived was 900 square feet and there were usually two children at home. To have a comfortable and extremely quiet home with an independent study, a huge desk (actually two together), book shelves along the walls, including a separate one exclusively for library books that I can keep at home for three months, was unthinkable to me. Working upstairs in my study and going down from time to time to make coffee, sitting outside in the garden to read something all make me relaxed and create an outstanding atmosphere that make work more pleasant and much more efficient.

During my work at UCLA I lectured, did a tremendous amount of research, and published a series of books on the complex history of Central and Eastern Europe from the end of the eighteenth to the early twenty-first centuries: one volume on the "long" nineteenth century (from the 1780s to the 1910s) *History Derailed* (2003), one volume on the first half of the twentieth century from the first to the end of the second World Wars, *Decades of Crisis* (1998), a third volume on the second half of the twentieth century between 1944 and 1993, *Detour from the Periphery to the Periphery* (1996). I actually started with the third volume, nearest to my exciting historical experience, and went backward in time writing the two others. Somewhat later I added a fourth volume on the history of the Central and Eastern European transformation: *From the Soviet Bloc to the European Union: The Economic and Social Transformation of Central and Eastern Europe Since 1973* (2009).

In some way this series, covering the entire Central and Eastern Europe and the totality of its modern period from the late eighteens century up to the present and offering a complex history that focuses on the interrelationship between social, political, cultural, and economic trends put into the broad international framework may be my trade mark work. Nothing similar exists in historical literature.

Untouched by the ideas of the Enlightenment, the region remained frozen in serfdom and other institutions of the aristocratic-noble society, in other words, in the Middle Ages. All of the countries of the region lost their independence between the fifteenth and eighteenth centuries and became incorporated into huge multi-ethnic Habsburg, Ottoman, and Russian empires. Modern ideas arrived from the West with Romanticism, a revolutionary cultural trend that actually carried the idea of nation and national independence. The small elite realized the backwardness of their "sleeping countries," and wanted to mobilize them to follow the West. Nation building began as a cultural and linguistic movement, and railroad construction followed. The liberation of serfs and a belated agricultural revolution inspired modern transformation. Agriculture multiplied its output and agrarian exports increased incomes but industrialization and urbanization hardly got started. Failed or semi-successful modernization characterized the entire nineteenth- and twentieth-century history of Central and Eastern Europe. Traditional social and economic features were preserved as well as social values and attitudes. Except for the Bohemian lands, the region remained predominantly agricultural until the mid-twentieth century, and illiteracy remained high.

When independence was restored or achieved at the end of the nineteenth and early twentieth centuries, the business of nation building remained unfinished. In the area often called the belt of mixed population, national homogenization did not take place, and ethnic conflicts and hatred led to waves of ethnic cleansing throughout the twentieth century. The independent states did not follow in the footsteps of the West but remained authoritarian and repressive. Under the banner of "defending the nation" governments engaged in territorial disputes with neighboring states whose population included ethnic "brethren." During virtually the entire period of the nineteenth and twentieth centuries, socio-economic modernization failed or remained unfinished. Integration into the international free trade system in the period of "first globalization" before World War I was as unsuccessful as the reverse policy, economic nationalism. Protectionism and autarchy, during most of the twentieth century under right-wing or communist regimes, were built into the Nazi-led or Soviet-led regional integration systems. With some fluctuation, income levels in the area remained less than half that of the West.

In the fourth volume I discussed the dramatic historical turnaround of the region. Post-communist transformation and admission to the European Union opened a new chapter and the hope of catching up with the West. The European Union, by building up its backyard to adjust to globalization, helped the region's transformation by strict requirements prescriptions, providing large direct investments and contributing a huge infusion of financial aid, which was double the amount extended to post-war Europe by the U.S. under the Marshall Plan. Dramatic structural and technological changes followed and opened the road towards catching up with the West in time. This process, however, was accompanied by dramatic social decline of certain strata of society and by large-scale social shock. Due to this, the region became a hotbed of right-wing populism.

In the first decade of the twenty-first century some Central European countries exhibit signs of economic success, while others seem unable to follow. Foreign participation opened the road to the digital age in the region by modernizing the backward telephone systems of the countries involved. In the late 1980s in the United States, 79 out of 100 households had telephone lines, while in Central and Eastern Europe there were hardly more than 7 lines per 100 homes, but this situation dramatically improved during the 1990s. Multinational companies established the first high-tech and medium high-tech industries in the region, and created competitive export sectors. Today a full third of the total of Hungarian exports is being produced by four multinational companies. Slovakia has become the world's number one auto producer in terms of number of cars produced per its inhabitant. On the other hand, it is true that several countries in the region paid a high social price, and are entirely or overwhelmingly dependent on foreign companies and can not develop their own research and development networks, which is the base of innovation. The role of small- and middle-sized local companies is minimal in most of those countries.

If they will not be able to stabilize their societies and, entering the higher stage, establish their own independent economic base, they may get stuck in dependence and a lower level of division of labor performing unskilled work in high-tech industries, and producing simple parts for sophisticated products. In this case their income level may remain permanently lower. Which alternative will be realized depends on each individual country. Slovenia, the Czech Republic, and Hungary, before 2008, exhibited positive signs of adjusting to the international production network and independent sustained economic growth. Others, mostly Balkan countries, have no other advantage than their low wage level. Which countries will be able to follow the Irish and Spanish "miracles" and catch up with the advanced West depends on their domestic strengths or weaknesses. When the last mentioned countries were accepted into the European Union in 1973 and 1986, respectively, they did not enjoy a higher level of economic development than present-day Central Europe. In the early twenty-first century, however, Ireland has surpassed the average Western level and Spain is approaching it.

The Central and East European countries, which became the backyard of the western members of the European Union during the transformation decades and as candidates and later members of the Union, in my view, gained a historic opportunity to break away from their traditional backwardness and become equal members of the European community. This opportunity, however, is not automatic. If their domestic adjustment is not successful, if they do not counterbalance social disintegration, their dependent status and lower-level contribution may stabilize without closing the gap between East and West. Whether they will catch up or lag behind depends on their domestic policy, performance and capability. The 2008–9 financial crisis clearly exhibited the fragility of transformation, not only in the Central European region, but even in Ireland.

These four volume series were extremely important for me: my personal historical experiences pushed me to discover the historical roots of the events that determined my life and the entire historical road of the region during my life-time, closely connected to my entire life experience. It felt this work to be my mission.

With this work, however, I also tried to change of the American public's knowledge and view of the region: Central and Eastern Europe was not on the intellectual map in the United States, except some oversimplified stereotypes. The term Europe was practically synonymous with Western Europe in American academia. As a clear sign of misunderstanding I often read studies and heard remarks on how difficult it was to overcome roughly half a century's communist denial of western values when transforming Central and Eastern Europe. In reality, major differences separated Central and Eastern Europe from the West not only during its post-war, communist period but across a far longer time, stretching farther into the past. Eastern Europe had been falling far behind ever since democracy and industrial society emerged in the West. Although the main slogan of 1989 was "back to Europe," the region more often distanced itself from Europe than wanted to follow it into modern times. In 1905, the prophetic-minded Hungarian poet Endre Ady published an outstanding short essay under the title *Morituri*, in which he called Hungary a "ferry-boat country," sailing to and fro between East and West, but with the East being more magnetic than the West. He complained bitterly that Hungarian society shared "the fallacy of a Hungarian globe… Ten thousand people had run ahead and become European. They are a running hundred years ahead of Hungarian society… My people, for a thousand years you have been in a permanent struggle against Europe." (Ady, [1905] 1986, 46–7) My scholarly work, in other words, was as closely connected with my Central European past as with my American present.

The motivation that led me to write the above mentioned series also influenced me participating in other kinds of projects. I never lost contact with the process of economic transformation in Central and Eastern Europe. Although I left Hungary in 1990, I followed closely the transformation that characterized the 1990s and the first decade of the twenty-first century. I continued the practical work and involvement in reform, serving between 1989 and 1993 as a member of the Blue Ribbon Commission, the international advisory group initiated by Professor Paul Marer of Indiana University and co-chaired by Sylvia Ostry, former chair of the Economic Council and multilateral trade negotiator of Canada, and Márton Tardos, the Hungarian dissident economist. The Commission's first major document, *Hungary in Transformation to Freedom and Prosperity* came out in the spring of 1990. In the debates during the preparation of the document I argued for gradualism and state regulation to guide the difficult process of transformation from state socialism to private-market system, and also suggested the building of an appropriate social safety net to offset the partly unavoidable negative social side effects of transformation.

In the early 1990s, these views were not popular among experts and governments. This was the time of the "Washington Consensus," worked out by the Washington-based international monetary institutions and the U.S. administration for Latin America in 1989. This blueprint was immediately adopted for Central and Eastern Europe when communism collapsed. It made recommendations, but in reality it forced instant marketization, trade liberalization, and privatization upon the countries involved. These views were shared not only by most western experts on the Blue Ribbon Commission but also by representatives of organizations such as the New-York based East-West Institute, and the newly established European Bank for Reconstruction and Development in London, whose meetings I often attended. It was easy to counter my arguments by declaring: "you do not understand the market system well enough." This may have been in fact true, but the other side of the coin was that they did not understand the transforming countries, their legacies, social fabric, and economic inheritance either. Furthermore, most of them were "religious" neo-liberals.

These debates inspired me to organize three major conferences on the topic, two together with the German Südosteuropa-Gesellschaft in Munich in 1993 and Weimar in 1996, and one in Milan at the International Economic History Congress in 1994. It took almost a decade before the otherwise avoidable mistakes, extreme economic decline, and human suffering made clear that the highly advertised and applauded "shock therapy" was a mistake as was the passionately advocated withering away of state intervention. Only later did new recognition, a "Post-Washington Consensus"

With Paul Zsigmond Pach in 2000.

concept, emerge about the importance of the state in transformation and institution-building during the period when a well functioning market was not yet in place. When these views were expressed by economists such as the Italian Domenico Nuti, the American Richard Portes, and especially the Nobel laureate, Columbia economist, and former chief economist of the World Bank Joseph Stiglitz, I felt, at the least, deep satisfaction.

To present a better understanding in the eastern half of the European continent also led me to accept an invitation from the British publisher Ashgate to edit a reprint series on Central and Eastern Europe in those years. I approached several fine Polish, Czech and Hungarian historians and initiated publications of their studies grouped by topic. I initiated and edited nine reprint volumes for the *Variorum* series, the first by my former professor and mentor Zsigmond Pál Pach, which appeared on his 75th birthday. The series helped to make known important studies on the region. For example, both Pach and Maria Bogucka of Poland selected excellent articles on the history of the anti-business, anti-commerce attitude of the Hungarian and Polish nobility. This important feature of the nobility's value system became a national characteristic because the nobility was as much hated as it was envied, and its attitudes and lifestyle were broadly imitated by other strata of society.

Having finished the first three volumes of the above-mentioned series, and before writing the fourth volume on Central and Eastern European transformation, I turned towards the bigger picture and compared six different economic regimes in twentieth- century Europe. In my book *An Economic History of Twentieth Century Europe*, published in 2006, and translated and published in Turkish, French, Italian, Korean, Greek, Serbian, and Hungarian, I analyzed and documented their similarities and differences. Here I did not use the traditional chronological differentiation between the two halves of the century, but discussed the different economic regimes. These systems were not only very different but also competed with and confronted each other. The authoritarian economic dirigisme, as I called the economic regimes of Mussolini, Hitler, Franco and others, waged war against countries with market economies and against the Soviet Union, which established the only non-market system in the world. In spite of theses confrontations, what I discovered and analyzed was the interesting influences they had on each other. First of all, all the alternative systems emerged from the experience of World War I, especially the successful German war economy, with its economic dirigisme, state-run, planned economy. People realized that the country's economic potential increased significantly and became capable of achieving much higher goals than a traditional market system without government intervention. As early as 1920, John Maynard Keynes, the century's most influential economist, called attention to the lessons of the war. Nevertheless, Benito Mussolini learned the same lesson and established the Italian Fascist regime accordingly, building up a huge state-owned sector of the economy and "nationalizing" the trade unions and subordinating them to the corporative system. At the other end of the continent, Vladimir I. Lenin also found the key to establish his socialist economy based on the German war economy. More surprisingly, after World War II, democratic Western Europe took over important elements from Mussolini's corporative regime and welfare institutions and from Keynesian regulations to Soviet planning, merging it all into what was called a mixed economy and a welfare state.

I have to confess I did not realize during my work on this book how strongly my own life experience influenced my writing. Let me quote a few sentences from the review of the Italian economic historian, Gianni Toniolo, who noted that influence:

The six chapters are structured around the prevailing ideologies of the times rather than according to the traditional political or economic partitions of twentieth century history. Thus, the first chapter deals with the pre-World War I "laissez faire system," the second with the decline of laissez faire and the rise of "regulated market systems," the third and the forth with the fascist and socialist regimes, the fifth with the mixed economy and the welfare state. The title of the final chapter is "Globalization: return to laissez-faire?"... [I]ndeed, *meminisse juvabit* (it is useful to remember) and Berend's book will help to inoculate readers against the current loss of memory of how heavily European history has been burdened by ideology as well as against the assumption that we are now living in a post-ideological world. (Toniolo, 2007)

The big picture of the European and world economy always interested and challenged me. One cannot understand a country or a region without putting its story into the big picture and compare. During the last decades of the twentieth century the world economy changed profoundly. Both the Central and Eastern European story and the radical change of the European economic systems were only parts of a global economic transformation, which multiplied international connections and somewhat undermined the authority of nation-states. This new phenomenon, globalization, dramatically increased foreign trade, foreign direct investment, and various kinds of financial transactions. Multinational companies outsourced production to less developed countries where wages were low and established hundreds of thousands of subsidiaries all over the globe. In old, established advanced countries such as the Netherlands and Great Britain, multinationals produced roughly one-third of industrial output around the turn of the new century, and in newly emerging or transforming countries such as Ireland and Hungary, this share reached 70 percent.

Globalization generated a heated debate and often even violent demonstrations against top globalizing countries and international financial institutions with views differing by 180 degrees. Pro-globalization arguments maintained that all participants profited from it; income differences would disappear, as would the use of terms like Third World countries, and core—periphery relations, the concept that backward regions, the peripheries of the world system, are dependent on the advanced core. As the European University Institute's historian, Bo Stråth stated in one of his studies, "Globalization became a new *Zauberwort*... (wonder-word) in the emerging master narrative on Globalization. Economy replaced Hegel's Reason as the blind force of history."

Opposing views, however, held that only the rich countries profited while the poor ones were exploited and lost their markets and resources. In several countries populist political forces are rushing to defend citizens and national independence. This trend strongly characterizes some of the transforming Central and Eastern European countries, most of all Poland, Slovakia, and Hungary in the first decade of the twenty-first century.

Recently the debate has become even more complex and confused: advanced countries also have begun complaining about outsourcing jobs, and the infusion of foreign goods into national markets. Disappointment is spreading since the benefits from most of the huge extra incomes from outsourced production are being reaped by a small group of society while real wages are falling behind. Suddenly certain political forces even in the United States have demanded restricting imports and cutting global ties.

Economic historians have much to say about those economic phenomena. As a life-long researcher of economic nationalism I also sought to participate in the world-wide discourse on the impact of globalization on Central and Eastern Europe. Everybody who knows anything about interwar Europe, and especially Central and Eastern Europe, knows a lot about the danger and harmful consequences of attempts to create national self-sufficiency, which characterized the entire interwar and state socialist periods, i.e., most of the twentieth century in the region. To be isolated from the world economy had much more harmful consequences than to be "globalized." The late nineteenth century, recently dubbed the "first globalization," also offers both a good comparison and lessons for the present and future.

In the later 1970s and early 1980s, when Gyuri Ránki and I were studying the economic performance of the southern and eastern peripheries of Europe, we realized that introducing modern technology and management in peripheral countries required foreign contribution. Relatively backward countries can never be technological leaders. They lack sufficient internal resources for research and development. Their only possibility to introduce modern technology and management is technology transfer. Foreign investments are the vehicle of these transfers, and consequently neither good nor bad by themselves. Their good or bad impact depends on the domestic social-cultural-economic environment, the potential to generate a spin-off effect to spread the technology and bring the domestic economy into the production network. The worst possible alternative is to remain outside the international economic network. The most striking lesson from various national experiences is that some countries are profiting greatly from globalization while others are paying a high price and lagging behind. The less developed countries are reacting in various ways to globalization. This was true in the late nineteenth century and the late twentieth century as well.

I argued in a similar way regarding the role of multinational companies in the transforming countries of Eastern Europe at the World Economic Forum in Davos in 1990 and 1991 and at the European Economic Forum in Geneva in 2000, organized by the United Nations. I argued against isolationism in several publications, interviews and even in a televised lecture in Budapest in 2005. Nevertheless, the globalization of neo-liberal de-regulation policy since Ronald Reagan and Margaret Thatcher opened the gates for the speculative, robber type of capitalism. In the short run, it helped to return prosperity because of the more flexible financial markets. In the long run, however, it created "bubbles" which burst one after the other, and, in the end, led to the 2008 international financial crisis.

It remains an important political and economic task to counterbalance the negative effects of economic globalization, to reestablish international and national regulations, to curb and halt the social disintegration of backward countries and regions of continents. In 1989, Francis Fukuyama, the conservative American political scientist triumphantly announced the "end of history" since "liberal democracy as a system of government had emerged throughout the world and conquered rival ideologies like hereditary monarchy, fascism, and communism." He argued that liberal democracy, as the ultimate form of human government, may constitute the end point of mankind's ideological evolution. (Fukuyama, 1989)

Unfortunately he was wrong. His theory seemed at first spectacularly right as dictatorial regimes collapsed one after another in Eastern Europe, Latin America, and South Africa. Liberal democracy and the West, however, failed to integrate the globe. Globalization has its losers and, as a consequence, a well-known source for extremism did not disappear. What we call terrorism nowadays has a socio-economic background similar to extremism in twentieth-century Europe or Latin America, but in a different geographical location. The methods are also different since they are rooted in different cultural-historical traditions. The huge gap between prosperity and poverty may reproduce deadly conflicts and confrontations. The "war on terror" cannot defeat it. I profoundly agree with, and also cited in one of my books, the way this was put by President Truman, who recognized these phenomena and gave expression to them in his famous "Truman doctrine" speech in Congress in the spring of 1947: "The seeds of totalitarian regimes are nurtured by misery and want. They reach their full growth when the hope of a people for a better life has died. We must keep that hope alive." (Truman, 1947)

Furthermore, the gap between rich and poor is broadening dramatically in the world and is dashing the hopes of many. During the last quarter of the twentieth century the growth of per capita income in the Western world reached two percent per annum. Although some peripheral countries reached an even higher growth rate, Latin America was characterized by one percent only, and Africa by 0.01 percent, which is equal to stagnation. The per capita income disparity between the richest and poorest nations, to repeat the shocking figures, exhibited a ratio of 1:10 in 1913, 1: 26 in 1950, and 1: 40 at the end of the last century. I presented these figures in my study on the impact of globalization on peripheral countries. History is continuing.

Teaching in Two Different University Systems

Research and teaching have mutually influenced each other and become inseparable in my life. In several cases I taught certain courses for years before working on a book on the topic. Such was the case with my four volume series on Central and Eastern Europe, which was born of a one-and-a-half decades long span of both teaching and research.

For a third of a century I taught in Hungary at the University of Economics, and now for two decades at UCLA at the History Department. The two universities may be six thousand miles apart, but the difference between the two countries and the two university systems is even greater.

The Hungarian university, like most of those in Europe, was bounded on a demanding high-school education that guarantees a strong basic general education. The eight year education offered by the *gymnasium* concludes with the *matura*, a comprehensive and rigorous examination comprising both written and oral tests in math, language, and literature for everybody, and oral alone in other subjects. All require deep knowledge of the entire curriculum, not only the last year's studies. The exam was the most illuminating part of the secondary education for me and I understood more mathematics than during the gymnasium years before. A good gymnasium education was not comparable to American junior and high school training because it practically covered the general education of the first college years as well.

This made immediate specialization at the university level possible. Students enroll in specialized fields of engineering, economics, philosophy or medicine immediately. During the postwar period, specialization was even more intense: the four- or five-year university training of that time offered immediately applicable skills. In the 1960s my university offered 36 different degrees for various economic activities. Graduate education, however, following the Soviet model, belonged not to the universities but to the Academy of Sciences.

The subject of Hungary's economic history was offered for freshmen at my university in two semesters. My lecture courses in the second semester covered modern times, from 1848 to the present, and I also gave seminars in European economic history. My freshmen lecture classes were enormous, with about 250 students. Beside lectures, the required reading was only a single textbook. This textbook policy has been a general practice of Hungarian universities, and an undoubtedly bad one too. At the end of the fourteen week semester, a four- week oral examination period followed. My policy was to examine hundreds of students, one by one, or in groups of three. I followed the example of György Markos, Professor of economic geography, who offered a cup of coffee to his students during examinations. He made a deep impression on me at my own first oral examination at the university, and repeating his example, I too offered coffee to students. Altogether about 10,000 students attended my classes, and every year I examined 100-150 of them orally. I liked oral examinations because they offered a unique personal contact with the students and a better possibility to understand their way of thinking, analytical skills and intellectual strengths or weaknesses. I always felt that the exams themselves were an excellent tool for further education. It was interesting to me that former students I met decades later remembered the exams, and often even the questions.

At Hungarian universities, during the decades of state socialism, a class-based affirmative action policy was introduced in early 1949 and remained at work until the 1970s. Applicant students from worker and peasant families enjoyed preference over those who came from intellectual, professional or middle class families, let alone the "class enemy" bourgeois families. One had to belong to the best if coming from an intellectual or middle class family to be accepted. Both my friend György Ránki and I were categorized as coming from intellectual families, but we performed well and were easily accepted. During the Stalinist and early post-Stalinist years, young people from the "class enemy" category, however, were not accepted at all. For example, my only beloved cousin, the daughter of my favorite uncle, was first rejected because her mother remarried after the war and her stepfather belonged to the category of class enemies. Fortunately, networking and connections always helped, and she ultimately gained university admission and became a chemist.

The affirmative action policy targeted the training of a new intellectual elite and had a major social impact. A special substitute one year preparatory course was established to prepare students for university training from worker and peasant families who had no secondary education. In 1949, 20,000 students were trained and enrolled in universities in this way. The regime launched an educational revolution.

Before World War II, most of the population completed only four or six years of elementary school. A smaller group of those who finished the four-year course embarked on another four years in a kind of dead-end higher elementary school that did not prepare students for higher education. Only about 10 percent of the age group between eleven and eighteen enrolled in the *gymnasium*, the elitist grammar school-type high school, and no more than one to two percent of those between the ages of eighteen and twenty-two studied at colleges and universities.

The postwar educational revolution made high-school training nearly universal, although nearly 80 percent of the students studied at vocational high schools. A higher level four-year apprentice training combined with some basic general education was one option, but this type did not open the door to universities. The other type, called *technikum,* offered training in a skill but also made going on to technical universities possible. In other words although even secondary education became over-specialized and produced medium-level skilled experts, only a limited general education was offered.

Higher education also developed into mass education in that period: instead of the prewar one to two percent, 10 to 15 percent of those between the ages of eighteen and twenty-one enrolled in colleges and universities. The expansion of university training in those years had a positive social impact but at the same time contributed to the decline of educational rigor.

Student attitudes, for example, were lax: many students just wanted to get a diploma and the grade did not matter much to them. In a 5–1 grading system when 5 was equal to "A" and 1 was the equivalent of "F," many students targeted the still acceptable 2, or "D." We called this attitude "D-ism." It was also true that roughly 10 percent of the students were excellent and made genuine efforts to learn as much as possible. They were grateful to professors who were ready to offer more to learn and also demanded more. Many of them volunteered to take special courses equivalent to honors work in the United States. I had several students from that latter group and our common work established life-long friendships. While the majority did not make too much effort, this minority was very rewarding for me and made teaching a great experience.

Close ties, friendly and professional connections with those excellent former students have accompanied my entire life and have been very important for me. It was heart-warming, for example, that in the politically exciting years of 1988–89, when I served as chair of the government's advisory committee, which initiated the transformation of the country, the Prime Minister, Miklós Németh, had been a star student of mine and later a colleague at the university. I recruited several of my former students to another committee I chaired on the first economic marketization and privatization plan for Hungary.

One Saturday morning in 1989 in Budapest, returning from a walk Kati and I were told by our cleaning lady of a strange telephone call. Somebody with a strong foreign accent but in fluent Hungarian claimed to be the President of Cyprus. Probably a joke, she added. Not at all. Georgios Vasiliu, then President of Cyprus, was preparing for an official state visit to Hungary the next week and wanted to spend some time with me. Iorgos, as we called him, somewhat younger than I, escaped from civil-war-ridden Greece in 1947, came to Hungary, and enrolled in our university. I was a tutor for his studies of Hungarian economic history and we became good friends. After graduation, he joined the faculty, but resettled in Cyprus when the dictatorship collapsed, established a consulting firm, and then turning to politics, was elected President of the island republic. We had not seen each other for quite a few years, and our talk did not touch the historical time but was personal: it was very interesting to hear about our changed lives and recent experiences. Other Greek students, later becoming friends and colleagues, such as Stergios Babanasis, also returned to Greece after the collapse of the dictatorship and became professors and political advisors, and remained close, good friend.

In 1991, when I was invited to speak at the World Economic Forum in Davos, Switzerland, I shared the podium with another outstanding student of mine, György Surányi, who was head of the Hungarian National Bank that time. And there were other similar experiences. One of my former students became Deputy Secretary General of the United Nations; another became famous as Minister of Finance in Hungary in the mid-1990s when his name was connected with a major transformation reform, and again another is running the Institute of Economic Forecasting. In the post-1989 governments several were elevated to high governmental and diplomatic positions.

During a recent visit to Budapest, mentioning a last and somewhat different example, we sat with friends in the Gerbaud coffee and pastry shop in the heart of town. When I asked for the check, the waiter politely informed me that it had been paid. I did not understand and raised my eyebrow in surprise. She explained: the manager was a former student of mine, and ordered her not to accept money from me. I meet former students everywhere and their warm, nostalgic, and friendly feelings are the greatest reward a teacher can have.

During those decades at a Hungarian university I acquired important, though extremely limited, experience teaching in the West. In Oxford, besides my research tasks, I tutored graduate students who worked on East European topics. More importantly, in 1978 at Berkeley's economics department, when I replaced one of the professors who was on sabbatical leave, I got a taste of undergraduate teaching in America. It was impressive to see the drive of the students, their ambition to learn as much as possible.

It was different from my experience at home. I was enthusiastic when I learned that at the end of the course students anonymously grade the teacher, and I returned to Budapest, as rector (chancellor) of my University, I wanted to introduce student evaluations. I failed. The idea generated a huge reaction among the faculty, which was grouped around the university's Party organization, and they transformed the proposal into a "political" question, maintaining that I wanted to discredit a politically involved faculty. The authorities succeeded in thwarting this policy.

Royce Hall, the trademark building of the University of California, Los Angeles (UCLA).

My teaching experience at UCLA at the turn of the millennium helped me to understand the reasons for the superiority of American higher education. As I am going to describe my impressions about one of the top American public universities, I certainly cannot offer much new information for those who know it from their own experience. I think, however, that a great many people in the United States do not exactly know the system of the University of California that differs significantly from the European, but also from private American academia as well. I warn my readers, however, and suggest to those familiar with this issue to skip the next couple of pages and proceed straight to the next chapter.

Compared to my previous experience, the most striking difference in America was the competitive attitude of the students. They want to get the best possible grades. Many times students who, having received an A-grade, ask me what extra work they should do to improve their grade.

Unlike in Hungary, grade is crucially important for them, and those who are successful often ask me for a letter of recommendation for graduate school. Of course, I have students who failed or got "C"s, but unlike in Hungary the majority work hard and aim for the best grades.

During my first year at UCLA I found out about another aspect of student competitiveness. One of my colleagues advised me that I did not have to be present when students are writing their tests in the auditorium because they do not allow each other to cheat anyway. Cheating at exams in Hungary was seen a virtue, but here, students regarded it as unfair advantage which, in a competitive system, is not tolerated. Of course I have found more than one exception to this assertion, but it has been sporadic. It has become more widespread later on, in connection with take-home papers when some of the students took advantage of the unlimited offerings of the internet.

My courses in European economic history, the history and political economy of the European Union, and on Central and Eastern Europe have led American undergraduate students into unknown territories. Most of the history majors have very little or no economics background and they know little about Europe and Central and Eastern Europe in particular. I enjoyed the students' eagerness to learn about an unknown area. Teaching undergraduates, in spite of their limited background knowledge, has been a pleasure for me. It has been like conquering a new, virgin territory.

Graduate teaching was a real novelty for me. In my time in Hungary, Ph.D. candidates were guided by a tutor, mostly for three years, and did not have courses but worked on their dissertation. In the United States, in the first two years, candidates are helped by very demanding courses to learn a vast number of literature and research methods. At a top research university such as UCLA, graduate students are very highly educated and extremely hard-working. American graduate education at the top thirty, and probably one hundred, universities is definitely the best in the world. I always felt that the graduate students who worked with me for five to eight years were my young colleagues, or even like sons and daughters. We had long conversations on various subjects, and I invited them for lunch to the Faculty Club to discuss an issue or another, or for dinner to our home.

However, among the roughly three thousand higher educational institutions in America only the top private and state universities produce high-level experts, and the country is not self-sufficient in training. A great part of the highly trained minds at work are imported from all over the world. This trend started during the 1930s when tens of thousands of great intellects emigrated from Nazi-fascist Europe. The influx, nevertheless, became continuous and now, besides Europeans, it includes tens of thousands of Chinese, Indians, and others.

Meanwhile, American universities offer education to the entire world. It was an interesting and a good feeling for me when I arrived that the graduate student body at UCLA was recruited from 85 countries. Beside Americans, I had Chinese, Korean, and Hungarian graduates, French, Dutch, Italian, and Turkish students. In Southern California the entire student body is extremely mixed ethnically. Among the undergraduates about 40 percent of the students are now of Asian background and the number is rapidly rising. The Latino students, mostly with a Mexican family background, comprise a significantly smaller group, while the African-American contingent is very low.

When I arrived at UCLA, affirmative action policy was still in place, although, unlike in Hungary when I was there, it was based on race and ethnicity rather than class. In reality, nevertheless, the racial and social (class) background, though not mentioned, was closely connected. It was responsible for establishing a new stratum of middle-class and professionals from the minority, mainly African-American and Latino, population. A kind of historical mission of restitution lay behind this policy, which I support because it creates an opportunity for those who, coming from poor, less educated families, with a weaker public educational background, would otherwise be unable to rise up. Affirmative action strengthened equal opportunity for everybody. Recently, however, affirmative action has been abolished, and I am sorry about this. Nevertheless, UCLA, regarding the diversity of the student body and the percentage of students from low income families is number one nationwide.

The teaching morale I experienced here was another positive surprise that I highly valued. Teaching discipline is strict, and professors have to be in class on time. Missing a class is almost unimaginable, and if a class is not demanding, most of the students are dissatisfied. Promotion and professional advancement strongly depend on teaching performance and student satisfaction. This is a natural requirement. At research universities like the ten campuses of the University of California system, research and high quality publication are basic requirements for employment and promotion.

I sat on the Council on Academic Personnel (CAP), the council that has virtually the final say in hiring and promotion. CAP is a fascinating institution of this public university system. I was invited for a three-year term to be part of the fourteen-member body, selected from the entire university, including the medical, law, business, and education schools, and of course, the entire college of sciences, social sciences and humanities.

I strongly felt the contrast to the "authoritarian" leadership of European universities where the department, due to the wide-spread German tradition, is almost a "feudal" estate of the chair, and the dean has autonomous power. Appointments and promotions were decided by them. In Hungary, without search committee and open applications, the department chair selects a single candidate, decides on his or her employment. Similarly, promotion of members of the department was not prepared by committees and accepted or rejected by the department by secret ballot, but was the decision of the chair who made the recommendation to the dean who had the right to decide. Committees and the faculty at large had no voice in that *modus operandi*. This system was almost the same in several European countries but started changing from the 1970s on and elements of the American system were adopted. The public university system is also in sharp contrast to the practice of private universities in the States. At our public University, appointments and promotions of the faculty are democratically managed.

Here every job is internationally advertised, search committees at departmental level examine all applications and invite several candidates and select the best three or four who deliver a "job talk." Luncheons and dinners allow other faculty members to get acquainted with the candidate, and at the end the entire department votes on the appointment by secret ballot. In the case of promotions, another departmental committee evaluates the candidates' research, teaching, university- and professional- service activities, and votes on the proposal.

At the beginning this procedure seemed strange to me. In every third or fourth year every faculty member receives a letter from the chair that he/she is eligible for promotion. Who might be promoted is not the chair's decision—the candidates themselves decide whether they want to apply.

If they think they have fulfilled the requirements, they write a self-evaluation, listing publications, teaching and service activities, and apply for the promotion.

Without sufficient productivity and high quality publications, and also without satisfactory teaching, tenure and promotion are not forthcoming. The Californian system is quite unique. To sum up briefly: an assistant professor who cannot accomplish satisfactory scholarly production in the first seven years of employment must leave the university—and in most cases, academia as well. In the case that acceptable scholarship does not continue, one may be stuck at associate level and never be promoted to a full professorship. Good scholarship and teaching, on the other hand, guarantee a permanent upward movement on the "ladder," which has nine grades to be climbed. Beyond that it is possible to continue to "above scale" or "distinguished professor" status, which offers salary increases. Since eligibility is granted only every third or fourth year, one must fulfill requirements over one's entire career to make progress. Exceptional achievement, however, makes accelerated promotion possible.

The democratic character of the procedure here does not end at the department level. As I understood and followed the procedure, the department sends its proposal to the dean, who also evaluates the case and sends it to the chancellor of the university. Now comes the role of the CAP, which is the basic decision-making body for personnel affairs at the university level. Each case is reviewed by the most professionally competent member of the fourteen-member council. He/she reads the entire file, the attached publications and student evaluations reviews, and the departments' votes and committee reports. In certain crucially important stages of the promotion (tenure, or honoring life achievements) several outside experts are also asked to write letters and analyze the candidate's achievements in scholarship and teaching, including foreign evaluators as well as former and current students. The CAP reviewer summarizes his or her view in a written report for the CAP plenum. Every member of CAP reads the file and then the Council discusses each case and votes for acceptance or rejection.

I have to say that I was highly impressed to see the thoroughness and high standard of these debates. I never experienced logrolling or lowering the bar. The body felt a deep responsibility to maintain a high faculty standard. If the body's voting is unanimous or backed by an overwhelming majority, the decision is practically final. Officially the chancellor and the vice-chancellor, responsible for personnel affairs, have the right to overrule the Council's decisions, but in my experience this happened only in cases when the voting was split.

Being a member of CAP is a highly respected service, partly because of the high responsibility, and partly because this is the most demanding service for the University. The Council has one all-day session every week, even in summer, except for one month, and every member reviews several cases, sometimes from week to week, which also takes several hours of work. During the three-year term, I have read about 5,000 pages of records and written 100 pages of evaluations.

In spite of the long and tiring sessions of CAP, I often felt satisfaction and was proud to be part of it. Several times I have also thought about what a lucky country the United States is. A huge percentage of the faculty whose cases we discussed during the three years came from abroad. A great many came from China and India, but also from Europe. In one of the sessions there were two Chinese scholars as well as one each from Japan, Sweden, and Finland who joined UCLA. American universities attract stellar scholars from all over the world mostly because they offer better working and research conditions than anyone else.

Academic freedom became another new personal experience during my CAP years. It happened that over a three-week period I had to present the three cases of genuine Marxist scholars but at issue was only the scholarly level of their work and not their theoretical or political orientation. This practice was in sharp contrast with my Hungarian experiences. The employment of an openly non-Marxist scholar was almost impossible in the 1950s and 1960s. In a somewhat similar way, as an irony of the situation, employing a left-wing Marxist nowadays in Hungary is also extremely difficult.

Another outstanding characteristic I appreciate about many American universities is the capacity for dual organization unlike most European universities, which are organized according to disciplinary principles only. The departments are disciplinary organized units. Based on a cross-organizational principle, however, interdisciplinary research centers have also been established. At UCLA we have regional and topical interdisciplinary centers as research and sometimes also teaching institutions. Latin American,

Japanese, Chinese, South Asian, European and Eurasian centers offer interdisciplinary framework for scholars and students. Medieval, Renaissance, Comparative History and Social Theory centers focus on special topics or periods. Most centers do not have separately employed faculty, but offer a second home for faculty of various departments.

For twelve years I had the privilege to run one of these centers, the Center for European and Eurasian Studies, as its director. I was appointed in 1993, three years after joining the UCLA faculty. It was a surprise for me, a newcomer who did not even know the university well, to be selected by a search committee and appointed by the chancellor of the university. That center served and recruited from fifteen departments in the social sciences and humanities. We organized lecture series, including a very successful book discussion series, with the author and one discussant participating. These events stimulated fine debates on newly published important works. Internationally known scholars were invited to talk and even teach as visiting professors. Workshops and conferences enabled faculty from various departments to collaborate. All sessions were open to students and the general public, and often attracted large audiences.

Sometimes that became a problem. Los Angeles has huge minority populations. Besides Latinos, the majority, it includes Iranian, Armenian, Russian, South-Slavic, and Hungarian communities. One politically heated topic, the Yugoslav civil war, attracted people of Serb, Croat, and Bosnian origins. Quite a few people who had lived in the United States for decades and even those born here remained Serb or Croat nationalists. At some of the sessions it was difficult to avoid fistfights.

Vogues also play an important role in American university life. I experienced that when I began reorganizing the Center. When the Chancellor appointed me, he also gave me the task to reorganize the former Russian and East European Center into one with a pan-European profile. After the second year, I initiated an undergraduate interdisciplinary European Studies program as well. Now students may major in European subjects on an interdisciplinary basis. According to the rules, all fifteen departments were required to discuss and approve the new orientation. At this time, multiculturalism was gaining ground. Western civilization, a central concept during the cold war decades, which contrasted the value orientation of the Western world with that of the Eastern Bloc, was being challenged in the post-cold-war period for of its one-sided orientation and "Eurocentrism." It was more than bizarre, therefore when one of the departments rejected the European Center's European Studies program by arguing that it is "eurocentric."

This work was fascinating and intellectually stimulating. The only painful aspect was the continuous fundraising responsibility. The university provides only minimal financial resources for these centers, covering salaries only for one or two full-time permanent employees and occasionally part-time graduate students. Outside financing was required for programs, invited scholars, student grants for extra language studies, research trips, etc., I had to work with federal grant institutions and apply regularly for federal financing. In addition, I approached European institutions—the European Union, the German, French, Austrian, Finnish and other governments—and they were ready to finance certain programs, conferences on the enlargement of the Union, and the introduction of the common European currency, etc. I also had to find private donors and attract contributors. All this was time consuming and demanding, especially for me who came from a country where the only financial source was the Ministry of Education, and resources were distributed automatically. Nevertheless, I learned the drill, and during those twelve years, I raised approximately two million dollars. At the end, it was an enjoyable part of my university work.

My Globalized Family

In my childhood, my large family was localized. I had five uncles and aunts and more than thirty cousins in the countryside, most of them in an east Hungarian village called *Hajdúhadháza*. In Budapest I knew several members of my mother's family. We often visited my uncles, my grandmother's brother and his family, and some distant relatives. Among them were five sisters who lived together, and although I did not know their exact relationship to us, they were considered part of the family. The oldest sister, Aunt Ilona, had had a stroke and stayed in bed all the time.

But we had no relatives outside Hungary, and having relatives who were living outside the country became important in the late 1930s when the heavy clouds of war and genocide were gathering. This offered the remote possibility of emigration. I did not realize it, but my father permanently thought about escape. I often heard about distant possibilities to go to far away countries. One day my father came home and jokingly used German word play: *Heute Haiti*, today Haiti. None of his plans was realized because we did not have relatives abroad who could have helped us obtain immigration papers. Some were more fortunate. One of my father's friends emigrated to Australia, and my uncle Andor departed for Mexico with the help of his wife's relatives.

The globalization of my family began after the war. I married in 1953, and my wife Rózsa had a large family. Her parents who lived in the Sub-Carpathians—that region was part of Hungary before World War I, and

History in My Life

With my first wife, Rózsa, and four-year-old Zsuzsa in Budapest.

then became part of Czechoslovakia, but was reoccupied by Hungary in 1940 (nowadays Ukraine)—were deported in the summer of 1944 and died in Auschwitz. One of her sisters immigrated to the United States before the war, and two others, having returned from the concentration camp, left for Canada. Her brother settled in Israel. When our two daughters were born in 1954 and 1966, they already had aunts and cousins in the United States, Canada and Israel. My "Mexican uncle" meanwhile divorced and married a Mexican woman, and in the late 1940s, their daughter Irene was born. I have never seen my Mexican cousin since the couple divorced. He moved to Venezuela, his wife remained in Mexico and I lost contact with them all.

This family globalization gained new momentum during the 1980s. My older daughter Zsuzsa, after finishing her studies in Budapest and graduating in economics and sociology, received a grant from the Soros Foundation and went to New York for three months in 1984. She decided not to return

My Globalized Family

My grandsons, Benjamin (right) and Daniel, in 2008.

to Hungary. Staying abroad without permission was considered an illegal and criminal act in Hungary. She applied to Columbia University and was accepted, received her Ph.D., and married one of her American colleagues. I met my new American family at their wedding in New York in 1989. Suddenly I had acquired an American son-in-law, Rogers. My first grandson, Benjamin, was born in Boston. Three years later the second one, Daniel, appeared in Los Angeles. Both grandsons are American children, but they are bilingual.

My younger daughter, Nora, also finished her studies in Budapest and received a B.A. in Japanese language and history. It was already 1990 and the doors were wide open. With a French grant, she received an M.A. in medieval history in Paris. Her application from abroad was accepted by Columbia University and she too, finished her Ph.D. program there. After her degree in medieval history, St. Catharine's College, Cambridge, offered her a postdoctoral grant, and then she became employed by London University and a year later by Cambridge University. In London, she met an American, Joe, and they married in New York, where their first daughter, Esther, was born. Their second daughter, Rebecca, was born in Cambridge. Through Nora, a mediaeval historian who became a British citizen, I have

With my daughters Zsuzsa (wearing sunglasses) and Nora, Nora's husband Joe, and 8-month-old Esther in Los Angeles in 2002.

one more American son-in-law and two granddaughters, one an American citizen, and both British citizens. My family has become global.

This, however, is not the end of the story. In 1989 I separated (two years later divorced) and began a new life with Kati. Her own family was extremely mixed though all her ancestors were born in the territory of the Kingdom of Hungary. Her mother's side originated in what today is Slovakia and most of her aunts and cousins do not even speak Hungarian. On her father's side, the family was Croatian, though their name took a Hungarian spelling, Radics. This family tree goes back to the famous Croat Radić family. Stjepan Radić was head of the Croatian Peasant Party, and was assassinated during a session of the Parliament in 1928.

This surprising family mix is not unusual in Hungary. Before World War I, the country, the Hungarian Kingdom, was three times larger than after the war, with nearly half the population belonging to Romanian, Slovak, Croat, German, and other minorities. In 1918, when Austria-Hungary collapsed, the northern section of Hungary became the Slovak part

With my granddaughters, Esther and Rebecca, in Los Angeles in 2005.

of Czechoslovakia, and later, in 1993, independent Slovakia. Croatia was also a part, and after 1868, confederated to, the Hungarian Kingdom until 1918, when it became part of the newly established Yugoslavia, and then in 1991 reestablished as independent Croatia. Considering the large Hungarian diasporas, it is also natural that Kati has cousins and other personally unknown relatives as far as Brazil.

This is still not the end of the history of my family's globalization. I "inherited" Kati's thirteen-year old daughter, Dora, from her first marriage, and in 1990 she came with us to the United States where she studied, graduated, and married. She became American, and English is easier for her than Hungarian. Now she lives in Seattle, and her husband, Shree, is Indian. His parents still live in India. They had a double wedding ceremony, one according to secular American way, the other due to Hindu cus-

With my wife, Kati, and my stepdaughter Dora in our Los Angeles home in 1996.

toms in a Hindu temple in Seattle, where I had to repeat an ancient text in Sanskrit after the Indian priest. Now we have a son-in-law from India too.

What crowned the globalization process of our family was our arrival in the United States in 1990. We are both working at UCLA; both of us have become American citizens, but have also kept our Hungarian citizenship. Since Hungary became a member of the European Union in 2004, via the Hungarian citizenship our entire family has "European citizenship" as well.

Globalization is not a historical development for me. It is not only multiple economic connections among nations and continents, shaped by the decisive role of multinational companies that dominate three-quarters of the world's manufacturing trade and employ hundreds of millions of people all over the world. Globalization is my very personal experience.

In the Establishment

My career was thoroughly grounded in academia. The University of Economics in Budapest offered me my first job and I spent a third of a century at the same University. My scholarly work and productivity paved the way for my advance. In 1953, I began as an assistant professor, in 1960 became associate professor, and then in 1964, with five published books, a full professor. When my mentor and the founder of the Economic History Department, Zsigmond Pál Pach, took over the directorship of the Institute of History at the Academy of Sciences in 1967, I followed him as the chair of the Department. After that we did not work together in the same institution but our connection did not weaken; it accompanied me through my entire life. He was my best fatherly-friend. His high moral standard remained a compass for me. His advice was always important, and I was sad when I realized that my 2006 book was the last one with his fingerprints still upon it. I had discussed my ideas and the structure of that book with him. He died in 2001 at the age of 82 and I felt that my father died twice.

I "inherited" his chair at the Economic History Department in Hungary. That was a small department and after the departure of Pach, I was the only one with a "second" doctorate, the habilitation, and the only full professor. Recommended by the dean, I was appointed by the rector.

In line with the German tradition, for a long time there was only one professor at a department. This custom, however, changed and the American system slowly gained ground from the 1960s on. When somebody became the chair of the department, nevertheless, as in the old German practice, it was not a rotating but a permanent appointment. I remained Chair for roughly two decades. Meanwhile, in the second half of the 1960s I was dean of the School of General Economics within the university. Deanships fortunately are not full-time jobs at Hungarian universities. One professor fills these positions for a three-year period, with the possibility of one reappointment. My daytime schedule was packed; every minute was filled by meetings, receiving faculty, participating in departmental meetings, and having discussions with students, but I spent only three days at the dean's office, and for the remaining four days of the week, continued teaching and doing research as before. These years taught me to organize my time and work effectively. Besides being good at organization, fortunately, I was always a fast reader and writer. I climbed stairs two at a time, walked up escalators, and finished a meal before everyone else.

In 1973 the Hungarian Academy of Sciences elected me Corresponding Member. This was a major scholarly honor. The Hungarian Academy of Sciences was established in 1825 by Count István Széchenyi, whom Lajos Kossuth called "the Greatest Hungarian". Széchenyi was one of the largest landowners in the country, a strongly reform-oriented man. He was an early advocate of the liberation of the serfs, the first to plan Hungary's railroads. Széchenyi had traveled to England and urged following the British example. He published several influential books promoting modernization.

The more than 150 years of history and the wonderful building of the Academy on the Pest side of River Danube next to the Chain Bridge (also built by Széchenyi, in 1849, as the first permanently standing bridge on the river) in Roosevelt Square, made the Academy one of the most prestigious institutions in the country. At my university, as department chair, I was member of the University Council. In the late 1960s, I had serious open debates with the rector and the leadership of the university, which, in my view, was shifting in the wrong direction of over-specialization.

It was in this situation that when the term of Rector of the University expired, the Minister of Higher Education invited me to his office and offered me the post. I was not enthusiastic about academic administration, being aware how time consuming it was. Nevertheless, I was deeply

In the front of the Hungarian Academy of Sciences building on Roosevelt Square in Budapest.

involved in university business, and I felt a sense of belonging to the University. I was trained there as a student, found my first job there, and was made one of the youngest full professors. As a good citizen I would not feel comfortable saying no.

I told him that although I was just leaving for Oxford again and it would be best if he found somebody else, if he did not, he could count on me. I was in fact in Oxford when I read in the Hungarian newspaper that I had been appointed Rector of Karl Marx University of Economics. Between 1973 and 1979, I indeed worked for two terms in that post. Though I tried to make a positive impact on the structure and content of education, results were only partial. I decreased the number of specializations and strengthened general studies of economics. I also tried introducing more alternative subjects and free choices by decreasing compulsory classes. I also succeeded in introducing a special training for the diplomatic service. Most of all, I succeeded in getting money from the government for a major reconstruction of the University building. At the shore of the Danube River, our building was a landmark, built by the most famous architect in the 1870s as Central Customs Office. During World War II, one of the bomb raids destroyed a great part of the structure. In 1950, it was rebuilt for the university in a rather poor way. The reconstruction in the 1970s was very successful and created a modern university building. Beside the reconstruction, I could also acquire another building nearby and construct a new library. Vested interests and political limitations blocked the way toward required radical change in the curriculum and faculty. Remembering those years, I see the results as limited compared to the investment in time and energy.

Since I remained chair of my department as well, that work also deteriorated somewhat. It happened in spite of the fact that I continued teaching with a full teaching load, and built important scholarly connections. Our Department established regular joint scholarly conferences with history and economic history departments in Helsinki and Warsaw. I made an agreement with Immanuel Wallerstein, head of the Fernand Braudel Institute at the State University of New York, Binghamton, and sent over some of my young colleagues to work with Wallerstein on his projects for six months or a full year.

There was not enough time to build the faculty in a successful way. Employment in that system depended on the chair. I employed young faculties and some of them later could not keep the high standard of the department. This probably had a negative impact on the future of the department, which two decades later was abolished as an independent unit and absorbed by the Department of Sociology. I was far away by that time, but still felt responsibility.

My standing with the intellectual elite nevertheless had risen especially when in 1979, the Academy of Sciences elected me full member, and soon I became head of the Academy Department of History and Philosophy and automatically member of the leading Presidium of the Academy. Serving in those capacities at that time, I became member of the establishment. Being the leader of the country's most important higher educational institution in economics naturally generated several invitations to serve on various national committees and economic advisory bodies. I was invited twice to the plenum of the Party's Central Committee when major economic programs were being debated. These sessions and committees had interesting debates and even struggles between conservatives and reform-oriented members. At one Central Committee meeting a year after the 1973 oil crisis, a conservative member of the Committee, the former Minister József

Veress advocated cutting economic ties with the West. I took the floor and strongly opposed this view. We could not escape from the world market, I argued, especially since it had begun to penetrate the Soviet Bloc's market as well. In 1949, Stalin established a common economic treaty system for the Bloc countries, the Council of Mutual Economic Assistance, or as it was called in the West, the Comecon. It wanted to be a parallel world market based on trade in kind where countries paid each other by delivering the same value of goods. Comecon used prices different from world market prices. The member countries agreed to mutually deliver goods and products for a five-year period. From 1950 prices were fixed on that year's world market price level and did not change at all until 1957. From the 1960s, Comecon prices were fixed "only" for five years.

The Soviet Union, the main oil supplier to the East Bloc countries, "suggested" changing the Comecon pricing system immediately after 1973. Instead of fixing the prices for five years (based on the average price from the previous five years), after 1973, the prices began changing every year, based on the previous five-year average. In this situation, I pointed out in my intervention, we had to adjust to the world market's challenge.

An interesting episode followed my Central Committee intervention on the required Hungarian response to the world market challenge. The next day the telephone rang. On the line was a diplomat of the Soviet Embassy seeking an appointment to discuss certain issues. Two days later two young members of the Soviet Embassy, Musatov and Rozanov, both fluent in Hungarian, visited me in my office. They began talking about the topic of my intervention, Western economic contacts and the new Soviet policy on oil prices. They were polite and friendly and seemingly did not want to pass any message or get any information. I thought they did not want anything other than signal that they were aware of my views and closely follow the debates in Hungary. In a quiet way they might be warning people to think twice about public discourse.

These debates and working on committees increased my interest in economic policy and gave further incentives for comparative research. I made suggestions and wrote critical analyses of government economic policy measures and the need for further reforms. In other words, all these efforts were closely connected with my research. Later I also published several of these studies in three small volumes, a compendium of my studies on contemporary Hungarian economic and educational policy issues. One volume, *Öt előadás gazdaságról és oktatásról* (Five Lectures on the Economy and Education), published in 1978, included two essays critical of the three decades of Hungarian economic policy in a historical context, and a third was a critique of the neglect of infrastructural development.

Two years later, in another small volume, *Napjaink a történelemben* (The Present in History), I reprinted one of my essays written on the tenth anniversary of the major economic reform that introduced important market elements into the system in 1968. I wrote this bitter piece of writing at a time of counterattacks against the reform and an attempt to stop it altogether. The leading Party economist, István Friss, also published an article on the anniversary and stated: "The tenth anniversary of the introduction of the economic reform... passed without major celebration in Hungary. The reason was probably that reform has long become everyday practice." (Friss, 1978, 25) I offered a different explanation: the "absence of festive balance sheets [suggests that] some of the basic principles of the reform have not, or have only partially, been realized." I described how, in spite of the success of the reform during the first five years after it had been introduced, it was halted between 1973 and 1975 because, as its opposition argued, it eliminated planning, revitalized capitalism and income differentiation, and hurt workers' interests in favor of the peasantry.

In this second volume two studies prepared for a major economic advisory body in 1976 and 1979 were also reprinted; the first on the erroneous structural development policy of the country, and, the other making recommendations for the 1980s. Finally, in a third small volume with the title of *Szocializmus és reform* (Socialism and Reform), I also presented an essay on the importance of Hungary's connection to the world market. Here I analyzed the gradual alienation of the new generations from the regime, a paper I presented at the Academy in 1980, and in two essays discussed the possibility of catching up or lagging behind. All these problems were highly debated in the country in those years.

There was a negative side to this involvement as well. I had to make compromises. I could not mention the central issue of Hungary's satellite status in the Soviet Bloc. For a long time, I did not touch the problems of the political system, and focused on economic reform instead. I went further only in the late 1980s, for example on the last page of my 1988 book on the troubled history of the reform I discussed the future prospects noting "what I discussed before makes necessary not only an acceleration of the reform process, but also requires complex changes not only in the economic arena but with regard to the social-political institutional system as well."

I found a convincing explanation, however, for this compromise in the historical example of nineteenth-century Hungary. Following the defeated revolution of 1848, the Hungarian ruling elite made a compromise with the suppressor of the revolution, the Habsburg Emperor Francis Joseph I, in 1867. They shelved several revolutionary demands that were unrealistic in the given situation to achieve a comprehensive modernization of the country. One of the leading members of the liberal elite, József Eötvös, Minister of Education in the revolutionary government of 1848, who became part of the compromise, took over the same portfolio again after 1867 and introduced compulsory free elementary education, teacher training and an extensive school building program, an educational revolution in the country. He noted in his diary in 1870 that the condition of the nation "required us to delay political progress for a while and concentrate with full strength on the development of the material (economic) and spiritual (educational) progress of the country." (Eötvös, [1870] 1971, 18) It worked. I admired the successful reformer generation of the 1860s in Hungary. Later when I became president of the Hungarian Academy of Sciences, which had a contemporary portrait of Eötvös, I asked to hang it on the wall behind my desk.

As part of the compromise I also had to package my critical remarks into an acceptable form. It was advisable to introduce a strong critical remark along with praise for certain positive achievements. For example, industrialization policy was important and helped modernization, but the method and direction of industrialization were wrong, partly because it led to neglecting services and agriculture or developing the wrong branches of industry. Instead of flatly rejecting Comecon trade within the Bloc countries as non-demanding and inappropriate for technological development, it was better to speak about the need of a more balanced trade pattern and significant connection with market economies.

Meanwhile, several of the books co-authored with György Ránki came out in the United States, Britain, Japan, and Italy. In 1984, Cambridge University invited me to deliver the annual Ellen MacArthur Lecture Series, which then was also published there in a small book, *The Crisis Zone of*

Europe. My position in the international professional community became more prominent, and I was elected Vice President of the International Economic History Association, and invited to the Bureau of the International Committee of Historical Sciences.

One thing generated another, and not only in the professional world. I was often invited by British and American ambassadors to dinners and talks where interesting discussions with various guests broadened my horizons. These embassies created a circle of Hungarian intellectuals and often received visitors from the States or Britain. Several times I met face-to-face with ambassadors who wanted to broaden their understanding of the country. Such dinner parties and receptions also offered interesting meetings with people who otherwise would not be within reach. I once had dinner with Richard Nixon in Budapest, long after his resignation. By that time he was a wise old statesman with a surprisingly broad knowledge of a great number of issues.

Some, like the American Ambassador Philip Kaiser and his wonderful wife, Hannah, became life-long friends. We met often and once they visited me at Lake Balaton where I had bought a small condominium and spent part of my vacations. They arrived with one of their own visitors, an American NATO general. Philip was an outstanding and interesting man, born in an immigrant Russian Jewish family and serving already in the Truman administration in his early thirties. He played a major role in returning the Hungarian crown to Budapest. The crown, originating from the eleventh century when the Hungarian Kingdom was established, was taken abroad by the escaping Fascist government at the end of World War II, and then captured by the American army. It was not given back to the communist government until the Carter administration decided to return it during Kádár's regime. This gesture symbolized the consolidation of the country's relationship with the United States. Philip, who also worked with the legendary Averell Harriman for a while, invited him to Hungary, and I got the opportunity to meet him. I kept his dedicated book as a precious memorabilia. For decades I would visit them in their home on Connecticut Avenue, Washington, D.C. Philip died at the age of 93 in 2007.

I was also close to all of his successors: Nicolas Salgo, and Mark Palmer and his wife, Sushma. Palmer was a rare type, an activist ambassador who often gave interviews, participated in demonstrations, and became part of the passionate political life of Budapest in the late 1980s. He was well known and popular. When Karl Marx University was visited by the first President Bush, and Secretary James Baker and other members of his team entered the auditorium before the talk, they were welcomed with polite applause, but when Palmer arrived, there was a standing ovation.

I played tennis with Mark on the embassy court, and when he left his post in 1990, he organized a huge farewell party at the Hungarian National Gallery. He asked me with Béla Király, the general and a military leader of the 1956 Revolution, who had resettled in Hungary in 1989, to make farewell speeches at the celebration. I also developed a friendship with Brian Cartledge, the British ambassador, formerly secretary to Margaret Thatcher, later head of one of the Oxford colleges. We still visit each other.

In 1983, I was in Washington, D.C., when I received a telephone call with George Soros at the other end. I did not know him at the time, and most of the world learned his name later when the Hungarian born multi-billionaire venture-fund owner and manager became world renowned as a leading philanthropist who alone gave more aid to Central and Eastern Europe than the American government. Let me quote Soros as he later described our relationship (in his letter for my application for the Green Card):

> I first met Mr. Berend around 1983 when he was a resident scholar at the Woodrow Wilson Center in Washington. We were introduced by Phil Kaiser, former U.S. Ambassador to Hungary. Shortly thereafter, I set up a foundation whose purpose was to destroy the monopoly of communist dogma by introducing an independent source of funding for cultural, educational and social activities…I maintained close contact with Professor Berend all through this period. When he was elected President of the Hungarian Academy of Sciences, I asked him to become co-chairman of the Soros Foundation–Hungarian Academy of Sciences joint venture… he was committed to the ideal of an open and pluralistic society. He took an active part in the reform process which led to the eventual transformation of Hungary.

George Soros was a formidable personality. He played an important role in the transformation of the region. I fully agreed with him when he argued for a Marshall Plan for the region in 1990. His idea to establish a Central

European University was extraordinary. Besides, I liked his non-pretentious manner, never playing the role of the rich uncle. When he invited me to dinner at his home on Fifth Avenue facing Central Park, he behaved like any other friend of mine. I greatly appreciated his attitude when we once arrived in Budapest and took a taxi from the airport together. When he got out of the taxi at his hotel, he paid for his half of the trip and I was happy to share the fee continuing the cab ride to my home.

I realize that I have already mentioned meetings with famous people, and cannot resist mentioning a few more. Let me add to the list immediately the interesting but somewhat uncomfortable dinner in the Vienna Burg, the Imperial Palace, with Kurt Waldheim, at that time president of Austria, and previously Secretary General of the United Nations. The occasion was a meeting of presidents of European academies of science. When the gathering received the invitation, most of my West European colleagues decided not to accept it. It was understandable: at that time a scandal had exploded around Waldheim's unveiled past as an officer in Hitler's army and the role of his unit in Greece. When we discussed our standpoint with my colleagues, I said that as President of the Hungarian Academy of Sciences, keeping in mind also the special relationship between Hungary and Austria, I was not in a position to reject the invitation. They understood, and I participated at the dinner, which became very intimate because there were few attendees. We had a good talk in the splendid environment. Dining in the royal palace of the Habsburg emperors, also kings of Hungary for four hundred years, was an interesting experience, and I did not regret my participation.

Meeting well-known people is interesting for most of us and one can find name-dropping in memoirs all the time. To counterbalance my own weakness in this respect let me repeat a story, told by a friend and fellow historian, Professor Charles Jelavich of Indiana University. He once said jokingly that he would write a memoir about his meetings and talks with world famous people. It would consist of five chapters on five meetings. The first chapter would bear the title, "My talk with General Eisenhower." The content would be as follows: as a young officer in World War II in Europe, I was walking in my military camp when I encountered a group of high-ranking officers. They stopped, I saluted, and I realized that among them was none other than General Eisenhower, who was visiting the camp.

He turned to me and said, 'Lieutenant, the upper button of your uniform is unbuttoned.' 'Yes Sir', I answered, saluted again, and they left.

The title of the second chapter, "My talk with Marshall Zhukov," contains the following: As a young officer who spoke Russian I was ordered to attend the Potsdam meeting of the Allied military commanders. My task was to stand behind Marshall Zhukov, the legendary Soviet military leader, and to help him if he needed anything. I was standing behind him when all of the sudden he turned around and said, 'Officer, shut the window, please!' I said 'Yes Sir,' and the conversation was over. Similar stories would fill the remaining three chapters as well. His part in the dialogue was always to say "Yes Sir!" I ask my readers: please remember this story when I mention my meetings with famous celebrities.

Most of my public activities were connected with the Academy of Sciences. A very interesting aspect of that job was connected with the national educational system. Soon after having been elected as a corresponding member, I was asked by the then President of the Academy to participate in a long-range project of the Academy of Sciences to establish a new high school curriculum. The Academy, as one of the most prestigious institutions of the country, offered a visible and influential forum for open debates about the major shortcomings of the Hungarian educational system. I already had a critical view on the existing over-specialization at all of the levels from highschool to universities. Here was a good forum to elaborate my views.

In 1976 and 1977, I was asked to speak about these questions at the General Assembly of the Academy. The 1976 lecture, delivered at one of the sessions of the regular scholarly conferences, which accompanied the annual General Assembly meeting of the Academy, was entitled "Economy, Culture and Social Sciences," and it discussed the close interrelations between economy and education. My point of departure was Gunnar Myrdal's powerful argument in his *Asian Drama* that the lack of appropriate education is the main obstacle that prevents backward countries from breaking out of backwardness. I continued with the revolutionary ideas of two American economists, which changed modern growth theories: Robert Solow's conception of the role of technological development and Moses Abramovitz's idea about "social capability" as a prerequisite for modern economic growth. I also mentioned the efforts of Dennison and Bertram to quantify the exact contribution of education to growth. In backward countries, I concluded, one of the most important prerequisites of modernization is the cultural-educational level of the country.

I strongly criticized the Hungarian educational system, which, in spite of the major quantitative development it achieved, remained behind modern world trends in education, even declining, compared to its earlier strength. One of the most visible weaknesses was the overly specialized, practical orientation of training, which drastically limited the basic general education on the secondary level, reducing the number of students studying in *gymnasium* to about ten percent of the age group, and channeling most of the students into a vocational and technical training combined with limited general education. This trend made secondary education rigid and unable, or at least too weak, to serve further education and retraining.

The following year, the President of the Academy asked me to deliver the single, most prestigious central lecture at the General Assembly, a forum which the Prime Minister and the entire political and cultural leadership routinely attended. I decided to speak about the Hungarian "Economic policy—in a historical perspective." In the second half of the hour-long talk, I concentrated on the connection between economy and education. I described the high level of the Scandinavian educational system in the late nineteenth century as the basis for the catching-up process of the region after the 1870s. I talked about Japanese education as the main factor in Japan's flexible postwar economic adjustment, and then I questioned whether Hungarian education had developed enough to play such a role. My answer was negative. The education of the entire postwar period in Hungary, I maintained, has concentrated more and more knowledge in a smaller and smaller field in order to be able to compete successfully with the increased accumulated knowledge of the age. The policy was wrong because it became skill-oriented and overspecialized, not providing the basis for the further education and retraining that a modern economy requires. With facts and figures I showed that Hungary's education was "going against the new requirements of the modern age... The key factor of a good economic policy is a modern educational system." This lecture was a call for major educational reform. All of the newspapers and the entire public media reviewed the speech extensively.

Those who have only a general notion of the "communist East," imagine an unchanged, continuously brutal dictatorship, a "totalitarian" system, which does not tolerate critical opinions. This was not the case in Hungary in the 1970s and '80s. First of all, state socialism, probably even in the Soviet Union, was not totalitarian. It was impossible to run the society from top to bottom. The regime needed legitimization from below and made serious attempts to gain it. More importantly, the post-1956 Hungary of the Kádár regime was different from the earlier regimes. From the early 1960s on, there was compromise; oppression lost its harshness, and people were not arrested for political views and critical talk. After a certain period, there were no political prisoners in Hungary. Two major amnesties in the early 1960s released all those who had been imprisoned after 1956. Criticizing the regime no longer required bold courage, though there were some basic taboos which remained utterly unmentionable, such as the Soviet occupation and the leading role of the Party in the political structure of the regime.

However, an important reservation must be added: the authorities had different measures for different people. Although those who were considered enemies of the regime—and in the late 1960s and the 1970s hundreds were on that "list"—were not imprisoned, much less was tolerated from them. Their homes were bugged and the secret police planted informers in their circles. They were under continuous surveillance, being followed and their connections checked. Sometimes they were not allowed to publish and were in permanent danger of their passport being confiscated and losing their ability to travel. Sometimes, though, just the opposite was the case—the political police offered free emigration. This new policy appeared during the 1970s. Even known dissidents, however, enjoyed some security, because their international recognition protected them from arrest or police abuse. This situation became especially characteristic after the Helsinki Agreement of 1975. The meeting of 35 countries agreed on various issues that were divided into three main groups (called "baskets"): security, economic, and the third (Article 7), "Respect for human rights and fundamental freedoms." The "third basket" established more intensive relations with the West and more cultural freedom in the East. Human rights became a sensitive issue with legal protection.

The best known Hungarian dissident, George Konrád, published his memoirs in the early 2000s, and honestly presents his story under the telling title *A Guest in My Own Country. A Hungarian Life.* The English version of this book, edited by my good and close friend Michael Henry Heim, came out in New York in 2007. It helps in understanding the extremely humiliating but complex and controversial situation experienced by dissidents living in Kádár's Hungary. I attach a few short quotations from his memoirs:

> From age forty to fifty-five I was a nonperson in my country, a person whose very presence violated the regulations. My response to the prohibition against working and publishing? An unchecked, internal, authorial freedom. I distributed my work in samizdat...
> ... In 1973 the political police declared me a suspect and carried out several searches of my apartment, confiscating my diaries, firing me from my job, and depriving me of the right to travel abroad for three years.

On the other hand, Konrád was surprised quite a few times that his works were published:

> *The Case Worker* appeared in 1969, the darkest book to come out during those years. I could not believe it was permitted to appear, so strongly did it call the regime's official self-portrait into question. In 1973 I finished my second novel, *The City Builder*... [The publisher first rejected it] because of its dark view of the world. It was ultimately published in Hungary, minus certain passages, after it had come out in German and French, without official permission, in violation of the law.

Let me quote another paragraph:

> In 1976 I received a fellowship from the German Academic Exchange Service, for a yearlong stay in West Berlin. My three year travel ban having expired, I wrote a letter to Premier János Kádár requesting permission for a one-year stay abroad. Unusual as it was in those days, not only I but my wife and two children received a passport with the necessary stamps.

These few paragraphs above clearly reflect the dark side but also the controversial and tactful game the regime played. (Konrád, 2007, 254, 256, 276, 281)

I have to add a very personal story to show how irrational the entire situation has been. I knew George Konrád, who is three years my junior, very well. I not only read all his novels and sociological publications, but once, when I was invited by the state television to run a program, I invited him and Iván Szelényi who, together with Konrád, co-wrote and published a work on delayed urban development in the country, to participate. Before the live program began, I told them the questions I would ask. Konrád suggested to skip one of the questions because we were not in agreement on that, and he wanted to avoid debate. I dropped the question. On another occasion we were invited to see him and Yvette Bíró, his partner at that time, at their apartment. We arrived and spent a long evening together. As we prepared to leave, he accompanied us to the ante-room and asked me, at that time Rector of Karl Marx University, to help another famous radical dissident, György Krassó, who had been expelled from that University roughly twenty years before, by letting him complete his studies and defend his doctoral dissertation. I promised and brought it about, and Krassó gained the doctor's degree. From a distance of six thousand miles, no one can understand those situations in Hungary, a part of the communist block.

But let me return to other elements of the irrational situation. In the fields of art during the Stalinist and immediate post-Stalinist era only "socialist realist" works were allowed and even subsidized, but everything which was "formalist," for example dissonant modern music, even important pieces by Béla Bartók, or "abstract" paintings were banned, and never performed or exhibited. The mid nineteenth-century Hungarian national drama "The Tragedy of Man" by Imre Madách, inspired by Goethe's Faust and regularly performed by the National Theater for a century, was banned as "pessimistic."

During the maturing Kádár era, the cultural tsar, György Aczél invented and introduced a bizarre system, called the "three T-s." In addition to the two categories of art, "támogatott" (supported) and "tiltott" (banned) that existed in Stalinist regimes, including Hungary, a third category, "tűrt" (tolerated) was also introduced. Using the Hungarian words, from that time on cultural policy was comprised of "támogatott – tiltott – tűrt (the three "T"-s) arts. This opened the door for modernism, abstract, and various kinds of "non-socialist" art and scholarship, which previously were labeled as alien and excluded. One no longer was required to be socialist realist or Marxist to get a place in Hungarian arts and scholarship.

The categorization, of course, was still authoritarian. Decisions made by "art bureaucrats" were often excessively subjective, but still a compromise was forged which promoted a more normal cultural life in the country while Soviet control was strict and conservative, and traditional communist values dominated.

Those who were not considered belonging to the opposition or being "neutral" outsiders, let alone "enemies", had more elbow room. Even when saying the same thing as a dissident, when said by others, it could be interpreted as being said for the sake of the improvement of the system and not intending its destruction. Hungary was not a *Rechtsstaat* with the rule of law protecting everyone equally. Except for a minority, however, the population felt relatively comfortable. East European societies had been rigid class societies before World War II and the broad majority, mostly from the peasantry, had been excluded from society. One may not forget that these people had never experienced real democracy and had never enjoyed high prosperity and a high level of economic advancement. The generations after the Great Depression and the war had a somewhat better life.

Most of the people, of course, remained cautious because the memory of the 1950s and post-1956 retribution was in the not very distant past, and there were no legal or political guarantees against its return. The population's reaction to the change was an enthusiastic consumer orientation and depoliticization. The regime did not require political identification with socialism or the system any longer. The "mind your own business" attitude was extremely comfortable for the regime, too. This became a common platform, a silent agreement between the people and the Party leadership.

This political environment provided fertile soil for those ready to fight for change and reform within the system's given framework, though it was not too easy. Those who wanted "socialism with a human face," those who maintained that rigid central planning and the abolishing of market forces were harmful to the economy, were not in an easy position. One could hardly forget that the most influential reform wing headed by Imre Nagy and his close collaborators were mostly, though not entirely, eliminated after 1956. The Party's agricultural policy from the mid-sixties on, although loyal to the Soviet orders for collectivization, affected a very independent mechanism for the activity of the collective farms and introduced market connections between state and peasantry.

The "agricultural tsar," Lajos Fehér, was nearer to Imre Nagy than to Stalin or even to Khrushchev. He was probably nearer to Nagy than to Kádár. In an angry outburst, Kádár once accused Fehér of opposing the return to collectivization, which was not only stopped in 1953 but allowed peasants to leave the collective farms. Between 1953 and 1958, especially because of the 1956 revolution, the Bloc countries did not return to forced collectivization, but in 1958 the Soviet leadership ordered it to be restored. Poland, however, did not follow the Soviet line. Lajos Fehér was also against it, and he wept when Kádár decided to follow the Soviet line. He did compromise, but directed the newly established collective farms in a very different way from that of the Soviet Union and other Bloc countries, allowing private activities and market orientation under the collective-farm umbrella and assisting agricultural prosperity in the country incomparable in the Bloc. Fehér became one of the targets of the vicious attack against the reform after 1972–73 when Kádár, probably half-heartedly, joined the hardliners and removed him from the top leadership. I had a high opinion of Fehér and his agricultural policy, which made a positive impact on the life of the population.

During my TV lecture series on twentieth century Hungarian history, I discussed Fehér's agricultural reforms in depth and highly praised them, although he had already been removed from his position. I was very happy when he came over to me at a reception and thanked me for my lecture. That was the only time we met. Next, I was only able to attend his funeral in the 1980s. Kádár stayed away.

Rezső Nyers, who gained the upper hand in economic policy and reform in Hungary in the mid-1960s, was also a genuine reformer. He was a modest man with an old European social-democratic education. A member of two generations of social democrats, he joined the Communist Party when the Communist and Social Democratic parties merged in 1948. European social democratic values strongly influenced his thinking. Once, when traveling together from Budapest to the United States, we had a long, intimate conversation in which he told me his political credo: he was a "Eurocommunist" which meant more of a Western social democrat than a communist.

It was possible to work for reform and even criticize the system, with the exception of certain taboos as long as one could put aside concerns over unsuspected and therefore unpredictable retaliation. Of course, this meant that reformers had to make severe compromises. I made mine too.

Not everybody was ready to accept this situation. After the Soviet Bloc's military suppression in 1968 of the Prague Spring, one of the most promising reform movements, certain groups openly opposed and criticized the regimes of some Central European countries, most of all Poland, but also Czechoslovakia and Hungary. Those who gave up the hope of reforming the system and wanted to unveil lawlessness and violations of human rights were called dissidents. Although several of them had been idealistic communists in the postwar years, they became deeply disappointed in "real socialism." First, they demanded the return to "real Marxism" and socialism, but then gradually lost belief in their former ideals and placed themselves outside the system by rejecting it.

Courageously they opposed the regime and were no longer willing to make compromises. They were watched and followed, their apartments were bugged, spies were planted among their circles to report on their views and actions. Their freedom of movement was restricted, and they were often not allowed to publish their writings. In many cases, but especially in Czechoslovakia and Poland, their attitude was particularly heroic with long prison sentences at risk, as in the well-known cases of Adam Michnik and Václav Havel. These dissidents deserved admiration. Although they did not hope to realize their democratic dreams, they had an important moral impact and in the long run undoubtedly contributed to the weakening of the regime. Several contemporary Western observers, among them the influential and brilliant journalist Timothy Garton Ash, gave credit only to the dissidents. In the Cold War confrontation this was understandable.

Disappointment could also lead to another possible reaction besides open confrontation: not joining the dissidents in their open political criticism, but remaining on the outside, uninvolved, withdrawn to isolation, and in some cases to the writing of scholarly works. In Hungary the most spectacular example of this behavioral pattern was that of János Kornai's. He was probably the best and most widely known economist of the state socialist system, and his path was interesting. Starting as an economic journalist at the Party's daily in the worst Stalinist years of the early 1950s and enthusiastically supporting the Stalinist transformation, as many young intellectuals did, he soon became deeply disappointed and, after 1953, one of the best scholarly critics of the Soviet type of economic regime. His first book on the critical analysis of over-centralization was a political sensation before the 1956 revolution. In the early Kádár years he was criticized as a "revisionist" and withdrew from politics, distancing himself from the regime, even during the reform attempts of the coming years. However, he did not join the small group of dissidents, but published a series of excellent and thoroughly analytical scholarly works instead. All of them were translated in the West. Later Harvard University invited him as economist but he also kept his post at the Research Institute of Economics at the Hungarian Academy of Sciences, spending half of every year in Cambridge, Massachusetts, and the other half in Budapest for the next twenty years.

He always refused to attend reform committees, and consistently remained outside practical reform efforts. He was proud of his status, as his recent memoirs clearly express. His scholarly work on the bureaucratic character of central planning, anti-equilibrium, and shortage economy had a tremendous impact, but he never made policy or reform recommendations, never participated in efforts to improve the situation. True, he was convinced and later in his works argued, that reforms may not improve the state socialist economy but make the system even more inconsistent, confused and ineffective.

His attitude was not at all unique. I recently read Thomas McCraw's excellent biography of Joseph Schumpeter, who worked on a huge book of the Business Cycles in the 1930s. The biographer compared Schumpeter's attitude with John Maynard Keynes' standpoint, who also worked on the problem of economic cycles and published his main work, *General Theory* in more or less at the same time. In the foreword of the more than one-thousand page long study, Schumpeter stated: "I recommend no policy and propose no plan… [Understanding is] the only service the scientific worker is, as such, qualified to render." Keynes, on the other hand, offered prescription of a cure for the Great Depression. That was what people looked for and welcomed. (McCraw, 2007, 275)

I understood and respected the standpoints, to join the opposition or remain outside in scholarly isolation and work for a better understanding. I also shared several of these views. Nevertheless, I did not follow either path. I wanted to contribute changes and promote reforms. The premises of my standpoint were twofold: First of all, I did not believe in the possibility of the collapse of state socialism in our lifetime or even beyond. The divided world seemed to be permanently arranged for a long historical period. The Soviet Union, the world's second superpower and military giant with a nuclear arsenal and advanced space and rocket technology, stood behind the regime and, if it was endangered, intervened militarily as happened in 1953 in East Berlin, in 1956 in Hungary, in 1968 in Czechoslovakia, or even in 1978 in Afghanistan. Opposing the regime or remaining "intact" outside, I thought, did not offer much hope for change.

On the other hand, I believed in the possibility of reform. This view was partly the consequence of my opinion that Stalinism was a malignant deformation and had nothing to do with socialist ideals, which had values for me. Consequently, I was not in full agreement with the dissidents, and I was also convinced that one has to adjust to reality to be able to change it. Working from within might be more successful than opposing from without.

From a historical perspective I have seen certain parallels between reforming and modernizing state socialism and the development of capitalism from its early "raw," oppressive and exploitative forms to its contemporary "matured" efficiency and welfare social-safety system. The political circumstances of post-1956 Hungary, unlike several Soviet Bloc countries such as Romania, Bulgaria, East Germany, and post-1968 Czechoslovakia, offered a better ground for reform. The attitude of the Kádár regime also did not exclude the possibility of gradual improvement because the bitter experience and fear of the radical revolution forced the government to take popular steps, create better economic, social, and even political situations for the population.

I thought that there was a much greater possibility to contribute some important change from within than to oppose from without. I explained to myself that this is a more rational attitude, one which will lead to a better outcome. Was it true, or flatly just lack of courage, a fear of becoming marginalized? I cannot entirely exclude this latter assumption. In addition to these considerations, looking back from the present I also see some of my psychological motivations of that time. My early experience of nearly lethal exclusion, although more instinctively than deliberately, influenced me: I did not want to be excluded again. My personal character might also have played a role: I do not like sharp confrontations and would confront only with the chance of positive outcome.

My political path was gradual social democratization because I recognized that Western social democracy came much closer to realizing the ideas that were important to me than eastern communism. I believed it was possible to move in that direction through gradual reform. I fully agree with Sheri Berman's view, expressed in her book, *The Primacy of Politics,* that postwar western social democratic parties discovered and realized a "third way" and successfully combined the requirements of competitive capitalism, i.e. efficient economy, with genuine democracy, which regulates capitalism to avoid the subordination of the society to the economy. The Nobel Laureate American economist, Paul Samuelson maintained about the West European mixed economy and welfare state in 1980 that its strength lay in its ability to mobilize the mechanism of the market for human ends and to police those mechanisms to see that they do not wander too far away from the desired common goals. Today even that kind of social democratic welfare capitalism is challenged in the conditions of globalized world economy, but this is a new phenomenon, which became manifest only towards the end of the twentieth century, and already challenged by the consequences of the 2008–9 financial crisis.

My western friends hardly understood the delicate situation we had grown used to. It did not fit into the stereotypical black-and-white Cold War view according to which you were either for the regime or against it. An episode from 1983 may illustrate the difference between Western thinking and Hungarian reality. I had been at the Woodrow Wilson Center in Washington, and, like all the fellows, prepared a lecture on some part of my research project. These talks were open for the public, and the diplomatic corps always received the Center's schedule. It happened that the Hungarian ambassador attended my lecture. In the question and answer period, I got into a harsh debate with the ambassador, who disagreed with me on the historical evaluation of postwar Hungary, which, of course, had direct political implications. I rejected his view and defended mine. After the meeting, one of the fellows, Walter Reich, later the director of the newly opened Holocaust Museum in Washington, whom I liked a lot, took me away, seemingly frightened because of my confrontation with the ambassador. "Won't you have political trouble when you return to Budapest?"

he asked. I explained that not at all—we just disagreed and such a debate implied no personal consequences. I told him I had status in Budapest, a relatively well known reputation abroad, which provided additional security, and I had no reason to worry.

Let me mention another example. A week after my strongly critical plenary lecture at the General Assembly meeting of the Academy in 1977, especially about the increasingly lagging educational system of the country, I received a telephone call: György Aczél, the mighty "cultural tsar" of the country, member of the secretariat of the Party, wanted to talk with me. He invited me to his office at the Party headquarters. After a brief introduction, he offered me the post of Minister of Education in the government. It was difficult to refuse this offer. I argued that the conditions for effecting what I saw as most important were not satisfactory. If I thought that I could realize at least ten percent of what I thought was required, I would accept the position. Knowing the situation, I said I was sure that not even the ten percent was realizable. Although not without some uncomfortable feeling, I remained firm in my position. In Hungary, especially in the late seventies, nothing remained a secret. It became known in intellectual circles that I had rejected the ministerial post. In Central Europe, where people never identify themselves with the government, to remain outside or in opposition was always more valued in modern times, so my refusal strengthened my reputation much more than my efforts to influence reform and change.

When the second term of János Szentágothai, Professor of anatomy at the School of Medicine and President of the Hungarian Academy of Sciences, expired, I was elected by the General Assembly of 200 members, by secret ballot, to replace him for five years in the spring of 1986. Although the Academy got its budget from the government, it was not a government institution, and its president, though belonging to the high echelon of the elite, had a relatively independent status.

I spent the next five years in a superbly elegant office on the second floor of the beautiful building facing the Danube. Some of the office furniture once belonged to István Széchenyi, the founder of the institution. On the wall hang his life-sized portrait, together with the portrait of József Eötvös, Minister of Education in the revolutionary government of 1848 and again after 1867, who created the modern educational system of the country, both larger-than-life figures and former presidents of the Academy. A few years later David Shipler of *The New Yorker* magazine interviewed me and described this office with the following words: "Berend received me in a huge office at the academy, a massive neo-Renaissance palace as ornate as a cathedral. Two crystal chandeliers hung from the ceiling; a large potted palm stood near his desk. We sat in easy chairs at a handsomely inlaid wooden table." I will have more to say about the interview later.

After 1948, the old Academy of Sciences was reorganized on the Soviet model, as the home of basic research, comprising thirty-six research institutes and several smaller research units at universities in all fields of science and scholarship. The entire system was financed from the state budget. Altogether it employed about 10,000 employees, including 3,600 research fellows. The members of the Academy research institutes did not teach, except in cases where they had a second part-time job at a university. The Academy, however, was connected with Ph.D. training, which was separated from the universities and concentrated on research without organized courses. Teaching and research were separated in the Soviet-type academies, which were a great mistake in my view, but this separation survived the regime and still characterizes most of the former socialist countries.

I was deeply honored and happy, but it was hard for me to identify with the post. It was a schizophrenic situation when I had two separate personalities, I and the President of the Academy. It took more than a year until I and the President of the Academy became one single person. János Kádár, following the established ritual of meeting face to face with the President of the Academy once every year, received me in his office one afternoon and offered whisky. (Moreover, with a strange gesture, when he saw that I already finished the glass, he refilled it from his own glass.) He had great respect for my predecessor, a medical professor about his age, but that was an exception. He did not like intellectuals in general and was suspicious of me. I was already fifty-five years old, but he asked about my father's skill or profession, and the area where we lived in my childhood. Next day, György Aczél telephoned me and asked the same question, informing me of Kádár's dissatisfaction with my answer. You did not answer his question about your father, he said. I remembered the talk, and, indeed, I could not answer his question, because the answer could not be given in one or two words. I had told Kádár that it was difficult to give a simple answer because my father had several skills and jobs. He asked about something else and I did not think I had to return to the issue and tell him that my father first was a cabinetmaker, and then a schoolteacher, a writer, a shopkeeper, a factory director, and an accountant in his troubled and difficult life. Kádár, the old Bolshevik, thought I had some reason to hide something about my social origins.

In 1987, after a lecture at a Hungarian–Soviet social science conference, I got a telephone call from Lénárd Pál, a physicist and member of the Academy, who recently had been appointed member of the Secretariat of the Party and was responsible for science and culture. At the beginning of our talk he told me flatly that Kádár asked him to inform me that the leading Soviet party philosopher, Academician Fedoseev, head of the Soviet scholarly delegation at the conference, had complained to him about the ideas I presented at the conference, and that he, Kádár, fully shared his concerns. For the next hour, Pál gave me a detailed list of remarks critical of my paper, which discussed the continuity between the economic policy of the Horthy regime in the 1930s to 1940s, and the Stalinist policy in the 1950s, both connected to war preparation and integration into a closed, self-sufficient economic system. During the Horthy period the Hungarian economy was integrated into Nazi Germany's *Grossraumwirtschaft,* a regional economic system; and during the 1950s Hungary had to participate in the Soviet-led Comecon, the East Bloc's trade system. By that time, however, the Kádár regime had become relatively liberal and he did not even require any kind of "self-criticism," which I wasn't about to offer anyway. He just suggested thinking about the points raised.

Nevertheless, the next year the entire intimidating "education" was repeated in a similar way. This time the reason was the publication of my new archive-based book on the troubled history of the market-oriented Hungarian economic reforms. In this work I openly described and interpreted the attacks generated by the conservative wing of the Party in 1972–73, and then backed by Kádár himself, which practically stopped and even partly destroyed the results of the previous reforms. I was not surprised, but again, I received only a warning.

At the Academy of Sciences, nevertheless, I found unlimited opportunities to express my views. The Academy also provided occasions for several experiences and extraordinary meetings, which belong to the most memorable episodes of my life. When the *Academia dei Lincei,* the academy which

Being received by Pope John Paul II when I participated at the festive anniversary session of the Academia dei Lincei, the Vatican Academy of Science, in 1986.

belonged to the Vatican, celebrated its anniversary, I walked together with the other guests, presidents of various academies of the world, through the wondrous rooms and corridors of the Vatican. Some of us were guided to the Sistine Chapel which we admired without hundreds of tourists. All the guests were received by Pope John Paul II, who spoke almost all the languages of the visitors. The photo shot when we shook hands became a valuable memento for me.

At the beginning of my term, I was invited to a meeting with Mikhail Gorbachev, who visited Hungary and wanted to meet intellectuals. No more than twenty people attended that meeting at the agricultural research institute of the Academy in Martonvásár, and I was very interested to see and hear him. It was also the beginning of his term, and I know nothing about him, except that he was the first head of the Soviet Union who was younger than me, though only by a single year. The meeting, however, was disappointing. It was not the Gorbachev we came to know later.

At the festive plenary session of the Swedish Academy of Science in 1987

He lectured in the familiar authoritarian style, maintaining that Soviet economists suggested reform but he would never allow market reforms, which might undermine socialism. The speech was addressed to Soviet colleagues, but it definitely targeted us, Hungarian reformers.

I met the Minister of Science of South Korea twice, once in Budapest, and once in Seoul. In his company in 1989, we went to see the newly built "city of science" near Seoul. Several research institutes were already active, while others were still under construction. The entire enterprise of building headquarters for research and development clearly signaled the attitude explaining the success of South Korea, a colony of Japan not long before. As a curiosity, during an official dinner party in an elegant restaurant, all participants, including the Minister and myself, were required to go to the podium and sing a song.

At the Academy I became part of the heated political fight in Hungary about the planned Nagymaros–Gabčikovo Danube Dam. This joint Hungarian and Czechoslovak project, already accepted by the government, provoked widespread opposition throughout the country and reverberated abroad. It offered a convenient platform for certain groups of the opposition because they could argue about the environmental dangers without engaging in a direct political fight. An environmentalist-political opposition forum called the Danube Circle (*Duna Kör*) was established. The Academy was asked by the government to form an expert committee to evaluate the environmental dangers. Expert members of the Academy and invited experts began working on the topic, and I chaired the experts' meetings. At the end, the Academy of Sciences and I personally took a position against building the dam. I was invited to the meeting of the Party's Politburo meeting on the issue in the summer of 1985 where I represented the Academy's view. Károly Grósz, who soon had replaced Kádár as Secretary General of the Party, angrily stated that "intellectuals are against us." In the end this struggle, led to the cancellation of the construction which had already been announced and earthwork prepared for the construction. This was a major political fiasco for the regime. The Danube Circle organized an evening demonstration and a torchlight procession came to the Academy's headquarters in appreciation for its role.

As President of the Academy of Sciences my position in the establishment became strong. Probably nothing can better illustrate that than the list published by the Corvinus University, Budapest in early 2007 of "The fifty most influential figures of Hungarian public life." To my greatest surprise, I was still on that list in spite of the fact that for seventeen years I had been living and working in the United States without any influence on Hungarian public life.

When I became member of the establishment in Hungary, a mass opposition movement emerged and attacked the establishment in Poland. A series of uprisings in 1956, 1968, 1976, and 1980 had accompanied the entire history of the regime, and during the 1980s the Solidarity opposition rallied the bulk of the population. This was the crucial factor that undermined and destroyed the Polish regime.

Hungary's was a totally different case. Here the opposition, which played an important moral role, much stronger than its numbers suggested, was still relatively weak and limited in numbers, especially in comparison with Poland. According to scholars of the subject, not more than 300 people belonged to it. As a Western historian maintained, "they could not fill a private restaurant." After 1956 there was no revolt against the regime, and several Western journalists supported the view of the British journal *The Guardian* that Kádár would be elected even in free elections held by secret ballot. In Hungary, unlike in Poland, a social-democratized reform wing, a stop-and-go reform process, and finally the radicalized reformers played the central role in the collapse.

But this long, sometimes painful, often interrupted and halted but still progressing, gradual reform policy actually worked. Hungary was the only country within the former Soviet Bloc where the economic system was near to a market economy when the regime collapsed. Hungary was the only country where foreign direct investments and the entry of multinational companies such as General Motors and General Electric had begun even before the collapse. Nowadays it is taken as a given that Hungary had an important advantage in post-1989 transformation because the process had begun earlier and progressed in a more organic and gradual way than in the neighboring countries. The PHARE aid-program, managed by the European Union, gave assistance to Polish and Hungarian transformation as early as in 1989, and in the first period of transformation Hungary gained half of the total investments targeted for all of Central and Eastern Europe.

Hungary did not have to use the devastating "shock therapy" because the road of transformation to a functional market system had already been laid. My belief in the success of reform was not empty daydreaming. It became proven by historical results.

If I maintain that the social-democratized wing of the regime's elite played the central role in undermining the system in Hungary, I do not mean that they wanted to destroy the regime. What they wanted was to reform it radically and one successful reform step often generated the next. The reformers were ready to go the extra mile to transform the country, hoping to keep their leading role. Professor Charles Gati, a Johns Hopkins political scientist and expert on Eastern Europe, wrote in a letter to me: "There are two ways to undermine a mild dictatorship such as Hungary's in the 1980s. One way is to reject everything… opposing the system 'from without.' Another way is to work 'from within'… where real results can be achieved…"

I know that everybody likes to remember his road and his work in a positive way. I do not speak about deliberate lying about the past, which sometimes happens, but about selective memory and the strange mix of real and imagined or desired facts. Memoirs are loaded with repainted pictures of someone's past.

In an attempt to counterbalance my self-interpretation and self-evaluation, let me attach a few outside views. First, I should like to add a small part of the writing of the well-known British journalist-historian, Timothy Garton Ash, a terrific author of several works on the Central and Eastern European revolution. His book *The Magic Lantern. The Revolution of '89* includes a chapter under the title: "Budapest: the Last Funeral." Describing the Imre Nagy memorial celebration at Heroes' Square, and mentions my name in a hostile, or at least unfriendly way.

To give a more complex approach to my role in the transformation, it might be useful to add his paragraph to my narrative.

Thus it was curious to watch, for example, the historian and President of the Hungarian Academy of Sciences, Professor Ivan T. Berend, prominently paying his respects before the coffins. To be sure, he was a clever man who had tried to get as near the truth as was compatible with making an impressive career within the official Kádárite establishment. He chaired the Party subcommittee which began the official rehabilitation of Nagy. There were many worse. But what would he have said just a few years before to a member of the Academy who proposed to say publicly what everyone was now saying? 'The time is not yet ripe.' (Ash, 1990, 54–55)

No doubt, that was the view about me and my role of several "dissidents," who accepted less compromise (also quite a few had to make some to be able to accept foreign grants and travel) and remained in opposition.

Timothy Garton Ash's characteristic method of collecting material for his works is a few personal information from members of those dissident groups. Nothing wrong with that, except that it is definitely one-sided, and as in the above-cited statement, was based on a mix of truths and gossip. Regarding his comment, I, of course, do not remember whether answering some question I said or not a few years before that the time is not yet ripe to say the truth. From my writings, and practical work, however, from the 1960s on, I tried to tell the truth and moving the reforms ahead, meanwhile making some compromise not to touch certain taboos that would eliminate the possibility of assisting reforms. The Hungarian 1989 "refolution" as T. G. Ash called the revolution in another study, expressing the combination of reform-revolution, proved that fighting for reform and telling as much truth as possible worked in the longer run. I felt some shame when I stood next to Imre Nagy's coffin—as I will return to this dramatic event—because I remained silent when he went to the gallows. But I tried to do what one could do in moving practical reforms ahead in an authoritarian regime.

Thinking about the past, I wanted to add an outside and not friendly view on the role I played. T.G. Ash, however, actually completed the above quoted sentences with the following: "Of course the fortunate Westerner is in no position to sit in judgment, for who knows how you or I would behave in such circumstances?"

Let's hear a few other outside, but much more friendly, views about my role in those years. I was in close connection with people I am going to quote below in the 1970s and 1980s; they knew my activities well, and were objective outside Western observers. I should like to warn my readers that the following parts of quoted letters are from letters I sought in support of my green card application. The writers certainly carefully crafted their letters and wanted to say good things about me. But if they agreed to write the letters they basically held a positive opinion of my activities. Otherwise, they could have made a polite excuse such as lack of time to avoid writing at all.

Philip Kaiser, American Ambassador during the late 1970s, wrote about our connections:

> I met Prof. Berend in…1977… Soon after arriving in Budapest I invited him to our residence. It marked the beginning of a friendship that continues to this day… Berend was a leading exponent of the reform movement begun in the late 60s… During my years as ambassador, I frequently discussed with him the economic and political problems relating to the reform process… he was one of the spokesmen for the reforms which culminated in the dismantling of the Hungarian Communism.

Bryan Cartledge, British Ambassador in the early 1980s, has written the following:

Professor Berend has been personally known to me for many years, both professionally and as a personal friend, and I owed much to his wise counsel while I was serving as British Ambassador in his native Budapest from 1980 to 1983... He was a leading intellectual force behind the process of economic and political liberalization which took place in the latter half of the 1970s and throughout the 1980s...

One of his successors, Leonard Appleyard, British Ambassador to Hungary between 1986 and 1989, added,

Professor Berend played an important and positive role in the process of reforms in Hungary which led to the emergence of democracy in that country... In taking such a prominent role at a time of considerable political uncertainty and risk, Professor Berend demonstrated his integrity and commitment to freedom...

And quote the following paragraphs from Mark Palmer:

From 1982–86 I was the Deputy Assistant Secretary of State responsible for U.S. relations with Eastern Europe and the Soviet Union. From 1986–90 I was the American Ambassador in Budapest. Throughout this period I knew of Professor Berend's activities and from 1986 onward we worked directly and closely together in a number of respects... He deserves personal credit for... vigorously pursuing democratic political and economic reform in Hungary.

In the Storm of Regime Change

Hungary, like all Soviet Bloc countries, was in a deep economic crisis by the end of the 1980s. This was not a new development but part of a continuous slide since the 1973 oil crisis. The last quarter of the century was a period of a new revolution in technology and communications. Although the oil crisis, with the significant inflation it generated, was a turning point after the highest prosperity and fastest economic growth in European history, the setback could have been only transitory since oil prices receded again in a few years. Of more importance was the appearance of the personal computer in 1974, which opened a new chapter in technology and economy. As the outstanding Austrian-American economist Joseph Schumpeter interprets the impact of "industrial revolutions," or as he calls them "a whole set of technological changes," such a new development caused a structural crisis, which has happened a few times in modern history. The technological change led to the decline of the old leading sectors of the economy, which were based on the old technology. Although new technology stimulates the rise of new branches of the economy, new infrastructure, and industries, it takes time until they replace the former leading sectors. Until that happens, a long, sometimes 15-to-20-year-long stagnation may be experienced.

These periods of stagnation or decline of structural crisis, sometimes called great depressions, are well known in modern economic history. The advanced countries, which have the intellectual, educational, scientific, and financial background, rush to invest and create new, cutting-edge technology sectors and consequently emerge gradually from the crisis. The less developed countries, however, are never in the front line of new technology and depend on technology transfers from the leading countries. They often suffer long-drawn-out periods of stagnation or crisis, since they are badly hit by the decline of the old sectors, but lack the resources to create new ones. If Schumpeter rightly said that the structural crisis is "creative destruction," since it not only eliminates the old sectors but clears the road for new ones, for less developed countries the destruction is mostly not combined with creation.

As sometimes before, especially in the interwar decades, the Central and East European countries experienced such a "peripheral," as I call it, crisis situation. In the 1970s, however, it was even worse. Their economic system was rigid, lacking natural market incentives and entrepreneurial interests. Their response to world market and technological changes was delayed or lacking entirely. Most important, the only way for adjusting through technology transfer—was also excluded. Technology transfer was banned for Soviet Bloc countries as early as 1947. A well organized economic warfare, initiated by the Congress of the United States and institutionalized by the Coordinating Committee for Multilateral Export Controls (CoCom), was based on a list of banned exports, called CoCom list, which contained all modern technological products, know-how, and information, which could be used for military purposes or to strengthen infrastructure and the national economy in the Soviet Bloc. These countries, for example, were unable to modernize their telephone systems and could not enter the computer age. In Hungary, only nine telephone lines served 100 people, while there were 79 lines per 100 people in the United States and 45 per 100 in Scandinavia. A major German company accepted the Hungarian order and was ready to modernize the telephone system, but soon had to step back and decline the job. The telephone system remained backward until the collapse of the regime.

Hungary, like all the state socialist countries, lost its previous dynamism. The country was no longer isolated from the West, and half its foreign trade was channeled to the free world market. This small, strongly foreign-trade-dependent country had tremendous losses in foreign trade. Import prices skyrocketed and in the second half of 1970s increased by

70 percent, while exports faltered and export prices increased only by 30–40 percent. Hungary's "terms of trade," the relations between export and import prices, declined by 30 percent. A huge deficit emerged. Economic stability was undermined and the rapid economic growth of the previous quarter century came to a halt: from the annual 3.5 percent between 1950 and 1973 it dropped to 1.2 percent between 1973 and 1979. Moreover, in the second half of 1980s, stagnation followed with 0.9 percent average annual growth.

The Kádár regime wanted to maintain the achieved living standards and consumer orientation, the basis of political stability, and turned to foreign credits. A huge amount of debt accumulated, and was, for the most part, consumed. Repayment, consequently, became difficult and required new credits, which became more expensive. Some of the state socialist countries became insolvent and hyperinflation undermined stability. Hungary had to spend 40 percent of the country's hard currency export earnings on debt service. The country lost control over inflation: after decades of relative price stability, in 1986 and 1987 five and nine percent annual price increases followed. Prices jumped 16 and 17 percent in 1988 and 1989. The government announced every year the return to normalcy, but it did not happen.

After several years of anti-reform policy, the regime was forced to return to reforms in 1979–80, when hidden privatization opened new opportunities. The bank and taxation systems were reformed, most prices became market prices, and the country, without "consulting" the Soviet Union, joined the International Monetary Fund. All those previous achievements, however, which guaranteed full employment, welfare institutions, and a relatively better and improving life, were undermined and endangered. The Party and government could not find a solution and lost public support. An aging Kádár inanely repeated in his public speeches that "we just have to work better." He seemingly did not understand the situation and had no idea how to find an exit. He lost his standing as a pragmatic leader, and lost his popularity.

In the sixties, because of his pragmatic policy and the improving situation, he was the hope for many, and seen as the guarantor of reform. This itself was surprising since after 1956 he was the most hated man in the country. In recent decades, historians have often compared Kádár's story to that of Habsburg Emperor Francis Joseph I, seen at first as the hated suppressor of the country's 1848 revolution, who also evolved into a kind of beloved father figure by the turn of the century. Unlike Francis Joseph, however, in the last years of his rule, Kádár lost support, and became an obstacle, rejecting the required "reform of the reform," a bold escape forward. The regime's elite lost confidence in him and demanded radical change and a safe exit from the deepening crisis. By the end of the 1980s, the economic crisis had ignited a political predicament. Even the generally loyal Party bureaucracy revolted against Kádár's leadership.

In this situation, the demand for an extraordinary Party congress was forced on the leadership. According to the rules, congresses were held in every fifth year. The previous congress was in 1985. The Party elite, however, did not want to wait until 1990, and in May 1988 the extraordinary meeting became the scene of open revolt. János Kádár and almost his entire Politburo, plus a third of the Central Committee were removed, though a few from the old guard remained. The reform wing of the Party, headed by Rezső Nyers and Imre Pozsgay partly took over—with the heavy burden of Károly Grósz who replaced Kádár in the position of secretary general.

At that crucial turning point, sitting in the chair of the President of the Academy, I was approached and asked to join the renewed Central Committee. That forum in the new situation opened a new area to work for change and I accepted. After my appointment was announced, the telephone rang and Gyuri Ránki's widow asked me "you know what Gyuri would have said?" Of course, I did. Over the years we had discussed my involvement in public affairs. He opposed it. On this question we did not agree. I thought that besides historical studies it became possible to contribute to historic political and economic changes. In this respect, I followed Friedrich Nietzsche, who stated: "we want to serve history only as much as history serves life." My main effort in writing history always targeted a better understanding of the present.

In a sense, I had become a public intellectual. This type of intellectual is much more common in Central and Eastern Europe than in the West. To be an intellectual actually means to be a public intellectual, otherwise you are considered to be a scholar or expert. This phenomenon has its historical roots. From the nineteenth century on, modernization, revolution and reform in Central and Eastern Europe was urged and led by intellectuals,

With Rezső Nyers, the "father of Hungarian reforms."

writers, poets, historians, and composers who played the role of the missing middle class. To be a public intellectual was not my preference or "decision." I did not even become one before the 1970s when I became involved in public debates and struggle for reform.

This time, however, I saw the possibility to succeed. I had the experience of a failed revolution and consequently cast my lot in with the reform. In this respect I accepted the view of the best known Hungarian historian in the interwar decades, Gyula Szekfű, on the relationship between revolution and reform. As he explained in 1919, revolution is not the normal or ideal course of history. It is a feverish situation, which is the consequence of failed reforms. Revolution is a high price to pay for abortive reforms. I learned this concept from my own experience. After all, in spite of all of the difficulties, Hungary had already made some progress on the road to reform. After 1985, when Gorbachev already announced his surprising reform plans, and introduced glasnost and perestroika, I thought the main obstacle to reform, the strict Soviet control and pressure, had been removed. Domestic conservatism, vested interest, and inertia were still major obstacles. In the early years of the Gorbachev era, we still felt an uncertainty over potential Soviet reactions. I was ready to take part in these conflicts.

Indeed those years were gradually marked by hope: in early 1988, Rezső Nyers Minister of State in the government, asked me to chair a committee and work out a plan for economic transformation. The program we prepared was published and contained a cautious but revolutionary three-year marketization, price liberalization, and privatization plan for the government. My concept about the targeted new economic system, as it was embodied in the published program, was based on the introduction of a mixed market economy along the model of the postwar West European powers. In the given situation, I thought, a gradual privatization was best, rather than an immediate and total elimination of the state-owned sector. I also advocated moving towards a Keynesian regulated market system, not a laissez-faire regime. This transformation from state socialism to market economy, I thought, would be more organic and less bumpy. I followed the same principles as chair of the Advisory Body of the government of Miklós Németh, which rapidly moved to realize these plans.

(Jumping ahead a few years, let me add that actually I did not change my mind after the regime change in 1989–90. I participated in the international "Blue Ribbon Commission" between 1989 and 1993, which advised the first freely elected government of Hungary. I continuously believed in gradualism to avoid the sudden collapse of huge sectors of the economy and the decline of major layers into poverty. By that time, however, it became ever more evident that the transformation would follow a different course. Poland and Czechoslovakia announced "shock therapy" and spoke about jumping into a laissez-faire system from one day to the next. This concept advocated immediate price and foreign trade liberalization and virtually full privatization. I opposed this rush and argued for a more gradual progress towards the same goal. In 1993, being unable to influence the Commission's concept, I resigned from the Commission.)

The political crisis in Poland and Hungary culminated in 1989. It was an exciting time, pregnant with historical change. Politics consumed my life: the Academy, advisory meetings, interviews, sometimes telephone calls from BBC journalists. One day, the British Ambassador, Leonard Appleyard, called me at the Academy. He asked to talk with me. I invited him over and he arrived at my office within half an hour. He told me that he had heard rumors about plans to elect me to the Politburo of the Party and he wanted to convince me to accept that invitation if it came. We had a good relationship. We often met at his residence and elsewhere in private. I considered him to be a friend. When he finished I turned to him and said: "I understand your argument, but would you suggest the same if I asked for your advice as a friend?" He looked at me and smiled "No!" It signaled that he was an honest friend and also that I had a line that I did not want to cross. I had no political ambitions and did not want to be a politician.

Nevertheless, debates on planning transformation and the future were exciting. Legal experts worked on a major amendment to the constitution which, in the fall of 1988, reintroduced private ownership and pluralistic political structures. One of the crucial debates occurred at the 10–11 February 1989 session of the Central Committee. Characteristically enough, the same session discussed the re-evaluation of 1956 and the question of free, multi-party elections. Even the agenda was remarkable, taking place, as it did, before the Polish compromise between the communist government and Solidarity. Poland's Roundtable Agreement a few weeks later approved prearranged, semi-free elections. Both parties agreed on strict limitations: Poland changed the parliamentary system by introducing the upper chamber, the Senate, and decided that all hundred senate seats would be freely elected. On the other hand, Solidarity accepted that two-thirds of the *Sejm* (Parliament) would remain unchanged, and only one-third would be freely reelected. Most important, due to the Roundtable compromise the posts of the president, prime minister and the ministers of defense and interior would remain in the hands of the Communist Party.

The Hungarian Party, a few weeks before the Polish Roundtable decision in early February, decided to hold free, multi-party elections within a year, i.e., in early 1990, without any prearranged guarantees to retain power. I participated in that session and I could feel that the air was filled with history. The unedited protocol of the Committee's 1989 meetings was published in two volumes in the early 1990s.

I will quote from the published protocol parts of my speech on the second day of the debate. First of all, I defended the re-evaluation of 1956 as a people's uprising and fight for independence, which I discussed in a document prepared as chair of a historians' committee. This re-evaluation had been criticized at the meeting. I rejected those negative views, which rejected the re-evaluation and used the lynching and the bloody role of the street mob as proof that the official label of "counter-revolution" was correct. The historical evaluation, I argued in the debate, may not be based on atrocities and lynching by the mob. "The mob is present on the streets, and in some periods dominates the streets in a revolution." That also happened during the 1848 Hungarian revolution, when anti-Jewish pogroms tainted the events. Without tragic and bloody confrontations, I argued, radical change in history, in certain circumstances is not possible. All the successes of the Kádár era, I continued, were rooted in the radicalism of 1956.

The debate on 1956 helped break out of a nine-month hesitation over how to proceed with the transformation. Arguing against those who rejected the re-evaluation of 1956 to "defend" the Kádár era in the two-day debate, I supported the rejection of "bigoted, narrow-minded continuity" and added that the Party, during the last eight or nine months had emphasized continuity to a damaging degree. I quoted a few sentences from the statements of the Justice Department at the Imre Nagy trial in 1958: "The investigation accomplished in the case of the leading personalities who, in active collaboration with imperialist circles initiated an armed counter-revolution in 1956." And after that from the verdict: "Imre Nagy and his closest criminal collaborators began a secret anti-state conspiracy in December of 1955 to gain power by violent actions and destroy the Hungarian Peoples Republic." I argued that nobody could advocate continuity with this past.

In addition, I proposed erecting a monument for all the victims of 1956, regardless which side they fought on. I also spoke about the need for a "civilized" law on free archival research, instead of personal decisions about who is allowed access to the archives and who is not, in spite of the fact that I belonged to the lucky ones who had gained access to several sources. Regarding the free elections I agreed with those who maintained that society was not yet prepared, but concluded that historical experiences of recent decades proved that "it is mistaken to preserve political structures, which lead to unquestioned personal power." Hungary had faulty political and decision making structures which deformed politicians as well. The best way to avoid this mistake is through a "pluralization" of power, i.e. multi-party system and the formation of coalition governments. (MSzMP, 1993, 104–8)

The resolution of the Central Committee declared the need for devising a new constitution. The "leading role of the Party" had to be abolished, and a constitutional state and guarantees for the independence and sovereignty of the legislative, executive and legal branches of government introduced. The decision, which was backed by the majority of the reform wing, also declared to hold free multi-party elections in a year.

Between June and September 1989, following the Polish model, the Hungarian National Roundtable was organized with the participation of all of the legalized parties, the governing and opposition parties, which agreed on the entire procedure of transformation. An important element of this process was the modification of the state socialist constitution, in reality, the acceptance of a new constitution, which was proclaimed symbolically from the balcony of the Parliament on October 23, 1989. Hungary was no longer a "people's republic," but a republic with democratic rights. In that month the Constitutional Court was also established.

In that agitated atmosphere the reform-communist government performed a huge, unintended service for the international community. As a symbolic act, the Németh government decided to dismantle the border fortifications which remained in place from the earlier period. They no longer had any practical importance since everyone had passports and could travel freely. Before President George Bush visited Hungary in the summer of 1989, the barbed wire fences and watch towers were destroyed and small pieces were sold by entrepreneurial people as souvenirs. This symbolic act, however, gained a tremendous practical importance for the tourists from East Germany who were forbidden to travel to the West and spent their summer vacation in Eastern countries. Hungary, especially Lake Balaton was a preferred family reunion place for East and West German families who could not meet on German soil. When at the end of August and early September they realized that they could pass into Germany via Austria, tens of thousands of German tourists decided to vote with their feet.

Hungary had an old agreement with all the Bloc countries to capture and hand over citizens who tried to leave illegally. It provoked a diplomatic crisis, but the Hungarian government decided to allow the Germans to move freely. Gyula Horn, Minister of Foreign Affairs, traveled to Bonn and made an agreement with Chancellor Helmut Kohl. The dramatic and enthusiastic events at the Hungarian–Austrian border were televised and mobilized the East German population. German tourists stormed West German embassies for asylum in Prague, and hundreds of thousands of demonstrators flooded the streets in Dresden, East Berlin, and other cities. Opening the Hungarian borders led to the collapse of the Berlin Wall and the fall of one of the toughest countries in the Bloc, the German Democratic Republic.

At the World Economic Forum in Davos in 1990, I sat in the huge auditorium and heard the speech of the main guest, Chancellor Helmut Kohl. The speaker's face appeared on a large screen above the podium. When he spoke about the Hungarian border event, the huge man was overcome with emotion, and tears ran down his cheeks. The domino effect that followed destroyed state socialism and the entire Soviet Bloc. The situation, of course, had been brewing from the early 1970s, but the Polish and Hungarian events and the unplanned consequences of the border opening ignited the *annus mirabilis*. In the chapter on the collapse of the communist regimes entitled "a revolutionary symphony in four movements" from my 1996 book I referred to the "revolutionary crescendo," the collapse of state socialism after the collapse of the Polish and Hungarian regimes in four other countries in six weeks.

The decision about free elections did not mean, of course, that the Hungarian regime's elite decided to give up power. The reform wing of the Party which had a good record during the reform process since the 1960s, and especially during the 1980s, and in the last two post-Kádár years, and led the country towards a peaceful transformation, was convinced that free elections would legitimize their power in a democratically elected parliamentary system. Hungarian history offered similar examples. In April 1848, the Hungarian parliament of nobility voted for the liberation of serfs and for the abolition of noble privileges. The ruling elite gave up its feudal power and privileges, but, boldly paying that price, preserved its leading social and political position in a transforming modern Hungary. This time, however, it turned out to be a miscalculation. The Socialist Party received somewhat less than 10 percent of the votes in the first free elections in the spring of 1990.

During the last one to two decades various publications and debates discussed the question, "who made the regime change?" One could read and hear various strongly differing answers to this question: The merit is Gorbachev's who let changes happen; the "street" took over in Central and Eastern Europe and the people destroyed the regime they always hated; the Polish workers and their Solidarity movement smashed communism.

All of these views have a certain truth. In my view, however, the regime collapsed in two countries, Poland and Hungary, and all the others only followed through the opened gate. This finally led to the collapse of the Soviet regime and state. While in Poland the street, the workers and Solidarity, were the main players, in Hungary the regime was undermined from within by the "social democratized" reform-wing of the Party. The opposition had an important moral role but little direct impact in the process, and the street hardly played a role at all. Did this reform-elite aim at what actually happened? Of course not.

What happened was historically not at all unique. It proved the truth of the German historical-philosopher, Georg Wilhelm Hegel, who recognized two centuries before that the actions of people in world history in general resulted in something other than what they targeted and aimed at, what they had directly known and wanted. Indeed, the Polish workers and their Solidarity movement nurtured the goal of an imagined ideal workers' democracy with the political power of the trade unions, worker ownership of the firms, and self-management in the factories. The Czech Charta 77 movement, and its famous founder, Václav Havel, who became the celebrated President of post-communist Czechoslovakia, in his famous essay, the *Power of the Powerless*, explicitly rejected Western consumerism and bureaucratic systems. He dreamed about an "existential revolution… a moral reconstruction of society" that creates a "human order" rooted "in the universe" and without "formalized organizations," with 'dynamically appearing and disappearing organizations." He explicitly spoke about a revolution that "goes significantly beyond the framework of classical parliamentary democracy," as he called it, a "post-democratic system." "As far as the economic life of society goes, I believe in the principle of self-management… the genuine participation of workers in economic decision making." (Havel, [1979] 1991, 209–13) Polish Solidarity and the Czech dissidents as well as the Hungarian reform-elite had idealistic or/and self-serving ideas when they opposed existing "real socialism" and acted to replace it. Looking back from the 1990s or later, we see that what happened in reality was beyond their goals and ideals.

Within a few months the Hungarian reform-elite took a step unprecedented in Central and Eastern Europe (but soon followed in all of the countries of the region) when it moved to dissolve the Party itself in Octo-

The peaceful Hungarian Revolution: announcement of the democratic constitution in 1988.

ber 1989. There was again an extraordinary congress, one of whose sessions I chaired. The Hungarian Socialist Workers Party was replaced by two parties; one kept the old name with a modified old program, the other became to be a Western-type social democratic party with the new name of Hungarian Socialist Party, soon accepted by the Social Democratic International. This Hungarian Socialist Party, although it lost the first free elections, actually won the second and regained power a third and fourth time. It became the first party in the country to win two elections in a row and so far has governed the country's transformation and led the democratic and market transformation longer than any other party after 1989.

In early 1989, nevertheless, nobody was absolutely sure about the Soviet reaction. When the Baltic republics demanded independence, Gorbachev did not hesitate to use military force. I was one who nurtured the belief that there was room for political maneuver, although I had no reason to be sure. My hunch was based on a meeting with Budapest intellectuals called by Alexander Yakovlev, Gorbachev's right-hand man, and probably the most important architect of perestroika. In a large room about eight of us sat around the dinner table with Yakovlev. He talked about his work as an investigator of the Stalinist purges and crimes. It was dramatic as he described that after long working days, he couldn't have dinner because he lost his appetite from learning about all of the horrors and personal tragedies during that era. Later in the discussion I asked him: what will you do if the socialist regime collapses in one of the states in the region? He looked at me and said "nothing. It is the domestic affair of the given country." The date was November 1988. Looking into his eyes, I believed in his seriousness and honesty, and for the first time, I believed that Gorbachev's Soviet Union had really changed, that the satellite countries had gained the freedom to move. I believed this, though some uncertainty remained in the back of my brain. Was that country really predictable? Was that leadership durable? Bronislaw Geremek, one of the leading Polish dissidents, Solidarity leader, and later speaker of the *Sejm,* stated even in 1989 that the limits of Polish actions were the movements of the Soviet tanks. One could not be hundred percent certain.

In the summer of 1989, two funerals signaled historical changes in Hungary: first the reburial of Imre Nagy, hanged in 1958 by Kádár. The exhumation of the remnants was not an easy task since he had been secretly buried after the execution in a mass grave where several others and various kinds of animals were also buried. I briefly and silently stood next to Nagy's coffin at the top of the stairs of the impressive turn-of-the-century Art Gallery building at Heroes' Square in Budapest. The memorial celebration was not an official government event. It was organized by a committee of former political prisoners, the Committee for Historical Justice. I was invited to stand next to the coffin by one of their leaders. We had been classmates at the university, and after he was released from years of prison after 1956, I offered him a research job at my department. I had mixed feelings: happiness that Imre Nagy at last became a national hero and that the country had embarked on a road towards Europe, but also shame. I was shocked when Nagy was executed, but remained silent. That was one of the compromises I made. On that occasion, my old Polish colleague, fellow historian and friend, later the first ambassador of democratic Poland to Budapest, Kozminski, introduced me to Adam Michnik, who came to the city for that occasion.

A few weeks after Nagy's burial, I went to say goodbye to an age, and to the person for whom I had felt first admiration and then disappointment:

I attended the funeral of János Kádár, who as in a scene from Shakespeare, lost his mind and died after his victim was buried. The bulk of my adult life has taken place between the death of Imre Nagy and János Kádár. At those two funerals I said farewell to an entire period of my life.

The year 1989 and the beginning of 1990 became the most hectic but also the most euphoric period of the stormy history of Hungary, and also of my life. In those exciting days when everything collapsed and everything transformed around me, my private life did not remain an exception. My marriage also collapsed. It did not happen from one day to the next. It was the outcome of a painful ten-year long process between 1978 and 1988. It was an extremely hard decision to make, but at least I did not have to destroy my family with my departure. My daughters were already adults, Zsuzsa living in the United States and Nora finishing university and living her independent life in her own home, which she inherited from my father after his death.

In January 1989, I left my wife and in the New Year, I began a new life with Kati. For private life, however, we had only stolen hours. Public life dominated with numberless events, invitations, and exhausting travel. As a consequence of my activities in the transformation, I received an invitation from the Aspen Institute to participate in a conference in Dubrovnik and lecture about Central Europe to American senators and congressmen. It was exciting to sit and discuss together with several famous senators. During the meeting, David Hamburg, one of the organizers approached me and asked to be a permanent member of the Aspen series for briefing leading American politicians. I happily joined and with Kati participated in the next conferences in Jamaica and then in Prague.

I met and talked with several senators and congressmen, Sam Nunn, Charles Schumer, Paul Sarbanes, Barbara Boxer, Nancy Johnson, Bill Bradley, Alan Cranston, and many others. I was impressed by their preparedness and knowledge. Cranston and a few others had just returned from a trip to Central Europe and understood a great deal about the ongoing changes in Poland and Hungary. Barbara Boxer told me that her ancestors had originated from Eastern Europe.

Among the guest speakers it was interesting to meet with Ms Gro Harlem Bruntland, former Prime Minister of Norway. I had rarely met politicians with such a high intelligence and knowledge. They were a different

With Kati, after having received an honorary Doctorate from Glasgow University in 1990.

type of top-level politician from the ones I knew in Eastern Europe. It was also true for West European "Eurocommunist" politicians. One of them, a permanent participant at the Aspen seminars and member of the European Parliament, was Giorgio Napolitano, one of the top leaders of the Italian Eurocommunists, a real European democrat. We established a close relationship and he invited me to participate in his election campaign in the early 1990s. I was not surprised that he recently became the president of Italy. This exciting *"annus mirabilis"* brought several honors for me in both 1988 and 1989. I was invited to deliver the festive keynote address at the general assembly meeting of the Austrian Academy of Sciences in Vienna. The same invitation was soon repeated from the Belgian Academy in Brussels. I was elected corresponding member of the British Academy, the Austrian Academy, and altogether six European academies. In February 1990, at the World Economic Forum in Davos, I talked about future economic roads for Central Europe.

Then Glasgow University privileged me with an honorary doctorate. The official citation delivered by Professor William Wallace, besides mentioning twenty books and more than a hundred studies, also praised my role in reform and transformation:

> In a society that came to recognize that its economy should and possibly could be reformed, whereas its politics could not, his economic elucidation was particularly apposite. He helped fashion the intellectual framework for the attempts that were made at reform from 1968 onwards... 1989 was the year of the great East European Revolution. But not even revolutions are sudden and spontaneous. They take the thoughts of many courageous people over many years. Ivan T. Berend as one of these... helped to create the political revolution.

I was invited to deliver the annual Panglaykim Memorial Lecture in Jakarta in August 1990. The impressive Manggala Wanabakti auditorium was full when I spoke on "Why has East European Communism failed?" It was an exceptional feeling to lay out a balance sheet about the transitory success and fatal failure of the regime, which determined my entire adult life, and now was part of history. In Jakarta, I already knew that we would leave Hungary, and our entire life there would also become history for us. One of those trips in 1989, a long roundtrip flight of altogether thirty-two hours between Budapest and Seoul, had a special importance for me. I wrote an extremely personal historical essay on the airplane for the Memorial Volume of György Ránki about Central and Eastern Europe in the "short twentieth century." It clearly expressed my way of thinking about past and future.

I spoke about Central and Eastern Europe's "two great revolts against traditional capitalism. Nazism and Bolshevism. Decisive though the role of the latter was in destroying the former, nonetheless, the reactions they triggered were interconnected and interacting." I welcomed, along with most people, the collapse of the revolts against the West that characterized the entire "short twentieth century" and the fact that the end of the century saw "the region returning, battered and disheveled, to a policy of pursuing the West's values and path of development."

When I welcomed that change, it did not mean the denial of my previous way of thinking and the values I cherished. I welcomed the turn to

Delivering the 1990 Panglaykim Lecture in Jakarta, Indonesia.

the Western path because Western Europe meanwhile had undergone an important transformation itself: Nineteenth century "brutal capitalism" with its class society, colonization, and warfare was replaced by a society "where the middle strata are expanding and the disappearance of the proletariat in the old sense warrants the description 'welfare society,' or a society moving in the direction of developed Scandinavian socialism." I quoted Joseph Schumpeter, the Austrian-American economist, who in 1928 prophesied the outcome of the current transformation of capitalism and the emergence of a new quality, about which "it will be a pure matter of taste whether one calls it socialism or something else." Schumpeter, one of my favorite economists, returned to this topic and in 1945 he added: "Government control of the capital and labor markets, of price policies and, by means of taxation, of income distribution... [transforms regulated capitalism] into a guided capitalism that might, with almost equal justice, be called socialism." "Sixty years on," I noted in my study, "one finds his prediction fulfilled." Moreover, a new type of West European capitalism led "economic multi-nationalism to the prospect of a questioning of national frames and a post-1992 Europe knowing no borders and using a common currency."

At the end of the essay I anticipated and discussed two possible scenarios "along a peaceful but by no means smooth and painless path" to the future. The successful one "leads to the development of a civil society of constitutional statehood and parliamentary, self-governing, public institutional democracy... wise international cooperation and steady, comprehensive integration with Europe." Another negative historical trend, however, cannot be excluded. I added the possibility of a "self-annihilating battle between opposing forces," and countries, which prove "unable to attain the desired development for an extended period." In that case integration into Europe is ruled out. Even if collapse is avoided, prosperity does not ensue and the gulf separating the West increases. The countries of Central and Eastern Europe still contain the extremes familiar from earlier periods, "varieties of 'left' and rightwing fundamentalism, populist nationalism...national and communal hatred and isolationist philosophies." In a few years, these extremes unfortunately destroyed a huge part of the Balkans: Yugoslavia exploded in a "self-annihilating battle between opposing nationalist forces." (In Memoriam Ránki, 1990, 226, 234–6)

A few weeks before the Berlin Wall collapsed, I went to West Berlin to visit the *Wissenschaftskolleg* in Grünewald. This was one of my last visits representing the Hungarian Academy of Sciences. The *Wissenschaftskolleg* is an advanced studies institution, modeled on the Princeton Institute. With Rector Wolf Lepenis we walked to lunch in a nearby Italian restaurant and during the meal I suggested to him to establish a filial of his institution in Budapest, together with the Hungarian Academy. During this exciting time there was no obstacle to realizing this improvised idea, which he immediately liked. He collected the money from various European governments, visited me in Budapest a few weeks later and the Hungarian Academy offered one of its best buildings in the Royal Castle area of Buda, at that time the Institute of Linguistics, and actually the workplace of Kati, as the Hungarian contribution. In one year, the Collegium Budapest was opened in the presence of the new Prime Minister and the new President of the Academy. My name was not mentioned at the celebration, except by Lepenis in an interview in a Hungarian daily.

In August 1990, I was also invited to participate in the Aspen Institute conference in Aspen, Colorado, to celebrate the fortieth anniversary of its foundation. The two main speakers and guests were the first President George Bush and Prime Minister Margaret Thatcher. I was one of the speakers of Plenary Session 2 on "Shaping a New Global Community," together with Paul Volcker, the former Chair of the Federal Reserve, and Giorgio La Malfa, head of the Italian Republican Party.

For each lunch and dinner, we were invited to the vacation homes of one of the richest men of America. One of the funniest episode of these visits was my meeting with Margaret Thatcher at one of those luncheon parties. When the host introduced me to Thatcher, she grabbed my arm and took me to a corner and asked me about the exciting events in Hungary. She, nevertheless, did not wait until I began speaking, and immediately started answering her own questions and explained to me what was really happening in Hungary.

It was much more interesting to discuss the striking parallels between the Spanish and Hungarian transformation at an intimate dinner party at the residence of the Spanish Ambassador in Budapest with Felipe Gonzalez, the Spanish prime minister who visited Hungary. Gonzales expressed a deep interest and an excellent understanding of what was happening in Hungary, and asked brilliant questions. I was engaged by the historical parallels and differences between the Spanish and Hungarian post-Franco and post-communist peaceful transformations. During my previous visit in Spain I made an agreement with the Spanish Scientific Research Council and, as one of the last activities I arranged at the Academy of Sciences, in May 1990 the two institutions organized a joint conference in Budapest on the characteristics of the transformation of the two countries. In my introduction to the debate I stressed the role of "common historical memory" of troubled and bloody twentieth-century history in both countries that helped forge a peaceful solution.

In these exciting times, among hundreds of events and interviews, David Shipler a leading contributor to *The New Yorker* magazine made a visit to Hungary and came to see me in my office at the Academy to ask about the ongoing transformation in the fall of 1989. This interview changed my entire life.

Shipler asked the question: "how did Hungary's communist party come to permit a transition to democracy?" In my answer, I explained,

> the last fifteen years saw a slow but gradual erosion… Economic problems were not resolved, actions were delayed, living standards started

to decline... Slowly the party intellectuals, even part of the apparatus, started to revolt...Political structure prevented resolution of the economic problems. We have to destroy it... the limitation was always the Soviet Union. When Gorbachev opened the door... the Kádár regime... didn't want to explore the possibilities... the reform wing started to attack the leadership.

I talked a lot about economic problems. Shipler, however, asked everybody for an opinion about a revival of anti-Semitism.

Most of those interviewed avoided a flat answer. When he asked me, I answered his question and he published this conversation in November 1989 in *The New Yorker*: "Anti-Semitism is strong in the Democratic Forum," he said, referring to the largest opposition party. He made it clear that he was not indicting the entire Forum but only a populist wing, dominated by nationalists. "They are counting the Jews in leading positions; they are counting the Jews in the mass media, and are saying they are destroying Hungarian culture... I should not say it is a decisive issue now, but it is penetrating the whole political atmosphere." (*The New Yorker*, 1989, November 20)

My statement was based on facts. During the regime change, between 1988 and 1993, vehement, open anti-Semitic attacks were launched by leading populists who belonged to the founders of the Democratic Forum. István Csurka, Vice President of the party, said in an interview reported by Shipler in the very same article in *The New Yorker*, that a particular Jewish-communist group monopolized the media. In a radio program he said that "the large ethnically pure masses of Hungarians cannot feel at home in their own country. Wake up Hungarians!" Csurka revitalized the old interwar right-wing racist-nationalist interpretation of "Hungarianness." As Ferenc Fejtő, the Hungarian writer who lived in emigration but visited Hungary frequently until his recent death, stated in his article in 1992: "Why isn't someone a Hungarian even if he is legally a Hungarian citizen, speaks Hungarian language, and adapts himself to Hungarian culture...?"

The newly formed Alliance of Free Democrats, the party of the former dissidents and anti-communist opposition was called a "Jewish party," and they were accused of plans to "fabricate a parliamentary springboard for themselves." The communist regime was interpreted by this group as "forty-three years of Jewish revenge." A member of the Presidium of the party, Gyula Zacsek, viciously attacked George Soros for supposedly helping the communists preserve their power to turn over to "cosmopolitan" (i.e. Jewish) dissidents. A worldwide Jewish conspiracy theory reminiscent of that of Hitler was repeated several times by these populists in those years. This was a small but noisy and dangerous group. In August 20, 1992, István Csurka, still vice-president of the Hungarian Democratic Forum and the leader of this extreme right-wing group published a political program in his weekly *Magyar Fórum* demanding the destruction of "Jewish-cosmopolitan continuity of power," which ruled the country behind rotating liberal and communist masks. He called this an urgent task to avoid the arrival of the "last hour" of the nation and for the "Hungarian resurrection." In this study, Csurka denounced the "agents of Paris, New York and Tel-Aviv" who were "giving orders" to certain Hungarian politicians. (Held, 1993, 105–33)

A political scandal exploded and led to a debate in the U.S. Congress, initiated by the Hungarian-born Congressman Tom Lantos, condemning the Fascist threat in Hungary. Prime Minister Antall, at last distanced himself and his party from Csurka after that incident. Csurka established his own far-right ultra-nationalist and xenophobic party. Nothing could prove better retrospectively that my statement in the interview was true.

(This ugly face of the past remained still around or resurfaced: in March 2007, the leaders of the Jewish Community in Budapest issued a declaration urging its members to stay home during the coming March 15th celebration of the anniversary of 1848 Hungarian revolution "to avoid disagreeable incidents." The same mob I became so well acquainted with before often ruled the streets of Budapest between October 2006 and March 2007.)

A few weeks after the interview was published in *The New Yorker*, I was called from a meeting to be told that the noon radio news had just made the following announcement: The Hungarian Democratic Forum had initiated a libel suit against me at the Pest District Court. They interpreted my statements in the interview as "libel, which strongly interfered with the interests of the Hungarian Democratic Forum." In the heated political atmosphere this became a nationwide sensation.

Before the ensuing first free elections in March 1990, I received a message that József Antall, head of the Democratic Forum (and soon the first freely elected prime minister of the country) himself wanted to talk with me to find a way to drop the legal case. I knew him since he had been a historian and director of the Museum of Medical History. On a Saturday afternoon in February we met in my office. He was accompanied by another leading representative of his party, Balázs Horváth. After a long "history lesson" about the historic character of the time, and also about the great reputation of the Academy, Antall suggested that I should make a statement that the American journalist did not express my statement appropriately and *The New Yorker* publication had misrepresented what I said. I rejected this suggestion. It is true, I agreed that from the 80 to 90 minute unrecorded interview, the selected and recollected parts expressed my views more sharply than I explained them in a broader context; nevertheless, it correctly reflected the essence of my views. At that point, Mr. Horváth, who was silent during the first hour of the discussion made another offer: the presidium of the Hungarian Democratic Forum would hold a meeting that next week, and we could make a joint statement. The presidium would condemn anti-Semitic views within the Party, expressing disagreement with them, and I would state that I gave an interview analyzing the political situation of Hungary and from a long discussion with the journalist; Shipler picked a few sentences out of context. I had no intention at all to offend or harm the Democratic Forum.

In principle I did not exclude the possibility of a joint statement. They promised to send the text after the presidium meeting. On March 13, I received the text of the suggested statement. To my great surprise, it was exactly the text first recommended, blaming the journalist for distorting my words. In my answer, I stressed that the text they sent was not a joint statement. I repeated what I had already told them, that they were asking for a false accusation of the journalist and an apology. I said I saw no reason for that and was ready to defend my views in court.

A few weeks later, in March 1990, the free multi-party elections led to an overwhelming victory for the Hungarian Democratic Forum. This party, a coalition of conservative, Christian and populist groupings, formed a coalition government with some other right-of-center parties and occupied sixty percent of the seats in Parliament. József Antall, the head of the Party, became Prime Minister of the first freely elected Hungarian government. Balázs Horváth, who represented the party in the legal case against me, became Minister of Interior. The entire police force belonged to this ministry. It was not a good omen for me.

In those weeks, the lower court made its decision in my "libel case" on March 21, 1990, maintaining that libel cases according to the Criminal Code's 179/183 paragraphs could be initiated only by a private citizen and that a political party cannot file a denunciation. Thus the court dropped the case. The Democratic Forum appealed and the appeal court accepted the legal argumentation. An institution such as a political party has the right to make such a case. In its decision on May 3, 1990, however, the appeal court concluded that the Constitution guaranteed the right to free expression of views and my statement was not slanderous, did not use abusive language, and could not be punished by legal action. The Hungarian Democratic Forum lost the case. Nevertheless, between December 1989 and May 1990, during the crucial weeks of historical change, it poisoned my life. It clearly expressed that certain influential groups considered me to be an enemy. It questioned everything I had accomplished and made the atmosphere more than uncomfortable for me. It was, I felt, unjust and intimidating.

The frightening episode of the "libel case," nevertheless, did not end with its ending. In those weeks, the entire leadership of *Time* magazine, its chief editor, publisher, and a few of its leading journalists visited Hungary. They sent me a dinner invitation from New York before they arrived. I accepted and appeared at the agreed time and place. The publisher of the magazine told me at the table that in the morning they had visited the headquarters of the Hungarian Democratic Forum where they were informed that if I was invited to the dinner, they would not send their representative. The correct answer of the publisher was, as I learned: "we are very sorry." In the end, the Democratic Forum did send a member of the presidium of the party, actually an old quasi friend of mine. At the end of the dinner I turned to him and told that I have heard what a storm my invitation stirred up in his party. He appeared uncomfortable and apologized "on behalf of his party." This unimportant incident clearly signaled that the Hungarian Democratic Forum considered me an enemy.

Even worse, several anonymous partly handwritten letters were thrown into my mailbox every day with ugly, fascist, anti-Semitic dirt and frightening messages. "You cannot escape, we will kill you." I still have them.

Fortunately, as I also realized, many people expressed solidarity and sympathy. I was not the only one who felt this way. The nominating committee of the Academy of Sciences, led by my predecessor, János Szentágothai, an unquestionable moral and political authority, based on personal interviews with virtually all of the two hundred members of the Academy, wanted my reelection for a second term at the General Assembly meeting in early May, 1990. Szentágothai informed me of this, and added his personal expression of complete support. He would recommend my reelection. In those days, it was known that his name was the very first on the official list of parliamentary candidates of the Hungarian Democratic Forum. He indeed, became a parliamentarian representing the new majority in the Parliament.

I also received a letter from the United States from Iván Szelényi, one of the leading Hungarian dissidents in the 1970s, who was practically expelled from Hungary in 1975. As a renowned sociologist, he became university professor first in Australia, and then in the United States. In 1990 he was the chair of the Sociology Department at UCLA, and is now a professor at Yale. He attached a copy of his letter, dated February 5, 1990, addressed to József Antall and expressing his concerns that my libel trial might establish a precedent for critical political remarks to be subject to legal retaliation. Szelényi underlined that he followed the activity of the Democratic Forum with sympathy, which he expressed multiple times in public, but "in agreement with Berend, I found some statements of a few politicians of the Democratic Forum easily misunderstandable to those who are concerned about the revival of anti-Semitism."

He asked Antall to convince his party to drop the case, recalling that in the 1970s he himself was a victim of legal abuse in Hungary, and that he had *The New Yorker* interview before him and found my statements matter of fact and tranquil. Next came the most important part of the letter:

> Ivan T. Berend was one of those very few scholars who boldly took a stand for me when I was accused of subversive activities in Hungary. I am also informed that he defended several other dissidents and even employed some and helped their publications and travel. He has enduring merits helping emigrant Hungarian scholars as well. I can send you a long list with names of colleagues living in the United States who would not be able to continue research in Hungary without his help.

These and similar views and expression of sympathy were more than important to me. But the entire situation was intimidating. It revitalized my war-time experiences and strongly influenced my decision about the future.

Leaving Hungary for Los Angeles

I have to return to the year 1989 when Iván Szelényi, and his wife Kati visited Hungary. For a few years, Iván and Kati were able to visit Hungary and planned to stay for longer visits there from time to time. We often met since they were forced to emigrate in 1975. Iván visited me in Oxford when I was at All Souls College; I reciprocated in New York, when he worked there. We had a long common history. He sat in my freshmen class in 1957. We became colleagues, sometimes visited each other's homes, but a special connection developed between us only in 1974 when he became a well-known dissident. Because of a manuscript he had written with György Konrád about the intellectuals' road towards power in state socialism, they were briefly arrested and offered what was called free emigration from Hungary. Konrád decided to reject such an offer and remained, but Iván had experienced enough insult and accepted the deal.

I was Rector of the University at the time, but was at a conference in Baghdad. When I returned, a deputy responsible for personnel affairs informed me that while I was away, she received a report about this affair and a message from the secret police to cancel Szelényi's part-time job at the university, which she had already done. I did not accept such an "order" from the police, and ordered Szelényi reemployed, stating that he could work at the university until he would leave the country. I telephoned the Department of Science at the Party headquarters; its head, Mihály Kornidesz was a historian and a university schoolmate of mine. I informed him about my step

With Iván Szelényi.

and he accepted my view. To play the game, you needed this kind of backing. Szelényi was reemployed and stayed until he left the country. Before his departure he visited me at my home where I was in the bed with pneumonia. We said farewell and wished each other all the best.

Then in the summer of 1989 Szelényi arrived with the following news: the history department of the University of California in Los Angeles was allocated a new position from the dean and would like to employ a historian of Central and Eastern Europe. They advertised the job in the usual way, and received thirty-five applications, but were not satisfied with the pool of candidates and were asking me to consider applying. "What do you think?" he asked me. "Would you come over and join the faculty?" That was probably the second time in my life after 1956 when I had to make a decision that would influence my entire future life. Strangely enough I did not see it as such. Inertia again proved to be the decisive factor. I was in the middle of feverish activity at the Academy, where the possibility of a second term had been informally offered. This was the most interesting and promising time in my life in my own country and so my answer, without really thinking about the alternatives, was negative. It would also be too late, I said.

I am fifty-eight years old. "Think about it" he suggested. As a real gentleman, he did not express his worries about my future in the transforming country, something I could not even think about at the time. He foresaw the troubles, however, and wanted to help.

In the following weeks I received an invitation from UCLA: "Come over, you do not have to decide anything yet. Let's see and talk about it." In late November, 1989, Kati and I received the air tickets and flew to Los Angeles. Professor Hans Rogger of the Department of History was waiting at the airport. We knew each other from our time together at St. Anthony's College, Oxford in the early 1970s. With his first sentence he announced that he had just read and liked David Shipler's interview in *The New Yorker*. We spent a wonderful week in Los Angeles at the university guesthouse in the spring-like weather of late November and early December. I met several members of the department, delivered a lecture, talk to the chair, the dean, and the provost. The Szelényis took us to the university's open air swimming pool, to the shore of the glorious Pacific Ocean, and to dinner in Westwood Village. It was an impressive visit to an attractive and superb department and university. However, I still was unable to make a final decision.

Meanwhile I received invitations from Rutgers University for a semester and from St. Johns University, New York, for a three-year visiting professorship. We took the Pan American flight and returned to Budapest. Then it was that the Hungarian Democratic Forum turned against me in the court.

Although my programs in January and February of 1990 remained continuously hectic, I became engrossed in my future plans. I was again lucky that my destiny in the shape of the UCLA, offered the possibility to make a final decision and I was able to control and change my life. On March 21, I wrote a letter to János Szentágothai, Chair of the Academy's nominating committee. In this letter, which was also published in the daily *Magyar Hírlap*, I announced that I did not want to be a candidate at the coming presidential elections at the Academy of Sciences.

"In your recent letter to me," I began, "you maintained that the majority of the members of the Academy, including yourself, would prefer the continuity of leadership and my reelection as president...A few months ago when the nominating committee approached me, I wrote a letter to you suggesting multiple candidacy at the coming elections at the Academy, and at that time I did not give a final answer about my availability. I asked some more time to make my final decision in the spring. Today is the first day of spring. In the past months I thought a lot about the situation and my plans for the future. I decided to give the coming years to quiet research work. I ask the majority of the members of the Academy to understand my decision when I announce that I do not want to be a candidate for the next term. I will look back proudly to the last half decade when I was able to serve Hungarian scholarship and the Academy of Sciences in a unique historical period."

I also accepted the invitation from UCLA where the History Department meanwhile voted for my employment.

In May, 1990, I presided for the last time at the General Assembly of the Academy of Sciences and gave my strong support to a new candidate for presidency. I recommended the election of the aging Domokos Kosáry, a leading historian. Actually his 1941 book on the Hungarian Reform Age before the 1848 revolution was the first scholarly book of history I ever read. Kosáry was removed from academia after the communist takeover in 1948 and became a librarian. In 1956, Imre Nagy asked him to collect documents about the revolution, which he did, and as a consequence, was arrested and imprisoned for years. Fortunately, in the later Kádár years he was released and reemployed as a research fellow of the Institute of History at the Academy of Sciences. It happened that he was the mentor of József Antall, when the latter worked on his dissertation, and was now Prime Minister. I was convinced that this excellent historian, with all those troubled years behind him, would be the best candidate for the Academy.

At this General Assembly meeting of the Academy which took place a few weeks after the regime change, Kosáry's candidacy was viciously opposed by another historian, Professor György Szabad, who was then the new Speaker of the Parliament and represented the majority Hungarian Democratic Forum. He accused Kosáry of collaborating with the regime. This was outrageous, and I could not resist taking the floor and informing the General Assembly how Szabad and Kosáry had become members of the Academy in the early 1980s. I was then head of the Academy's Department of History and Philosophy. According to the bylaws of the Academy, two members of the Academy must write letters of recommendation for the candidacy of new corresponding members. These letters are published in the official journal of the Academy before the election by secret ballot. In the case of Szabad, the nomination letters were signed by two leading Party historians, Erzsébet Andics, a high Party official in the Stalinist 1950s, and Dezső Nemes, a member of Kádár's Politburo. On the other hand, Kosáry's candidacy was sharply opposed by conservative communist historians, who maintained that he was anti-Marxist.

I made an appointment to meet with György Aczél, member of the Politburo and Party secretary responsible for cultural and scientific affairs, arguing that Kosáry was internationally renowned and a better historian than Szabad; Fernand Braudel and the Annales historians highly respected his works. To elect Szabad *instead* of Kosáry as corresponding member would be inadmissible. I said that if Kosáry was rejected I would oppose the Szabad candidacy. In the end I was able to avoid the Party's veto and convince the members in the debate so that both Kosáry and Szabad were elected by the Academy.

This entire story was what I told at the General Assembly meeting. Szabad left the session in a fury, and Kosáry was overwhelmingly elected President of the Academy. Three years later he was reelected for a second term. The new President of the Republic and the Prime Minister participated at the session. It was an exciting and nerve-wracking time but a good and appropriate farewell to the Academy.

We began packing. UCLA generously financed the shipping of all of our furniture, books and other belongings, which were on their way towards the port of Rijeka in a container bound for Long Beach, California. We bought the air tickets and on September 27, 1990, at Budapest Ferihegy Airport, boarded the Pan American airline flight to Los Angeles.

I picked up a few current papers at the airport to read on the plane. As an "appropriate" farewell message, in one of the journals I read a nationalist, anti-Semitic article by Sándor Csóri, a poet and one of the founders of the Democratic Forum, in which he stated: "the last moment when the Jews could identify themselves with the national problems of Hungary was the pre-World War I period; but today… liberal Hungarian Jewry is trying to 'assimilate' Hungarians to its style and way of thinking." (Csóri, 1990) The old racist stuff—recycled. Outraged, I put down the paper, shut my eyes and thought about closing a huge chapter of my life and opening a new one. From that very evening I was joining the large contingent of "Hungarians abroad."

From the country of ten million, altogether about two million people left Hungary in various waves, during the last century. The first wave a hundred years ago, consisted mostly of landless peasants. After World War I, then in the 1930s, again after World War II, and after the 1956 revolution came wave upon wave of mostly political emigrants, sometimes from the left, sometimes from the right. Among them were a great many highly educated people, and this group of intellectuals, who became successful abroad, was a permanent topic of discussion in Hungary, and a source of national pride. Many émigré Hungarian scientists, intellectuals and artists, indeed, became extremely successful and world famous. A surprisingly large number became Nobel laureates. The list is long and the fields varied. Paul Lendvai, himself a successful Hungarian exile who lives in Austria published his book, *The Hungarians. A Thousand Years of Victory in Defeat* in 2003 discussed the "geniuses and artists," Hungarians abroad on nearly forty pages in the last chapter of his book.

Although some of them were already famous while working in Hungary, and almost all educated in Budapest, most of them could not have adequate research or artistic opportunity and never could have achieved Nobel Prize-level scholarly work, or international artistic fame, had they stayed in Hungary. Among the more than a dozen Hungarian Nobel laureates, only two received the prize when working in Hungary, and almost all of them became successful because they worked abroad. Most of the success stories of Hungarians abroad give little reason for national pride. In a popular Hungarian journal I read an article in 2007 on world famous Hungarians abroad. The article concluded in the following words: "Is it the destiny of Hungary that its society does not understand its genius sons, and they have to go abroad to gain understanding and incentive?"

Why did I think about this during my flight towards Los Angeles? Of course, I did not consider myself being even near to the above mentioned exquisite group of artists and scholars. Moreover, what happened to them characterized a different age. Now, when I moving from Hungary, the world has significantly changed and made movement more common and natural. I did not feel that I was going to emigration. I continued to teach in Budapest at the Central European University, and remained a member of an international advisory body for the government for a few more years. When we left we planned to spend a quarter of each year in our Budapest apartment. However, I felt a certain similarity: I was leaving Hungary and was going to reestablish myself and a new career in a different world and linguistic environment. It was never easy, but for many very successful. I would not have to worry about the future. First of all, the new world was not unknown for me, I was not jumping into an uncertain situation, and I was going to continue what I did before.

The examples of the successful Hungarians abroad made me optimistic. I knew and established friendships with a few of the Hungarian-born British and American economists. We visited each other in Oxford, Cambridge, Washington and Budapest. I had long talks with them. When I considered their amazing life stories I was encouraged. Many years ago I had also read an interview with Lord Thomas Balogh, who was asked about the "secret" of his and some of his emigrant colleagues' successes abroad. He maintained that as a Jew in interwar Hungary he learned that he had to work twice as hard as everyone else to be a success, and after emigrating he was convinced that he had to work even twice as hard as before. Immigrants must be hard working to compensate for their disadvantages. Chinese immigrants were more successful in business and science in their new countries than at home for a long time. Another fact: while the nationwide figure for college graduates is roughly one quarter of the given age group of the population in the United States, it is nearly two-thirds among Indian immigrant families. That looked convincing to me.

We arrived in Los Angeles on a sunny September afternoon. Iván and Kati Szelényi were waiting at the Los Angeles airport and since they were about to leave for Europe for three months they offered their apartment and car for that first period. Their apartment, the last building on Sunset Boulevard facing the Pacific Ocean, was not only a beautiful place to stay for the first months in our new life, but a wonderful symbol of friendship and solidarity. In Hungary, Iván and I belonged to different parts of the political spectrum of society: I was part of the establishment; he was a renowned dissident before 1989. But we both felt close human and political ties, and we reached over to help each other when needed. When a Hungarian friend learned that we had bought an apartment later, and left the

Horse riding in the Sierra Nevada in 1995.

Szelényis' place, she expressed her sorrow that we had moved out. As she noted, what exemplary loyalty, friendship, and humanity was symbolized by our stay at the Szelényis. We found friends in Los Angeles. Besides the Szelényis, my old schoolmate from high-school, Alfred Pasternak, who left Hungary in 1956 and settled in Los Angeles, lived nearby. He had become a successful gynecologist. We had stayed in contact. He often visited Budapest and I visited him twice in Los Angeles in previous years. Many others followed soon. We were surrounded by new colleagues and established new friendships.

I found my home on the UCLA campus as well. Here too, in the first few months I used the office of a colleague who was on sabbatical, but soon moved into my own sixth-floor office in Bunche Hall, facing the sculpture garden. I always loved the spacious American campuses and found the student body similar all over the world. The department, one of the largest history departments in the world with 80 professors, seemed a wonderful place with many excellent and friendly colleagues. Those months were my honeymoon with UCLA.

However, I had to learn many new things. The university gave me a computer, which I had never used before, and I stopped writing my manuscripts by hand. I had to decide about insurance and incomprehensible healthcare policies, choose doctors and dentists, and learn everything about the new environment. Surprisingly, I felt immediately at home.

Nevertheless, the real turning point arrived when we bought our own, new, two-bedroom, 2,000 square feet condominium in Westwood and our own car, a second-hand Ford. We were on our own. We were standing on our own two feet and had really begun our new life in the United States. Even more symbolic, when we moved in and unpacked our furniture, which had waited in a self-storage, we also had to buy additional things like bookshelves, beds and pieces of small furniture. And so we bought several things, and rented a truck, and on December 11, my sixtieth birthday, for the first time in my life, I drove a truck from the store to our home. It symbolized a new beginning, a renewal, an unlimited possibility to start again in a new place on a new continent, six thousand miles away from my other life. As another symbol of unlimited possibility for a new start, I soon experienced the terrific feeling of riding a horse for the first time in my life through the beautiful foothills of the Sierra Nevada, at the ranch of our new colleagues and friends, Cindy and Gary Nash.

Our first home, according to one of our friends, was a "European" apartment in the Westwood area where mostly three-level condominium buildings surrounded the streets, and walkways offered space for traffic. After six years, however, we moved to a semi-attached townhouse in the hills of Upper Bel Air, with a small garden, overlooking Benedict Canyon. It was the same distance from the University, seven to ten minutes by car, but without public transportation, surrounded by wilderness, free from city noise, regularly visited by a deer family, coyotes, owls, bobcats, even rattle snakes in the middle of the Los Angeles agglomeration of nearly sixteen million people. This was already a typical Los Angeles home.

America

Even though it has stretched into two decades, our life in the United States has been an endless discovery of a new world. I certainly cannot tell an American reader anything new about the United States. My impressions, however, might represent an outside perspective on very well known subjects that, just because they are "natural" for Americans, are not always obvious or given deliberate thought. Moreover, my viewpoint is of both that of an insider and an outsider, since it is based on better and deeper knowledge than visitors may have, but nevertheless with an eye still fresh. Actually I am in a somewhat similar position nowadays when I visit Hungary, which I do almost every year for a week or so. That is a place I know thoroughly, but the life, the entire world has changed so greatly that I see everything from a different angle. I have become an outsider there too, though still with an insider's experience. In other words, I am partly American there and partly Hungarian here. This position may give me some advantage in seeing and comparing the social-cultural phenomena that are natural for long-time citizens. Even if it is not new for a born American, it might be interesting to look at known problems from a different angle.

There are, however, some limitations to note. Working at a university is an atypical and privileged situation. A tenured position, unlike most other American jobs, is totally secure. We have excellent health care, provided by the University, and a superb University's hospital and clinic with outstanding doctors. Academics may not be millionaires, but we are relatively

On one of our tours to "discover" America: in Bryce Canyon, Utah, with Kati in 1997.

well paid and enjoy the freedom of long summer vacations, opportunities to travel, and the satisfaction of doing work we love. I work during the entire summer as well, but that is my choice. I do not have to spend my whole day at the office, and I may work at home a few days per week even when school is in session. I typically spend three days a week working at home. This does not mean that I work less than others. I start my workdays in the early morning and sometimes finish late at night. To me, there is no such thing as a fixed and regulated work day. But working ten to twelve hours per day is my deliberate choice and I do it because it is a pleasure for me. At the same time, I realize that I see things from a privileged perspective.

Coming from a small country in Central Europe, I indeed see an entirely different and in many senses, surprising America. This is true for the physical environment. Although settled and working, living the life of the people of this country as if I am one of them, I have retained the commitment of a genuine tourist and still make the conscious effort to go and to see.

Nature in the United States not only differs from that of Europe but has a different function too. The explanation I read in the Gene Autry Western Heritage Museum in Los Angeles seems convincing: In America, national parks are a substitute for ancient ruins, medieval churches, renaissance palaces, and the missing millennial history. I felt that exactly in the Sequoia National Park as I walked through the two-thousand years-old giant trees towering like the most beautiful cathedrals. The stone arches cut by streams and natural forces in the Arches National Park in Utah, the giant Rainbow Arch at the end of Lake Powell, or Bryce Canyon with its pillars created by nature compete with Europe's masterfully built ancient buildings and their ruins, while the Grand Canyon's chasms open the globe to exhibit the endless layers of the earth.

Walking around the geysers in Yellowstone, smelling the sulfurous air, watching the punctual schedule of Old Faithful, one can understand medieval visions of Hell and imagine the earth in the making. Yes, America's national parks symbolize the youth of this still new world. If one walks on the stone-hard lava in the Big Island of Hawaii, and observes the permanently flowing red lava, or climbs on Mount Saint Helen where the last eruption of the volcano a quarter of a century ago left an environment that seems as if it happened yesterday, the same feeling wells up—this continent is not yet finished.

The great variety of deserts are amazing, from the sand dunes of Death Valley to the incredible stone formations of the high desert of Joshua Tree National Park. This arid environment always remains as exotic for us as the Pacific Ocean.

When I consider the physical environment of our new home with Kati in Los Angeles we are struck by an urban landscape entirely different from that of Europe. L.A. is certainly one of the least European cities in the world. Here downtown is not a real city center, though we see the legacy of the turn-of-the-century beauty of Art-Deco American urban architecture. Half of the downtown area is old, mostly run-down, crowded, full of cheap shops—one block for jewelry, another one for underwear—a flower market, a Mexican food market—and it is crowded all the time. The other half is twenty-first century modern, with a landmark concert hall and hundreds of office buildings, few shops or pedestrians because residential space is lacking. It is impressive, yet without people in the streets it is dead. People go downtown only to visit city offices, courts, concerts, operas, and theaters, and is not part of the city as a whole. This uniqueness, however, makes downtown Los Angeles so attractive for me, and also for all of my foreign guests who I always accompany to proudly show this amazing city.

Each district has its own "village," a center for shopping and sitting in restaurants, separate from the other. Public transportation hardly exists: several parts of the city, including our neighborhood in the hills can be reached only by car. In many places, there are not even sidewalks. Throughout this huge agglomeration jammed freeways cross each other. People either hate it or love it. I belong to the latter group.

The mentality of the people is as different as nature and urban landscape in America. The mood of the country is no less surprising to me than its physical environment. The United States has a calm, well organized everyday life. People are not nervous and do not "educate" each other on the streets or in public places and shops, which was a common practice in Hungary and several other countries of Europe. Here strangers prefer to smile and even greet other pedestrians. Shop clerks ask the stereotypical question "how are you," and even if nobody waits for an answer, immediately a friendly atmosphere has been created. Communication and exchange are smooth and polite. This attitude made a powerful impact on me when we came to the States because it represented exactly the opposite of what I had experienced before.

In sharp contrast with the historically highly developed culture of negativism and complaining predominant in Central Europe and several other European countries, American people are basically calm, balanced and have a positive attitude towards everything. In Hungary, if you are not cautious and ask somebody "how are you," you have to be prepared to hear a detailed answer about a bad health situation, accidents, death in the family, and troubles at the work place. People are inclined to see the negative side of everything. That which is wrong attracts their interest. In conversation with others, you often feel that life is miserable. People are very often irritated. So we were surprised to hear people in the United States being interviewed after some terrible natural catastrophe, earthquake, fire or hurricane that leveled their home and destroyed all their belongings speaking about how lucky they were to have survived, and how they were and going to rebuild what had been destroyed. People want to find positive lessons and outcomes from bad experiences. I like this attitude, probably because this is the way as I look to things as well. The different patterns of behavior are extremely visible. Václav Havel, the former President of the Czech Republic, in his memoirs compared the American political class that is "good-natured, calm, handsome and charming" to the Czech situation and asks: "Why is it that we Czechs are always so harried? Always so irritated?"

"Why does this country have such a pleasant atmosphere?" Kati and I used to ask each other. As a historian I easily found an historical answer: Because it is a fresh country with self-reliant and entrepreneurial people. History has formed it in this way. The pioneer attitude, the "it has to be done and we can do it" mentality still dominates. A typical feature of this attitude is the Home Depot hardware store's advertisement "you can do it, we can help you." The Barack Obama campaign in 2008, represented hopes and change, used the slogan, repeated thousand times at rallies, "we can." The richness of the country, it's excellent (though recently eroding) infrastructure and well-oiled service are the factors strongly determining this atmosphere. Virtually everywhere, even in remote gas stations in the middle of nowhere, restrooms are clean and well kept. Before the cell phone was introduced, you could telephone from any place to any another, at any time. You may ask the post office to hold your mail if you are away. The university libraries have an open-shelf system and you find works that you did not even know existed.

It happened more than once that Kati and I returned after a few weeks spent in Europe or Asia late afternoon or in the evening. We were tired, and had emptied the refrigerator before we left. We went to bed early, but being jetlagged, we woke up at three o'clock in the morning, looked at each other and said "let's go shopping and fill the refrigerator." One can shop for twenty-four hours a day, during weekends, even on Sunday. Europe defends its workers, America prefers its customers. In other words, we experienced the highest level of consumer infrastructure to promote both business and comfortable life.

No less important is the feeling of freedom. Nothing is compulsory and you may do what you want. At least, this is how most people feel. Of course, there are strict limitations created by one's financial situation, including long workdays and short vacations, but you still have a liberated feeling. While traveling through the country you do not fill questionnaires at hotels. At the university nobody tells you what you teach. One has to teach a certain number of courses and, another attractive feature for me, it is equal for beginner assistant professors and renowned full professors, but no one has a word about its content. This freedom of teaching is granted by the tenure system. Your advancement does not depend on one boss. If you don't want to go to a meeting, nobody will ask you why you did not come.

The American people's mentality, if generalization is possible at all, was in many ways surprising for me. Americans are more naïve than their European counterparts, and ready to believe in others, taking what is said at face value. Politicians on the campaign trail change their political position on certain issues when they realize that their previous position did not have popular support. That may be natural, but what surprised me was that they were able to convince voters by simply saying something that was the opposite of what they did or said a year before. People believe in positive changes.

In Europe, people do not like to mention their bad habits, even in the past tense. They assume that if they confess that they once were alcoholic, others will not believe that they have changed. In America, they believe it because positive change is always believable. The same attitude causes many people to become victims of swindlers. They do not assume that the stated words might be false and that somebody wants to cheat. This naïve and benevolent attitude is much more widespread here than in Europe where suspicion is the norm. We see this naïveté also in the widespread admiration for celebrities while fame and infamy are often confused. Many Americans seem wedded to fairy tale stories of romance. Being known sometimes establishes a sort of celebrity status. The media plays a significant role in this phenomenon. As I write this memoir a typical case has emerged as illustration. The thirty-nine-year-old Anna Nicole Smith was found dead in her room. This former Playboy model became notorious a few years ago when she married a ninety-year old multimillionaire, and after his death, launched a protracted fight with his family for the inheritance. Nothing about this scandalous person was significant, but the media discussed her case every day and for weeks.

This is one of many cases that could be mentioned that illustrate the bad influence of the sensation-hungry media on a public that exhibits similar attitudes. Happy marriages and scandalous divorces of "known" people regularly gain central place in news and attract major interest. Hollywood also plays a role in this phenomenon. Idealization of tough, heroic gangsters and "bad guys" is an integral part of the history of the American motion picture industry.

As a historian, I easily understand that history does not play a big role in people's way of thinking in America. History, of course, plays an important role in American lives, but people do not turn to history for explanations. In Europe, stormy history strongly penetrates private life and consequently, habits and thought. This is especially true for the adult generations of Central and Eastern Europe. To explain something, it is natural to turn back to history. When a crisis develops, intellectuals look to the historical roots of the events. I mentioned before that in the late 1980s when a complex economic and political crisis emerged in Hungary, I was asked to chair a history committee to analyze the reasons that led to the crisis. People in 1956 turned back to the 1848 revolution to strengthen themselves. Historical symbols help mobilize the population. The people of Central and Eastern Europe look back more often than forward.

The huge difference played by history in the way of thinking does not mean that Americans are not interested in history. At my university, the nearly 30,000 undergraduate students take roughly 29,000 history courses every year at our History Department. This does not mean that almost all the students study history, because quite a few take more than one course in a year, but is a surprisingly large number. History, nevertheless, is not at the forefront of interest in a forward looking nation.

Is it the consequence of the relatively short history of the United States, compared with the histories of other countries that stretch back a thousand years or more? That may be one of the reasons, and for a long time I thought this was the main one. A colleague and friend of mine, however, offered a deeper explanation. America is a nation of immigrants who sought to escape from religious or political oppression, from lack of land and work, from poverty and minority status. Most of the immigrants wanted to forget history and focus on the future ahead. In other words, the history of the country explains the lack of historical thinking.

It might seem surprising to others, but even American consumerism, although it is common knowledge, also surprised me. I grew up in a poor environment. What we consumed was what was needed for everyday living. The bulk of my parents' income was spent on food and basic necessities. I always inherited my brother's clothing. I never had more than one pair of shoes. Consumerism was unknown to me and to most people in Hungary. Standards of living and access to consumer comforts improved during the 1960s to the 1980s in consequence of the government's deliberate policy—albeit designed to pacify the population following the 1956 revolution—to make the economy more consumer-oriented. Consumerism, nevertheless, was modest and limited.

When I began traveling in Western Europe in the 1960s, those countries were just becoming consumer societies. Postwar German journalistic jargon invented special terms to characterize certain stages of postwar consumerism: first they talked about a *Fresswelle* or gobbling wave, followed by the *Kleidungswelle*, clothing wave, and then the *Reisewelle*, or traveling wave. Homes became mechanized, household machines were widespread, and the car market was saturated because virtually every family had a car. For decades before arriving in America, I was familiar with this Western European consumerism.

But passionate American consumerism is something else. I know from history that this trend is relatively new here too, and emerged gradually after World War II, especially from the 1960s on. However, for a newcomer it looks like a "natural" habit. Holidays are over-commercialized. Each is connected with major sales and becomes an occasion to buy things. In my experience the only exception is Thanksgiving, the most friendly and intimate festivity, celebrating the forefathers' own celebration that they had enough to eat after a difficult first year in the New World. Interestingly enough, this was the festivity I immediately internalized. I also like the custom that people invite to their table those who have no place to celebrate—visitors, students, and newly arrived people. Kati and I like and have cultivated this custom from our very first year here.

Yet in terms of naked consumerism, as a marked example of the contradictory impulses in American life, "Black Friday," i.e. the day after Thanksgiving, is the biggest sale and shopping day of the entire year. Indeed, it marks the beginning of the Christmas sales and consumer feeding frenzy. The shops open as early as 4:30 AM to long lines of people who have already formed outside, waiting greedily to gobble up bargains. Companies predict their entire quarter's profit estimates based on the sales receipts of Black Friday. A virtually unlimited selection of goods and new products, continually increasing portions at restaurants, a powerful advertising industry, and retail infrastructures are the vehicles used to inspire consumption and generate a passionate obsession to shop and to spend. Because of this feverish obsession to consume, the richest country in the world has accumulated no savings in recent years because the population spends more than it earns. Shopping became an entertainment.

This habit is also related to naïveté. Millions of people are buying with money they don't have, using credit cards without thinking about the usurious interest rates that many will be unable to repay. In similarly rich countries such as Norway and Japan, I have witnessed very different habits, inherited from the poorer past but retained as a national characteristic. In Norway, people with puritanical traditions are thrifty even in eating. When Kati and I traveled along the exceptionally beautiful fjord-line in Norway and stayed at bed-and-breakfast farm houses, we took every opportunity to talk with people. We learned about their puritanical eating habits—having a piece of yellow or brown cheese for breakfast and a piece of salami on Sundays. Savings is a moral responsibility in Norway as well as in Japan, and roughly one-fifth of the nations' income is saved and accumulated.

Friendly informality is also a characteristic feature of American mentality. Strangers who have never seen you before call you by your first name almost everywhere, even by phone. Informality in clothing, with some regional and occupational differences, gives almost everybody a similar appearance. This is especially true in California, regardless of whether you visit a friend, or go to a theater or opera performance. You can not differentiate between poor and rich based on clothing in most cases. I have adjusted to this comfortable custom, although the adjustment did not happen at once. For years, I wore a suit or jacket and tie to class. At one point a student even commented in the student evaluation form that "this professor is a gentleman, like only a European can be." Unfortunately, or perhaps fortunately, I changed. However, I still dress "appropriately" for a concert or opera as an expression of respect. But I no longer dress formally for class or for visiting friends, nor even for a familiar small theater or restaurant. Interestingly enough, in such an informal environment, it has become uncomfortable to be formally dressed, and I have learned to prefer informality.

American informality has several other faces and elements. One of them is the lack of dining etiquette. Most people cut their meat, then put down the knife and eat with their fork only, and often use their hands to take out something stuck between their teeth. In Europe, Americans are easily recognized because table etiquette does not allow this behavior. Cell phones are used in public places and people talk loudly about private matters, although increasingly this is becoming an international phenomenon.

Driving mentality in America can be surprising as well. When my father-in-law visited us he asked to stop on the bridge over the freeway, telling us later that watching the endless flow of cars, the white and red chain of lights in the evening, was one of the most memorable experiences of his visit. Even our German guests were impressed when I picked them up at the airport and drove home on the freeway, with its five lanes in either direction. But for me, the most surprising fact about California's traffic is its discipline. The majority of drivers obeys rules; waiting for pedestrians before they step down from the curb, and allowing each other to go. Drivers rarely honk to "educate" other drivers if they made some mistake. This discipline is especially surprising because such a premium is placed on personal freedom and individuality in America. Personal freedom, self-reliance, lack of governmental or other regulations have a high value in this country and people behave accordingly.

Individualism influences personal behavior. I do what I like to do and do not care too much about others. Once, visiting Berkeley in the mid-1990s, before the scheduled meeting at the University, Kati and I walked from our hotel to a nearby, popular coffee house to have breakfast. To our great surprise, two naked young women were walking in the same direction, and they stood in front of me in the line for coffee. Actually they were not absolutely naked because they had straw-hats on. No one was surprised or signaled any sign of it. No one made any remark. They were asked about the order and served. In public places, people march straight through doors without regard for anybody else who might be waiting to enter. For instance, a group of women was surprised when, according to the European custom, I let them go first in to the elevator or a room even though I was there before them.

Nevertheless, on the Californian road one experiences a highly disciplined and polite attitude, much more so than in Europe. Reckless drivers, of course, exist everywhere. People do a lot of things in the car, including shaving, reading, doing make up, and almost always using their cell-phone to make calls in preference to "wasting" time sitting in the car. These habits are the result of long distance driving on jammed freeways on a daily basis. In some areas people spend two or three hours in a car every day. It is true in large parts of the country as well. "Such a vast country," often the first thing Europeans notices upon arrival. It was hardly believable how much open, uninhabited countryside exist in several states, how many hours one can drive on and on and on just for an intra-state trip. I felt it several times beside California, in Arizona, Nevada, probably most of all in Montana. The vastness of America and the enormous scale of the freeways that traverse it influence driving habits.

The majority of drivers are extremely polite in California—compared to Germany, France, Belgium, let alone Hungary. They are the most polite with pedestrians, not nervous, and even allow impatient drivers to pass first and squeeze their cars back into a line of waiting cars in front of them. They do not speed between lanes as Italians do, do not race on the freeway and do not tailgate to force you to change lanes as is customary on the German autobahn. We have found American drivers on the West coast to be much safer and more polite than most of their European counterparts. It did not fit into the picture of the America I had in my mind when we first arrived. But soon I began understanding the reasons.

Among them are disciplinary adjustment to the huge number of cars on the roads, and early driving experience. Regulations are much stricter, moreover, and control by the police and parking enforcement officers is much more frequent than in Europe. One might drive in various other countries for two to three weeks without meeting or even seeing a police car. In America one cannot drive 30 to 100 miles without encountering them. Getting a ticket means trouble, much more than in Europe. You cannot escape by paying the fee on the spot. The story does not end with the traffic cop but only begins with it: the ticket remains on your record and increases your insurance fee. Getting a ticket may be excessively expensive, especially if you accumulate two or three of them and established insurance companies refuse to insure you. This happened to a friend, who collected three tickets in a row. Because one may not drive without insurance, he had to turn to a special small robber-insurer. Those three incidents ended up costing him an additional $3,000. All these factors combined with the fear of being sued convince the vast majority to be careful and disciplined while driving.

The reception of newcomers in this country is also surprising. Immigrating to a country and integrating into its society can be a difficult process. People have to learn the language and to change deeply rooted habits to be able to adjust to a different society. In certain communities it never really works. It is not a festive march in the United States and hostility against illegal immigrants is emerging, especially in certain parts of the country. But in big cities in the coastal regions integrating is probably the easiest in the world. It is definitely connected with the history of the country, a country of immigrants where millions of nationalities became Americans in the "melting pot."

Today the melting pot idea has mostly been replaced by the concept of "multi-culturalism" and cultural diversity, the cultivation of ethnic and national heritage. But America nonetheless remains a melting pot. The majority of Americans living in big cities are still willing to accept newcomers. Urban America is still a genuinely welcoming and friendly social environment. In spite of the sometimes hysterical and hostile reaction to a possible quasi amnesty for the 11 to 12 million illegal immigrants, a poll in the summer of 2007 clearly reflected that the majority of the population is receptive and ready to accept hard-working newcomers.

For Kati and me, integration went smoothly. The factor contributing most to our fast-track adjustment was the university environment. UCLA, as is true of most American universities, is an almost independent township within the center of the Los Angeles agglomeration. UCLA is a one-campus institution. During the first years of the twenty-first century, besides the nearly 40,000 undergraduate and graduate students, 3,000 faculty members, and even more numerous staff, thousands of people visited the campus where every day 60,000 cars are parked in nearly forty parking structures. The campus is "self-sufficient." It has several places to eat, a faculty club, a number of cafeterias, several shops, theater, movie, and concert performances, and hundreds of public lectures every day. American university campuses are the best places in the world for me.

The university has been made especially receptive not only by its immense size but also by the strongly multi-ethnic character of both student body and faculty. At the turn of the twenty-first century, forty percent of the undergraduate students have Asian backgrounds and, along with the Hispanic students, they now represent the majority. The *New York Times,* in which one rarely finds expressions of admiration for Los Angeles, praised UCLA in October 2007 as one of the most receptive twenty-first-century universities in the country. Graduate students come from eighty-five countries, and the faculty is also extremely mixed with a great number of scholars from Chinese, Indian, Latin American and European backgrounds. All of these factors make newcomers an organic part of the university community in an instant. I was immediately accepted by and integrated into the faculty of my department, and have developed friendships among an even broader circle. Acceptance and adjustment would have been exceedingly more difficult, if at all possible, in Middle America or in a small town.

Friendship, however, has some special characteristics in Los Angeles. In Budapest, we were accustomed to enjoying close human relationships between friends. You did not even have to call somebody before dropping by, and meetings were frequent. This kind of spontaneity is hardly possible in Los Angeles, not the least because of the vast distances and time-consuming drives. Even close friends do not see each other for months on end, and one has to organize a meeting well in advance. More often people go out together to have a lunch or dinner. It took time for me to understand that human relationships, in spite of less frequent meetings and a different behavioral pattern, can be equally strong. I am grateful to a few close friends, first of all to Peter Reill, who taught this lesson to me.

Another shocking experience was the role of religion. The United States is the most religious country in the advanced world. On top of that, religion plays an important political role, in contrast to deeply secular Europe. According to a recent poll two-thirds of the population would not want to elect a president who did not believe in God. The religious Right has a "king-making" power. In presidential elections, candidates of the Republican Party have to adapt to the religious agenda, or risk losing the primaries. Churches are able to mobilize people, which may be decisive in the country where active registered voters represent a much lower share of the population than in Europe.

Religious organizations can influence education and force the introduction of alternative teaching of evolution and creationist concepts, since evolution, according to them, is "just another concept." Sporadically, but this is even true in higher education, and permeates even the academic scientific community. Some academically trained scientists with pedigreed PhDs from Ivy League schools, and the like, are adamantly opposed to evolutionary theory, and believe instead in a fundamentalist interpretation of the book of Genesis.

I have had a little taste of the countryside. I was surprised to find that the villages, or really small townships that have hardly more than one main street, are strikingly similar, with the same type of car dealerships, fast food chains, and banking institutions. At a rodeo in the foothills of the Sierra Nevada, I observed how very different the people in those areas are from those I know in L.A. While Kati and I were visiting our friends Cindy and Gary Nash there at their ranch, it was always an education to walk with them through the settlement. Pointing out a house, Gary might comment "this family home-schools the children." I learned that such home-schooling is a widespread phenomenon in Middle America, an effort to avoid the "evil" influence of school, which teaches Darwin's evolution theory instead of the creation concept of the Bible, which they hold sacred and valid in a literal sense. Urban settlements and those of the countryside are different everywhere, but significantly less so in Europe than in the United States.

At a debate of the Republican presidential candidates at the end of 2007, a young man asked the candidates whether they believed every world of the Bible. Most of the answers were a definite yes, maintaining that the Bible is the revelation of God. One or two of them risked to say that some statements are metaphoric. Elisabeth Dole, the Republican senator, sought to disqualify her Democratic rival in 2008 by screening a paid ad, suggesting that her rival is an atheist who does not believe in God. The Democratic candidate appeared on TV to confirm her belief in God. Religious American political life is very dissimilar to secular European one.

Churches are also strong social institutions, especially in smaller communities. Going to church on Sunday morning is, to an equal extent, a religious and a social event. One has to turn to history for an explanation. Europe was in a state of dramatic transformation from medieval to modern in the early modern centuries when the first immigrants left and arrived in America. Many left Europe so they could practice their religion freely. The Bible and the church preserved their intellectual values, ruled their views on the universe and life, and determined their personal behavior. They left Europe before the secular and scientific culture became dominant there. As one historian of early America explains, six generations of colonists lived continuously in the older religious framework in America and determined the pattern of life here. Perry Miller states: "without some understanding of Puritanism ... there is no understanding of America."

Black churches are particularly special institutions because of their major social, cultural, and entertaining functions. One of my most enduring and heart-warming experiences was our visit with Kati in a black church in New Orleans—long before the Katrina disaster. That church was located in the middle of the ghetto, an unfriendly neighborhood from the outside, but with the friendliest atmosphere inside. Without exaggeration I can say that I have rarely experienced such friendly hospitality and interest. We were the only white people there and were seated in the front row. Service and collective cultural entertainment were the same and inseparable. All the people had their role in the outstanding performance, singing, dancing, applauding, actually not only participating but living in the service-performance.

In connection with characteristic mentalities, I also realized the importance of certain *deeply rooted myths,* cultural beliefs about certain features of American life that are considered to be unique to this country. For instance, Vice-Presidential candidate Joe Lieberman frequently pointed to his Jewish origins during the election campaign of 2000, saying that his candidacy was possible "only in America." This uniqueness was a myth since several European countries with mixed political legacies elected Jewish political leaders including postwar France and Austria, and Lieberman, in the end, was not elected. Reality never plays a role in existence of myths.

Let me talk about some other myths that, in my view, are deeply rooted and belong to American identity. A myth that everybody is responsible for himself or herself and the country offers unlimited opportunities to everyone. If someone cannot exploit it, it is his or her personal mistake and failure. In Los Angeles, as in many other American urban centers, parts of the city are inundated with homeless people. Coming from Budapest where this phenomenon did not exist until 1990, I was shocked to see this. I had seen somewhat similar sights in Paris, and very recently in Tokyo, but the huge number of homeless people here who have dropped out of work and society is unique. On Ocean Parkway in Santa Monica, one of the most beautiful streets, in one of the richest cities and countries in the world, one bumps into homeless people at every step. How did it happen? The

United States introduced important welfare institutions during the Great Depression when President Franklin D. Roosevelt considered welfare policy as responsibility of a democratic state. The Kennedy and Johnson administrations went further by introducing important new welfare institutions, but the United States never became a welfare state as did virtually all the European countries and Canada.

Because of the missing social safety net, it is relatively easy to drop out from the society. Misfortune, illness and, most of all, mental illness may lead to joblessness and loss of homes that may throw people to the streets. During the Ronald Reagan administration, thousands of mentally ill people were dismissed from institutions and landed on the street. The traditional American philosophy that everybody is responsible for himself or herself created a social atmosphere that rejects establishing and running appropriate institutions to shelter the homeless. Similarly, the introduction of general health care to the entire population failed several times. America was an ideal country for the neo-liberal economics and philosophy that rejects regulation and state intervention and believes blindly in the self-regulating automatism of the market. Since the Reagan era, no one challenged this view, which became a sacrosanct doctrine and Reagan the most beloved President. During the Iraq war, the news strikingly unveiled the fact that in some cities a quarter of the homeless consisted of war veterans. Some 47 million people have no health insurance. These facts points to the country's imperative need to take care of its veterans, sick, and unfortunates, and, if possible, reintegrate them into the society, or place them into institutions that offer them care and human comfort.

The myth of the unlimited possibility and mobility to be elevated to the richest echelon of the population is a commonly shared view. Europe still carries the legacy of the old nineteenth-century class society and the poor envy and are angry at the rich. This is not so in the United States. Most of the poor admire the rich and believe that the gate is open for them too. This habit of admiring rather than hating the rich is deeply rooted in American history, though it may change with time. American society was the first in the world to become a middle class society from the early 1960s. During the postwar decades, white-collar workers gradually became the majority. The rapidly rising economy elevated the income level of the entire society. Moreover, between 1949 and 1979 the income of the bottom 80 percent, and especially the very bottom 20 percent of the population, grew faster than the income of the top one percent. After 1979, from Reagan's presidency onward and between 1980 and 2005, this trend dramatically changed and the top one percent increased its share of the national income from 8.2 to 17.4 percent.

The Cornell University economist, Robert H. Frank, pointed out in his recent book, titled *Falling Behind*, the realities giving rise to the sense of "falling behind" which emerged among the middle class. Frank described an "arms race of consumption" in which everybody wants to keep up with the level of those just above him or her. A symptom of this is the increase in the median size of newly built houses from 1,600 to 2,100 square feet, although the median family's income level hardly increased at all. The rich set the norms of consumption, and it stimulates tremendous material ambition from the non-rich. It is not accidental that the TV program called "War on the Middle Class" became extremely popular.

This attitude may be explained by the frontier individualism that naturally emerged in early American history, a residue of which we still see in American culture today. People had to solve everything themselves in virgin lands and without an organized state. "Building society in the wilderness," or colonial capitalism, as historians explain, offered the greatest possibility for entrepreneurial businessmen, adventurers, merchants, and speculators. The guaranty of success was a winning personality. A loser had nothing and nobody else to blame but himself for his misfortune, so the myth ran.

The other side of the same coin is widespread philanthropy: Rich people believe—and the tax policy allowing the deduction of donations strengthens this belief—in their mission to solve social problems through charity. Although evidence also indicates that, the very rich give *proportionately* less than those with middle class incomes, as was documented many years ago by an analysis of Forbes magazine, written about the philanthropy of the Top Ten. It was interesting to read Andrew Carnegie's *The Gospel of the Wealth* written in 1900. He belonged to the first multi-millionaires who established the habit which became a kind of compulsory behavior in the country. He recognized that free market capitalism, the engine of the "progress of the race" was leading at the same time to steeply growing inequality and to the formation of "rigid casts." "Human society," he complained, "loses homogeneity." The solution, he argued, lies in the correct "management of wealth:" in the foundation of universities, hospitals, and donations toward the society's well being. In this way, "the ties of brotherhood may still bind together the rich and poor in harmonious relationship." (Carnegie, 1989, 653–65) Both ways of thinking are alien to most of the European countries.

Of course, there are still several examples to "prove" the existence of unlimited opportunity. In America's recent past, for example, a university dropout named Bill Gates, emerged as the world's richest man. Not long afterwards, a couple of young people had a great idea, founded Google, and became multibillionaires virtually overnight. I myself know two immigrants from Eastern Europe who each arrived in this country penniless, with only a suitcase, and went on to achieve financial success. George Soros is one of them. He is running a hedge fund but also follows the philanthropic traditions of America. I also met with Milan Panic, who once invited me to speak in Costa Mesa at the annual meeting of the top managers of his pharmaceutical empire. He arrived from Yugoslavia to Los Angeles in the 1950s with $20 in his pocket, but became a multimillionaire in a few decades. There are similar stories about unlimited opportunity.

Nevertheless, this is more myth than reality. The Organization for Economic Cooperation and Development, as reported by *The New York Times*, compared social mobility in various countries and found that the United States is far behind Denmark, Austria, Norway, Finland, Sweden, France, Spain, and Canada. In the United States, if somebody belongs to the bottom 20 percent regarding income, more than 40 percent of his children will end up in the same layer. The reason is the much lower "investment" in children's education and much less government assistance, while in Denmark 75, and in Britain 70 percent of the children of the same income group rise into the higher echelons, while only a much smaller layer remains on the same level. The historically-based and deliberately cultivated myths are, nevertheless, deeply rooted. The popular nineteenth century writer, Horatio Alger, published dozens of novels about the realization of the American Dream, of getting rich and successful via hard work. The "self-made man," Booker T. Washington and his admonition to African-Americans to "pull themselves up where they stand," i.e., work their own way up humbly to earn their position in society, rather than directing their political energies into fighting the system for that position.

Among the things I would like to mention that surprised me the most is the myth surrounding gun ownership as a token of freedom, human rights, and personal security. America is armed to the teeth: according to a report 270 million of the world's 875 million weapons are in the United States. On average, nine guns for every ten people. The tragic repeated shooting sprees in high schools and universities, employees taking revenge against innocent co-workers for any kind of real or imagined insult or injustice at the workplace, and the troubling statistics on murders committed with guns apparently cannot convince the majority of population to ban firearms. The mistaken concept of self-defense with personal weapons rarely works but often leads to tragic manslaughter.

A few years ago, a Japanese exchange student was invited to a party. He knocked on the wrong door, waited, but nobody answered thus he turned back to leave. The owner of the home, warned by his wife that a stranger wants to come in, opened the door and shot him. A similar episode of "self-defense" occurred more recently when a 34-year old man accidentally locked himself out of his house, and was shot dead by his neighbor through his neighbor's door as he knocked on it for help.

Coming from Europe, we find this passion for guns extremely odd and incomprehensible. What is its reason? The tradition stemming from pioneer times when ownership of arms in Europe was a noble privilege and became here a symbol of freedom and equality? At the time when the constitution and its clause legitimating arms were originally formulated, this was meant for the purpose of armed local militias, which were an absolute necessity in a new nation with no police or even standing army in a frontier situation. People indeed had to defend themselves. This constitutional clause has become utterly obsolete nowadays, but remained integral both to the gun lobby's calculating legitimization of gun ownership, and for too many everyday Americans' "frontier mythology" of gun ownership as a part of individual self-defense and "rights."

Among the various myths, the strong belief that America has always had the most democratic political system has an important place. The constitution as the founding fathers crafted it is indeed convincing evidence of the American democratic tradition. Nevertheless, it was shocking to watch documentaries on Southern segregation and the struggle for desegregation during the 1960s. Nazi racism and World War II belonged already to history by that time, partly because the United States played a major role in their destruction, and defended democracy in Europe. But Presidents Eisenhower and then Kennedy had to send troops to Arkansas and Mississippi to defend desegregation from the passionate southern population. Virginia had chosen to close public schools rather than let African-American children enroll. Civil right advocates were murdered, and black churches burned. Southern whites had their own interpretation of democracy. The recent "Jena Six" case, an episode of violence that began with white students hanging nooses from "their" schoolyard tree when black students tried to sit under it, exhibits the remnants of that legacy. Noose hanging, as it was reported, occurred even in the last two-three years about 50 to 60 times in the country.

It was equally striking to learn that Jews and women could not get academic jobs before World War II, and country clubs continued practicing exclusion for quite a while even after the shock of the Holocaust in Europe. The road toward democracy in America was quite bumpy. When watching documentaries and talking with colleagues who knew American universities in the old days, I have a strong feeling that today I am living in a very different America. The change is as admirable and as striking as is, in retrospect, the abuse of democratic principles half a century ago, and its resurgence from time to time. The 2008 presidential elections with the impressive victory of Barack Obama signal historic change. As one of the journalists phrased it, the civil war ended now, after one-and-half century.

The myth about personal responsibility, and the condemnation of "socialized health care," consequently the lack of a universal health care system in the world's richest country, was also shocking. Even more startling is the provincialism of neither knowing nor caring about other countries' practices and experiences. Several fellow citizens believed what pharmaceutical and other lobbies broadly advertised when the Clinton Administration worked on the introduction of a reform: The general health care system is not viable, may ruin the country, or ruin the quality of health care, or both. I have heard and read several times that "we have the world's best health care system." This statement is true regarding the unique medical technology and medical service level for those who can afford to pay for it. It is also true that the United States has the highest health spending in the world, more than 15 percent of the national income, while most advanced

West European countries' and Canada's health expenditures are around 10 percent of their GDP. The high spending, however, reflects mostly the skyrocketing price of medical services, and ignores the fact that 47 million people are uninsured, and insurance companies have the right to drop people if they get seriously ill. In the last twenty years, America's average life expectancy rate at birth declined from the 11th place to the 42nd among countries in an international comparison. In some urban ghettos, African-American life expectancy is similar to Bangladesh. The United States is not among the first 25 countries with lowest infant mortality, and regarding child health, it occupies the 21st place. It is striking that relatively poor countries such as Hungary, Poland, Greece and Portugal have better situations in this respect. But the traditional American viewpoint internalized the neo-liberal concept that was best formulated by Milton Friedman, who advocated that a competitive free market and private, individual responsibility create the best healthcare, schooling and pension systems. If you failed, the failure was certainly the consequence of your mistakes; you simply not try hard enough or do well enough.

I was surprised that many people knew very little about the Canadian and European systems. For many, the world outside America is non-existent. I have realized for years that in my university classes on twentieth century European economic history and the political economy of the European Union, students have no knowledge about the European welfare state and policy and do not know that the most generous Scandinavian welfare state is also economically the most prosperous, fastest growing and competitive.

Attempts to introduce new welfare institutions are viciously attacked and recently generated a presidential veto by President George W. Bush against Congress' child healthcare initiative. A large part of the population, indoctrinated by neo-liberal economic views, believes that welfare institutions are brutal interventions into personal freedom. Milton Friedman compared social welfare to "sending policeman to take the money from somebody's pocket." The welfare state is considered to be a "Robin Hood" institution, taking money from the rich (or the middle class) and giving it to the poor. According to meticulous calculations, however, this is just not true. The European welfare states are mostly "piggy banks," using Nicolas Barr's term, as roughly two-thirds to three-quarters of the welfare expenditures are the outcome of a mechanism for redistribution over the life cycle. The tax money spent for pensions is redistributed from the middle to later years of life, free education similarly redistributes from the middle to the earlier years. In other words, what one pays to the state, one will get back in a different period of one's life. The view that health insurance, pensions, and educational expenses are a private responsibility is mistaken, since information is limited for a person, uncertainty and risks are too big, and the lack of a safety net easily leads to exclusion from society. The emerging depression, however, led to the recognition of the majority of the people that America has to establish a general health care system, and voted for the candidate, Barack Obama, who advocated it.

The broadly advertised and deeply rooted myth that government is not the solution but the problem, the widespread anti-tax and anti-government attitude differentiate the United States from all of the countries I know, visited, and studied. The bulk of the population believes that higher taxation and higher social expenditures might ruin the country. This myth, as myths in general, is unrelated to the facts. It is intimidating and irritating to me, as an economic historian who deals with comparative history, how facts are swept away in discourse on these subjects. Seemingly, nobody cares that Sweden, the pioneering and model country of high-taxing welfare state reached and is still reaching the most dynamic and high growth performance for a century. Myths, especially if propagated by the most sophisticated media machinery, and held as a doctrine by the entire political class, easily neglect facts and reality that contradict the myth. It is a painful intellectual experience. The international financial crisis that spread from the United States in 2008 may close an era, the unchallenged reign of neo-liberal doctrine. The most anti-tax, anti-state intervention, and unregulated free market government of President George W. Bush had to run and bail out the banking system using hundreds of billions of taxpayer's money, and even nationalizes parts of the financial institutions. The former head of the Fed, Alan Greenspan was "surprised" that his belief in the self-correcting mechanism of the market did not work. Europe seemingly learned the lesson. A new regulatory system may reestablish a healthy market situation.

I discussed mentalities and myths that differentiate American everyday life and beliefs, as I experienced them after my arrival from another continent and world but became an American who spent more than one-fifth of his life in his new home country. Let me turn, at last, to a third bunch of *economic, political, and legal phenomena* that surprise someone who is looking at and living the American life at the same time as both insider and outsider.

The world looks to America as the embodiment of efficiency, prosperity, and modernity. All of the generations in the twentieth century outside the United States, shared this view. The nineteenth century belonged to Britain, but towards its end the United States began emerging as the leading economic power of the world. The past century, without doubt, was an "American century." In the present, however, frightening signs signal an ongoing change. As an economic historian who closely follows economic trends and has an obsession to read statistics and economic news, I realized striking new phenomena.

Let me start with the fact which was already recognized by the world's very first economists such as the French Anne Robert Jacques Turgot, and the British Adam Smith, that relatively high capital accumulation is one of the key factors of economic growth. America exhibited the custom of high savings and accumulation in its entire history. Many signs reflect the beginning of change. Besides dramatically declining savings and the spreading habit to spend more than is being earned, as I discussed before, one of the most frightening new trends is the sharp decline of the value of the dollar and its endangered position as a world currency. In the nineteenth century, the British pound, with its unchanged value and stability, was equal to gold and accepted by the entire world as such. After World War I, the British pound began losing its world position and was ultimately superseded by the American dollar. This replacement was emblematic of America's leading position in the world economy.

The European Union introduced its common currency, the euro, a few years ago at the turn of the century. At that time, it was intended to have equal value with the American dollar. But it almost immediately lost part of its value and became equal instead to 0.80 dollar cents. With an unprecedented speed, however, the euro was quickly elevated in status to a second world currency. Before the 2008 crisis, a euro was equal to $1.56. One fifth to one-quarter of the world's financial transactions is already using the euro instead of the dollar. This dramatic change is closely connected with the huge American indebtedness and deficit. The United States, when I am writing these lines, has an enormous deficit of $791,510 million, compared to the European Union's mere 28 million. The United States, the world's banker since the 1920s, has suddenly become a capital importing country, moreover, the second biggest among them. Its roughly $100,000 million capital inflow is twice as much as the Mexican, Brazilian, and Russian capital imports combined, and one-third more than the Chinese. Foreign capital inflow keeps finances in balance. The world's leading power, however, is dangerously dependent on foreign countries buying American securities. Isn't it odd that the United States depends on Chinese, Japanese, and Russian capital exports and that two out of the three main creditors are less developed countries? If these countries stopped buying American bonds, the sliding of the dollar could dramatically accelerate. This process had silently begun. As the Japanese Daiwa Fund reported, in one single month, October 2007, individual Japanese investors removed $4 billion from the United States and invested $17.5 billion into emerging, mostly Asian markets. The 2008 crisis, at least temporarily, stopped this process. One may not know what will follow.

I check statistics from time to time. How disappointing that the media, sensitively following the stock market's daily movements, hardly shows any interest, and does not inform the population, about one of the central economic questions of the country. Initially, true, the decline of the dollar mostly hit only American tourists abroad. In the summer of 2007, Kati and I spent a wonderful time in our favorite parts of Britain, London, York, and the Cotswold, and we experienced that the trip became 50 to 70 percent more expensive than in 1993 when we made it the last time. The low dollar, however, is starting to negatively influence domestic consumption as well since we have to pay more for imported goods in cheap dollars. Every time I fill the tank of my car, as everybody else, I feel it. Domestic consumption is traditionally the driving force of the American economy. Together with the unfolding real estate crisis, the low dollar and its deleterious effect on domestic consumption may generate a recession.

What is happening? Is it a consequence of mistaken government policy, reckless spending, tax cuts for the upper one percent of the population and an expensive, counterproductive war? During the long presidential campaign during the last year of the George W. Bush administration, I have heard about these issues often. America's defense spending, about

$10 billion per month, is extreme. Indeed, it exceeds the total expenses of the next ten highest defense spending countries combined, including China, India, Britain, France, Germany, Italy, and Japan. This is definitely a part of the problem.

The United States is losing ground in world trade as well. America's share in the world export of goods is less than nine percent of the total, while Germany alone has a nearly 10 percent share, and China—with one fifth of the GDP of the US– has a share next to that of America with eight percent, and it is growing. The euro-zone, the countries that use the common European currency and share roughly the same aggregate income level as the United States, is ahead of America by nearly 50 percent. The same is true regarding foreign direct investments. In the early twenty-first century, the United States had a somewhat more than one-fifth share of the total, while Western European investments comprised about 40 percent. As a consequence—to place these figures in an international context, something that I always do in my economic history research—in the first decade of the twenty-first century, no less than 50 countries have had higher growth rates that of the United States.

A third of a century ago the world entered into the age of new globalization. This question gained a prominent role in my scholarly work in recent decades. Several critics have maintained that the term, "globalization" was a euphemism or just a more acceptable name for old-fashioned imperialism since the rich advanced countries were profiting from globalization. In reality, as I studied the process, I realized that it is not true, and globalization may be advantageous for those less developed countries that were able to adjust flexibly to its requirements. Backward countries with low wage levels were able to attract huge amounts of investments if their labor force was well educated and efficient and if they developed the required infrastructure. They profited from investments, outsourcing jobs, and contracting out production from advanced countries. I have heard American public complaints about it quite often. Some of the formerly backward countries were able to join the international production network.

Several Asian countries, first the "small tigers," then huge elephants such as China and India, and then most recently some of the Central and Eastern European former communist transforming countries have speeded up and reached 9 to 10 percent annual growth. The world economy is in a

My home and refuge in Los Angeles for the last thirteen years.

state of transformation and rearrangement. The European Union, China, and India are emerging as economic super powers.

On the other hand, some of the early beneficiaries of globalization, among them the United States, are facing increasing competition, losing jobs, and accumulating trade deficits. As a surprising new phenomenon, some economic and political groupings of the "globalizers" who were traditionally advocates of free trade, are now turning against it. Indeed, they are suggesting the defense of their national markets against imports from the less developed but fast growing and exporting countries. Have we entered into a new period of the world economy? A backlash to globalization? Are we facing the end of the "American century"? There are certain signs of that.

Turning to another central problem of American life, the system of justice also amazed me. I have learned a lot from a legal case my wife and I faced. To sum up briefly, our house is part of a homeowner's community of more than 300 houses and is facing a picturesque canyon. It happened that the canyon's steep slope had slid somewhat, and the homeowners' association decided to rebuild its edge. When heavy earth-moving machines removed the upper level of the slope, they discovered a leak into it that was originating from our neighbor's garden. The board of the association decided to sue three members of their own association: the owners of the three neighboring houses, including us. These homes have a common sewage system. The accusation was superficial: we had not taken care of the underground sewage pipes, and that omission might have caused the leak and consequently the slide of the slope as well. The association wanted the three families to pay for the rebuilding.

We had to hire a lawyer, whom we paid by the hour. Before the case came to trial, however, an arbitration process took place involving the representatives of the four parties, namely, the Association and the three homeowners. Two lawyers represented each family, those whom they had privately hired, and the lawyers of the companies who insured the homes. A retired judge was hired and paid by the hour. The parties sat in separate rooms and the judge went from room to room. First, he asked each party the same question: "what amount are you ready to pay?"

No one examined the truth of the accusation; no one investigated what caused the slope to slide. Our lawyer said that we were not responsible, that nothing proved our responsibility and we were not going to pay a cent. "That is not very helpful," the judge said, and left the room. After quite a while, he returned and asked the same question. This time the lawyer of our insurance company said that he was authorized to pay a certain amount but not more. The judge left again. We did not know what the answers of the other "co-defendants" were. The insurance companies, as the lawyers explained to us, have a policy to pay in order to avoid trial, which is more expensive. Certainly all the insurance agents offered a certain amount. The Association's lawyer accepted the amount and the case were closed. There was no trial, but also no investigation to discover the true cause and responsibility. We knew that the Association heavily watered the slope. It did not matter. We paid our private lawyer, a payment partly recovered from the insurance company. Our insurance company paid everything, but immediately increased our insurance fee for five years, so at the end of the day, we ourselves had paid for everything. The real shock was to learn that roughly ninety percent of all civil cases are being settled in a similar way, i.e. through arbitration, with no real investigation of the truth. Everybody and every insurance company want to avoid the high cost of a trial. The fee for a lawyer at that time was about $350–$400 per hour. I was astonished to learn that suing somebody is an everyday occurrence in the United States.

One of our friends, to mention another example, caused a minor accident on the freeway. Her car was damaged because she changed lanes without looking back and a huge SUV hit the side of her car. The SUV was not scratched, but the owner, whose husband was a lawyer himself, sued her claiming, among other things, that she had headaches and, as a result, could not have sex with her husband for two weeks. That was too much, and the Court rejected her claim. Justice in civil cases has become a big business with smart and ruthless lawyer-entrepreneurs.

An even more dramatic revelation of American justice came when I learned from the news that from time to time people are released from prison after fifteen or even twenty-five years, after having spent a great part of their adult life in jail, because their innocence was retroactively proven. Major crimes, such as the murder of civil rights activists in the 1960s, on the other hand, went unpunished at the time, and predators were indicted only forty years later, if at all. These crucial mistakes form one of the main arguments against the death penalty. But "mistakes," especially in the past, sometimes have a common root, racism. Blacks were and, arguably, still are easily accused and sentenced without convincing proof, as one of the best American novels and movies, *To Kill a Mockingbird,* well illustrates. This old problem is still haunting the justice system in various ways.

One extreme naturally generates another, as the notorious O.J. Simpson case demonstrated. Political correctness often deforms the outcome of sexual harassment accusations. The fact that these kinds of abuses were non-issues for so long has generated an opposing attitude now. On the other side of the coin, we see how deeply the democratic traditions of the country run. When the Watergate scandal shocked America, some of my American friends told me that indictment and impeachment were unavoidable. At that time I was still living in Hungary, and argued vehemently that it would never happen. I just could not imagine a criminal case against a sitting president. In Hungary and other countries of Europe, such a case would never reach that stage. It was a surprising and positive experience to learn that I was totally wrong. On the other hand, the impeachment process against President Bill Clinton, which I followed closely, was not only disgusting and a violently partisan action disguised in moral and legal clothing, but unveiled a hypocritical attitude. A large part of the otherwise prudish section of the population, in a perverse way, loves sex scandals.

The guilty verdict in the high-profile Enron corporate scandal case as well as the Lewis 'Scooter' Libby case, both of which had broad repercussions, showed once more, however, the strength of the democratic base. In the latter case, the chief of staff of Dick Cheney, the most powerful Vice-President the country has ever seen, was openly condemned. For many, it was a moral as well as legal condemnation of his boss as well, because they wanted to compromise Ambassador Joseph Wilson who clearly unmasked the contrived reason to go to war. For this very reason, they leaked out that Wilson's wife, Valerie Plame was a CIA operative who arranged the travel of her husband to Africa to unveil the lie the government used to go to war.

It is true, however, that after the verdict, President Bush "commuted" the prison sentence, thus virtually pardoning Libby. The inherent contradictions in the handling of the above-mentioned cases and their aftermath reveal certain contradictions in the American juridical process in general. The jury system, with its deeply democratic foundations, nevertheless deserves admiration. As I see it, people feel a responsibility for society and believe in their juridical duty as a major part of citizenship's responsibility. The "twelve angry men," however, are often strangely selected. They may not have any previous information about the case. Well-informed and opinionated people who read newspapers are often excluded from the juror-body during the selection process. The system ultimately has several shortcomings from the selection process of jurors, inconsistencies based on racial or other prejudices, to the whole oddity of the American practice of perpetual suing and countersuing, and the extremely widespread practice of arbitration.

Another surprising experience about the American life was the meeting with cases of corruption, and consequently the collapse of my belief, my myth about the lack of corruption here. I experienced a great deal of corruption in my previous life in Hungary and the neighboring Central and East European countries. There were certain periods when people bribed shop clerks for goods in short supply, and paid "tips" to medical doctors for better care and hospital beds. The shortage economy was a hotbed of corruption that was a petty everyday phenomenon. This kind of corruption is naturally non-existent in America. It does not mean, however, that corruption is non-existent.

Corporate corruption is widespread and not petty at all. The Enron scandal and other cases provided a rare opportunity to view the lurid truth of

American corporate corruption. Although legalized by Congress, I find it equally corrupt that under the umbrella of the American Jobs Creation Act of 2004, according to a newspaper report, big corporations gained billions by bringing foreign-held profits back to the United States with sometimes an 85 percent deduction from the regular taxation rate. The report listed one hundred corporations which received a $90 billion gift in 2005 in this way. The giant drug company Pfizer gained $36 billion, but dismissed 8,000 workers. Hewlett-Packard repatriated nearly $15 billion, and laid off more than 14,000 workers. All of that happened under the name of the job creation project though those companies did not create jobs at all.

To my great surprise, certain forms of political corruption are also legalized because various lobbies and lobbyists can legally corrupt politicians who cannot win elections without huge donations. These kinds of contributions are mostly banned in Europe, but belong to a political mechanism in the United States that is legal. It made a big splash when recently a leading lawmaker resigned from his seat so as not to wait for two years, as a new law regulated, before he can join the lobbyists' moneymakers.

The CQ Money Line reported that 37 former senators and 158 former representatives of the House are among the ranks of lobbyists exploiting their political contacts, as one of the authors of the medical drug subsidy bill did, when he became a lobbyist of the pharmaceutical industry. The picture is more troubling if one also counts sons and relatives of active politicians among the lobbyists: as the retiring senator's sons were already lobbyists during their father's terms, more than two dozens relatives of senators and members of the House are lobbyist or government consultants.

Insurance companies, the pharmaceutical industry and other lobbies are able to influence political decisions by their unlimited financial resources. Congressmen regularly "arrange" lucrative investments or subsidies to buy donations from their constituency. Supplying the army and rebuilding Iraq was also spoiled by corruption as it was unveiled quite a few times in recent years. Money speaks—sometimes too loudly and too much. This kind of corruption becomes especially dangerous when the same party dominates all branches of government. The framers of the constitution wisely built checks and balances into the American political system; in certain areas, however, this has not worked, and gaping legal loopholes make pervasive corruption possible and unchecked. Democracy, however, works. People may and do vote mistakenly, against their own interest, but in the longer run, bad governments, parties, and politicians lose their standing and are replaced by better ones. The system corrects itself, as it happened in 2008. In this last chapter, I used the word "surprise" quite often. I could have phrased my impressions in a different way. Since history played the central role in my life, history, in this case American history is the lens through which I understand America.

Settling in America and integrating into its society, but seeing everything parallel from within and from without, has led to an endless process of discovery. My angle is automatically comparative, something which helps understanding both the great advantages and the shortcomings. I feel lucky to be integrated in our new world where I feel at home, and with my work, teaching, writing, appreciating and disagreeing, criticizing and using my citizens' rights, try contributing to the healthy progress of the country.

References

Ady, Endre, [1905] 1986. "Morituri," in Ivan T. Berend and Éva Ring (eds.), *Helyünk Európában. Nézetek és koncepciók a 20. századi Magyarországon,* Vol. I. Budapest: Magvető.

Ash, Timothy Garton, 1990. *Magic Lantern. The Revolution of '89 in Warsaw, Budapest, Berlin, and Prague,* New York: Random House.

Berend, Ivan T. (ed.), 1989. *A Gazdasági Reformbizottság programjavaslata,* Budapest: Közgazdasági és Jogi Kiadó.

Bibó, István, 1986. *Válogatott tanulmányok,* Vol. II. Budapest: Magvető Kiadó.

Carnegie, Andrew, 1889. "The Wealth" ["The Gospel of the Wealth"], *North American Review,* Vol. 148. No. 391.

Csóri, Sándor, 1990. *Hitel,* September 26.

Eötvös, József [1870] 1971, "Napló," *Történelmi Szemle,* No. 7.

Erdmann, Karl Dietrich, 2005. *Toward a Global Community of Historians,* New York: Berghahn Book.

Friss, István, 1978. *Társadalmi Szemle,* No. 6.

Fukuyama, Francis, 1989, "End of History," *The National Interest,* Summer, August 27.

Gati, Charles, 2006. *Failed Illusions. Moscow, Washington, Budapest and the 1956 Hungarian Revolution,* Washington, D.C.: Woodrow Wilson Center Press.

Grass, Günther, 2006. *Pealing the Onion: A Memoir,* Translated by Michael H. Heim, New York: Harcourt.

Havel, Václav, [1979] 1985. *The Power of the Powerless. Citizens Against the State in Central and Eastern Europe,* London: Hutchinson.

Held, Joseph (ed.), 1993. *Democracy and Right-Wing Politics in Eastern Europe in the 1990s,* Boulder; East European Monographs.

References

In Memoriam György Ránki. Modern Age—Modern Historian, 1990. Ed. by Ferenc Glatz, Budapest: Institute of History, Hungarian Academy of Sciences.

Konrád, George, 2007. *Guest in my Own Country. A Hungarian Life,* New York: Other Press.

La Stampa, 1993, November 2.

Matthews, John P.C., 2007. *Explosion. The Hungarian Revolution in 1956,* New York: Hippocrene Book.

McCraw, Thomas K., *Prophet of Innovation. Joseph Schumpeter and Creative Destruction,* Cambridge, Mass.: Harvard University Press.

MSzMP, 1993. A Magyar Szocialista Munkáspárt Központi Bizottságának 1989.évi jegyzőkönyvei. Vol. I., Budapest: Magyar Országos Levéltár.

Németh, László, 1943. in *Szárszó. Az 1943. évi balatonszárszói Magyar Élet-tábor előadás- és megbeszélés sorozata,* Budapest: Magyar Élet. 43.

Népszabadság, 1975, January 8. Éva Terényi's article.

{The} New Yorker, 1989, November 20.

New York Times, 2007. Sunday Book Review, July 8.

Quinn, William W., Colonel, [1945] 2000. *Dachau Liberated. The Official report by the US Seventh Army,* Michael W. Perry (Ed), Seattle: Inkling Book.

Reich-Ranicki, Marcel, 2001. *The Author of Himself: The Life of Marcel Reich-Ranicki,* Princeton University Press.

Sanders, Ivan, 2006. "I was Not a Soviet Agent—János Kádár's Address to the Central Committee of the Hungarian Socialist Workers' Party, April 12, 1989." *The Hungarian Quarterly,* No. 183. Autumn.

Schumpeter, Joseph, 1976. *Capitalism, Socialism and Democracy,* London: Allan and Unwin.

Szabad Nép, 1956, October 23.

Társadalmi Szemle, 1975. No. 6. Imre Szabo's article.

Truman, Hary S., 1955–6. *Memoirs.* Garden City: Doubleday.

Weber, Max, 1978. *Economy and Society. An Outline of Interpretive Sociology,* Berkeley: University of California Press.

List of Photos

The first photo of me, at age three, in 1933	6
With my mother, father, and brother Ervin in 1935	7
My grandmother	10
The last photo with my brother Ervin	12
36 Akácfa utca in Budapest (Photo: Szilvia Pető)	27
Dachau, where I spent the terrible winter and spring of 1944–45	32
In cast from head to hips in 1961	36
The Gebirgsjägerschule in Mittenwald	41
Budapest in ruins when I returned from Dachau in August 1945 (Photo collection of the Metropolitan Ervin Szabó Library, Budapest)	45
The 1956 Revolution in Budapest (Photo collection of the Metropolitan Ervin Szabó Library, Budapest)	63
The Jewish Gymnasium, my high school in Budapest (Photo: Szilvia Pető)	76
The Budapest University of Economics (Photo: Szilvia Pető)	79
With Eric Hobsbawm in his garden in London	114
With colleagues and György Ránki	121
With Paul Zsigmond Pach in 2000	149
Royce Hall, the trademark building of the University of California, Los Angeles	160
With my first wife, Rózsa, and four-year-old Zsuzsa in Budapest	170
My grandsons, Benjamin and Daniel, in 2008	171
With my daughters Zsuzsa and Nora, Nora's husband Joe, and 8-month-old Esther in Los Angeles in 2002	172
With my granddaughters, Esther and Rebecca, in Los Angeles in 2005	173

List of Photos

With my wife, Kati, and my stepdaughter Dora in our Los Angeles home in 1996	174
In the front of the Hungarian Academy of Sciences building in Budapest	177
Being received by Pope John Paul II in 1986	199
At the festive plenary session of the Swedish Academy of Science in 1987	200
With Rezső Nyers	211
The peaceful Hungarian Revolution in 1988–89 (Photo collection of the Magyar Távirati Iroda)	218
With Kati, after having received an honorary Doctorate from Glasgow University in 1990	221
Delivering the 1990 Panglaykim Lecture in Jakarta, Indonesia	223
With Iván Szelényi	234
Horse riding in the Sierra Nevada in 1995	240
In Bryce Canyon, Utah, with Kati in 1997	244
My home and refuge in Los Angeles for the last thirteen years	268

For Product Safety Concerns and Information please contact
our EU representative GPSR@taylorandfrancis.com Taylor & Francis
Verlag GmbH, Kaufingerstraße 24, 80331 München, Germany

T - #0017 - 200326 - C0 - 229/152/16 - PB - 9789633867013 - Matt Lamination